Nowhere

Walking the Wainwrights

Andy Grigg

SIGMA Leisure

Published by Sigma Leisure - an imprint of
Sigma Press, Stobart House, Pontyclerc, Penybanc Road, Ammanford, Carmarthenshire SA18 3HP.

British Library Cataloguing in Publication Data
A CIP record for this book is available from the British Library.

ISBN: 978-1-85058-983-9

Typesetting and Design by: Sigma Press, Ammanford.

Cover photograph: The Skiddaw Massif © Tania Grigg

Photographs: © Andy and Tania Grigg

Printed by: TJ International Ltd

FOREWORD
by
Alan Hinkes OBE

I don't mind admitting that I intend to bag all the Wainwrights.

What a fantastic experience to do them all together as a family and this book recounts the routes, anecdotes, highs and lows, along with a few gems of history and geography.

When I first started fell walking I didn't know about Mr Wainwright and his wonderful guidebooks, I was more interested in gnarly routes – rock climbing and scrambling on the more craggy fells. I aspired to the Alps and the Himalaya, climbing the highest mountains in the world.

My mountaineering began in the fells of northern England and I have an innate love of the Lake District. Map reading and geography is a passion for me and when I finally discovered the Wainwright Pictorial Guides I was captivated.

Just like Andy I feel that the Lakes are the 'right size' – you can have a great adventure in a day or even half a day – rather than a month in the Himalaya.

This book gives a lovely snapshot into a six-year family challenge to complete the Wainwrights: starting on Pavey Ark and finishing on the often-overlooked Catstycam.

This is a fabulous family achievement, with memories that will last a lifetime.

Alan Hinkes

For Tania, Will and Tom

CONTENTS

Conversion on the road to Keswick	7
False start October 2004	13
The Wainwrights April 2007	17
Standing Tall April 2008	23
The Challenge April 2009	29
The Rainy Season August 2009	49
Regret is Forever April 2010	66
Philosophical Wanderings August 2010	86
Milestones October 2010	103
Halfway February 2011	117
High Days and Holidays April 2011	128
The Glass is always half full October 2011	152
Dreaming of a White Christmas December 2011	161
If at first you don't succeed April 2012	167
Some Fells are bigger than others July/August 2012	179
Changes October 2012	197
The Beginning of the End December 2012/January 2013	208
Senses working overtime February 2013	215
Walk out to Winter March/April 2013	224
Completion May 2013	239
Index	247

CONVERSION ON THE ROAD TO KESWICK

"It is a truth universally acknowledged, that a single man in possession of new walking boots must be in want of a mountain"; well not necessarily! I start this book about walking with the statement that I was no fan of the outdoors; walking or scrambling. In fact I was no fan of anything that really involved effort, perspiration or dressing like a Geographer.

As a child I had enjoyed walking; my father was a geography lecturer and we spent many family holidays in Cornwall, Devon and various other parts of the country, looking at ox-bow lakes, raised beaches and other assorted geographical features. When I was nine, we all climbed to the top of Snowdon. I can still remember the excitement and exhilaration I felt at reaching the summit, thinking I was on top of the world, and being delighted when I was told that I was the highest person in England and Wales. I also remember racing up to the top of granite tors, and being amazed by Wistmans Wood on Dartmoor; the dwarf oaks and long hanging lichens made the whole place look magical, like something straight out of a tale by Tolkein.

This early taste and enjoyment of the great outdoors was, however, fatally diminished by life as a student. I freely admit that I was keener on strutting and posing, rather than striding out and wearing a cagoule. The joys of a weekend away in a mountain hut, paled into insignificance compared to a weekend of drinking and general debauchery at the University bar. Friends on my course (Geography) tried to persuade me about the joys of walking, God forbid climbing, and even worse camping, but I chose a path of comfort and indoor pastimes; anyway it's hard to enjoy the outdoors when you are scared that the rain will flatten your hair!

So imagine my trepidation, some years later, now a teacher, and being persuaded that a long weekend in the Lake District would be fantastic! To show willing I had purchased a new pair of walking boots. I say new, they were, but I had never owned a pair before. I say walking boots, that's stretching the definition a bit; I tried on some sturdy looking boots, but they just didn't look right, so I chose on the basis, not of comfort, suitability for the job in hand or durability, but on the basis of which boots made me look the least like a rambler (more on this wise choice later). I also invested in a waterproof, not really a sensible or accurate description of said coat!

On the journey up to The Lakes I was less than excited. If I had been heading for London, Leeds, or quite frankly any city, I would have been feeling a little brighter. The journey was without incident, if a little slow; my old mini was not used to long distances. I had been promised that I would love the Lakes and be captivated by the landscape, the beauty, the views; but this was October, the hour had just gone back and everything north of Birmingham was in darkness. The outlines of mountains were pointed out to me, but I was damned if I could see them.

Now, there are some things in life that even at the time you know are life changing moments, even I have had a few; meeting my wife for the first time, the birth of my children, hearing *This Charming Man* by the Smiths! Little was I to know as I slept that one of those moments was about to occur.

We stayed at a small Bed and Breakfast in Braithwaite. On arrival we were shown to our pleasant modest room and crashed out into deep sleep. Morning was revealed by sunlight flickering around the curtains, and the sound of an alarm that the previous resident had forgotten to switch off. Tired, but excited to have arrived and be on holiday, I pulled back the curtains. I now know that I was looking at Skiddaw, the fourth highest mountain in England at three thousand and fifty four feet. What a view, from Dodd up to Carl side, the summits of Skiddaw and Skiddaw Little Man, Lonscale Fell and Latrigg, all bathed in the red, orange, yellow and the brilliant white light of a glorious sunrise – it was stunning, it was beautiful, I was captivated, and what's more I couldn't wait to get out and about.

Today walking and the Lake District are a big part of my life. When I walk I feel relaxed and I feel content, perhaps it is some primitive desire to be free to roam wherever you want, without any constraints; to be at one with nature, to experience the elements, to feel the wind on your face, to breathe the air and to feel alive. The Lake District is also a vital component in my love of walking. Since my first trip I have visited many other prime walking and climbing areas, but there is something about the Lake District that makes it, for me at least, the best place in the world. I think it's the range of landscapes in a relatively small area, the fact that you can gaze up at the heights and still know that the summits are all achievable. I love the Alps, but the scale is daunting, somehow the Lake District is the right size.

Any journey to the Lakes is no longer filled with trepidation, but with longing, longing to arrive, to walk, to experience the sheer joy of being immersed in the landscape. I usually visit the Lake District a few times a year, and although it's still a long drive, as I presently live in Devon, I always get excited on the journey up the M6. I always get a real buzz as the first mountains come into view, and I am always thinking about when I can return as I leave.

So what is it about the Lake District that can bring forth such strong emotions? The Lake District, or Lakes, or Lakeland, is 885 square miles of mountains, valleys and lakes. It lies entirely within Cumbria, shared historically by the counties of Cumberland, Westmorland and Lancashire; it is one of England's few mountainous regions. All the land in England over three thousand feet lies within the National Park, including Scafell Pike, the highest mountain in England. The sheer variety of scenery is truly impressive; ice-carved, wide U-shaped valleys, many of which are now filled with the lakes which give the area its name. These lakes include the deepest and longest lakes in England. The upper regions contain glacial cirques or hollows and they are typically filled with tarns. The higher fells are rocky, with lower fells being open moorland covered with bracken and heather. Below the tree line, native oak woodlands sit alongside pine plantations. The Lakes also feature picturesque towns and villages, a rich history, a unique culture, and warm and friendly people. What's not to love?

Now what do I love apart from walking and the Lake District, well my family. It sounds obvious, but talk to people, it isn't always the case. I first met my wife after I had discovered the Lake District, but I was very fortunate. Some might say that I was fortunate to find someone full stop, but I was fortunate in many ways. Tania loved walking and the Lake District and me. Not a bad combination.

We first visited the Lake District together not long after we met. I remember climbing Helvellyn via striding edge, although in a spirit of true gallantry I also remember abandoning Tania and summiting the mountain on my own. We spent a very wet week in Ambleside for our honeymoon in 1994, and spent a beautiful wintry, white Christmas in Little Langdale in 1995. Our family grew, William arrived in 1997 and Tom in 1999. Living so far away from the Lake District meant that but for an excursion on a fieldtrip in 1998 (I forgot to mention that I became a Geography teacher, but don't say I look like one!), we were unable to visit the Lake District for a fairly long period. I didn't want to visit and not be able to walk anywhere, money was tight and options were limited. What I did want to do was take the boys to the Lakes when they would be old enough to do some walks themselves.

We returned with the boys in autumn 2004 and had a fantastic holiday, and we have kept returning with an ever increasing frequency. As the boys have got older, the walks have got longer, higher and more adventurous. Before we knew it we had completed several summits together. The boys managed to climb Scafell Pike and Coniston Old Man at a fairly tender age, and we got to thinking about what our next challenge would be. Now I love the Lake District, but when I thought about it I hadn't really covered much of the area. I think you tend to fall back on places you are familiar with and concentrate on well known and famous summits. Tania and I put our heads together, what should we do next? What could be our next challenge as a family? It seemed all too obvious; we should try and climb all the Wainwrights, all 214 summits featured in *Wainwright's Pictorial Guides*. It would make us explore the whole of the Lake District, it would allow us to see and experience old, new and hidden places that we would otherwise not visit, and it would be a great achievement that we could complete as a family.

The fact that I have already written a few hundred words about the Lake District, and that this is the first time I have mentioned Wainwright, is unbelievable. Wainwright and the Lakes are forever interlinked. I first became aware of Wainwright when I first visited the Lake District. Despite my ill fitting boots and suspect clothing, I did manage to climb Scafell Pike and Helvellyn. I was very impressed with myself; as mentioned before I was not a walker, I didn't think I liked walking that much, I was unfit and the only thing I had on my side was youth. Walking around Keswick I was looking for a souvenir of the trip, and that's when I came across Wainwright's glorious *Pictorial guides.* I stood in a bookshop and devoured Wainrights chapter on Helvellyn in *The Eastern Fells.* Like thousands of others I was captivated by the exquisite look of the *Pictorial Guides*, the combination of sketches, hand drawn maps and a very precise and personalised account of the fells. As I read the chapter on Helvyllyn, I also relived the experience of the walk. Wainwright lovingly produced the books for the days when he would no longer be able to climb the fells. His plan for himself has been a gift to us all. I relived the very footsteps of the walk, saw the views again and experienced all the joys and sense of achievement of the actual walk. *A Pictorial Guide to the Lakeland fells, Book 1, the Eastern Fells*, became my souvenir. In-between my first and second visit to the Lake District, I read it over and over again, to keep my memories alive and to whet the anticipation of a return.

At this stage I must tell you a strange story about that first visit to The Lake District. Despite a frankly rubbish pair of boots and suspect clothing, I did possess an OS map and a compass, and consequently as a geographer didn't once doubt that I would be able to successfully navigate myself around the Lake District. Even the summit of the highest mountain would not be an issue. Imagine my surprise; it was genuine, despite that fact that I have little real sense of direction and always seem to get lost; when not far from the summit of Scafell Pike, the mist came down and I couldn't work out where the summit was. I now know that I was somewhere on Lingmell Col. I was completely confused about which direction to take, so I thought I would ask someone. I spotted a solitary figure, sitting, sheltering between some boulders. As I approached, a large group of walkers descended out of the mist from what I now know to be the summit of Scafell Pike. Before I had said anything the man spoke to me, "Look at them" he said. "The noise, the colour, bright red jackets, they shouldn't be allowed on the fells, people should respect the fells, they should blend in". He was obviously not happy about the situation, I reviewed my situation. I was lost or at least as I like to put it, temporarily unaware of my exact location, and I was going to ask this somewhat grumpy man the way to the top of a massive landmark, the highest mountain in England. He would think I was an idiot! He was however extremely pleasant and polite, he knew where I should be heading; he didn't make me feel like an idiot and wished me well.

At this time I didn't know who Wainwright was or what Wainwright looked like, now I do and this man was the spitting image. Was it the great man? Well possibly. What an encounter, my first mountain and I think I could have met the person most closely associated with walking in the Lakes. If it had been two days later I would have known much more about Wainwright, I had seen his picture by then and I would have instantly recognised him. I don't know what I would have done or said differently, but I could at least have shaken him by the hand and thanked him for his wonderful legacy. I would have been absolutely delighted, but I'm not so sure he would have been.

A family challenge, the Wainwrights! You may well be thinking, "What say do the boys have?" Do they really want to spend days walking in the cold and the rain and the wind? Well I know that some people won't believe me, but the boys really like walking. They enjoy the challenge, and if they didn't the experience wouldn't be the same. Mind you, to give a little incentive, not that it was needed; we promised the boys a pound a summit!

FALSE START
October 2004

The first fell we climbed as a family was before we had any idea or plan that we would climb all the Wainwrights, the first Wainwright we climbed was also not a Wainwright! Confused? So was I after the walk when I checked my facts. However I am a little ahead of myself.

The first time we visited the lakes as a family was in October 2004, and we spent a week in Kendal. The holiday in Kendal was the result of a house swap. House swapping isn't for everyone, but as a family we have had nothing but positive experiences. House swapping basically involves swapping a house with almost total strangers. Now I think about it, it's a bit of a scary idea. A colleague at work had told me about this as an option for holidays, and a week in a caravan in Ilfacombe, convinced myself and Tania that we needed to find an alternative, but equally an inexpensive type of holiday. The idea is that you register on line and contact like-minded people. You write to people in houses and areas that you would like to visit, people write to you, and if you find someone who wants to stay in your house, and you in their house, you have a holiday with no accommodation costs. Now it's sounding like a good idea again.

We have travelled to some fantastic places doing house swaps, staying in amazing houses in the UK and abroad. Apart from the free accommodation, you have a whole house to yourself, no need to be living on top of each other; you get to stay in areas away from the crowds, and we have met and stayed in touch with some really lovely and interesting people. When the children were really young we always tried to swap with people who had children of a similar age, our boys would then have lots of toys to play with when they started their holidays. We have visited Canada, The USA, Germany, France and Italy; we have also stayed in the Lakes, the Cotswolds and numerous other locations in the UK. Our house and often our cat and car, have always been really well looked after. In lots of ways I feel happier knowing that someone is in our house and looking after it, than I would be if the house was left empty for weeks on end.

The house in Kendal was lovely; it had originally been two houses and still retained two separate staircases. William got to choose his bedroom before Tom, and he was very excited about having a TV in his room - such indulgences were not allowed at home! The house was located a few minutes away from the high street in Kendal, and a few hundred yards away from the delightful Brewery Arts Centre. The house was on a slightly elevated position, and had great views towards Kendal castle.

Kendal is often seen as the Southern gateway to the Lake District, being only around nine miles from Windermere and around thirty miles from Keswick. The other lakes are all within an hour or two's travelling by car from the town, as are locations for a variety of walks and rambles. Kendal's most famous export must be Kendal Mint Cake, a favourite for walks with the boys. The boys are in good company. Joseph Wiper came up with the original recipe, and it was used by Edmund Hilary and his team on the first successful conquest of Everest in 1953. Hilary said that it was the teams' favourite high altitude ration. Kendal was also the home to Wainwright, where he worked at the Borough Treasurer's office.

The boys had been walking on Dartmoor, but this was their first real walking holiday. We spent the first morning kitting them out in their own brand new walking boots. They looked pleased as punch, standing proud in all their gear, ready to walk. For our first visit to the Lakes with the boys, we are really indebted to Nick Lambert and his excellent book *South Lakeland walks with children*. The walks vary between about two and six miles, and they are all accurately described in fantastic detail. The descriptions include notes, and interesting facts and features for children to spot on route. We completed several of these walks, but our absolute favourite was Elterwater, the Forces and Little Langdale.

Although I love being up in the mountains, some of the best views are to be had from low level walks, looking up at the imposing heights. This walk started from the centre of Elterwater and passed through some of the most attractive countryside in the Lakes. The walk starts by taking you towards Little Langdale, with views up towards Lingmoor Fell. We stopped and had a great lunch at the Three Shires Inn in Little Langdale, a pub in which Tania and I spent Christmas Eve on our first winter expedition to the Lakes. I remember it being really snowy and icy, and consequently slipping and sliding my way to the pub that winter, which makes a change from slipping and sliding on the way home! The walk continued through grassy field and oak woodlands, until the sound of a waterfall came into hearing. This would have been Colwith Force, then it was on again to the very impressive Skelwith Force; it carries more water than any other waterfall in the lakes. The walk continues to Elterwater, the smallest of the sixteen lakes of the Lake District. Eltewater means 'the lake of the swans', and as we arrived with the sun setting, two swans swan into view; the sunset, the swans and the Langdale Pikes in the background, you would be hard pressed to find a more wonderful or beautiful view. It was a magical moment! Neither of the boys had ever walked so far before, about six miles, but they both loved it. Consequently, we thought they were ready to attempt their first Wainwright. Thanks Mr. Lambert!

Saturday 30th October 2004

Wansfell Pike

Height: 1588 feet (486m)
Route: Troutbeck via Nanny Lane

I don't know who made the mistake – it was probably me, but the idea was to see if the boys could cope with climbing a fell. We checked Wainwright, decided to climb Wansfell, and then promptly planned a route to the top of Wansfell Pike. It was the last day of our first family holiday to the Lakes, the weather was crisp and clear. We parked in

Troutbeck and took a public foot path that runs up a narrow rocky lane (Nanny Lane). The first short stretch runs due west up a hill. After the initial straight climb, the lane swings right and then left, we followed this lane as it ran between two stone walls. Using a ladder stile to cross the wall, we continued to head towards the summit of Wansfell Pike. We need not have worried about the boys, our initial fears were unfounded as Will and Tom made easy work of all one thousand, five hundred and eighty eight feet of the Fell. Tania and I found it hard to stop the boys running off as the summit came into view and they raced each other to the top. From the summit there were glorious views down into Lake Windermere and beyond. Many people regard Wansfell Pike as the true summit, because of its superior views. But unfortunately for us it is not the true summit, being lower than Wansfell by about twenty feet. William was seven years old, Tom was only five (and nine days), and they had both climbed their first Fell. We descended the same way we walked up the Fell, and headed for 'The Mortal Man' for lunch. Fantastic pint and steak sandwich by the way! For a long time, more than I care to admit, we thought of Wansfell Pike as our first Wainwright. But, one thing you can't do when completing a challenge is cheat. It was a great walk and a really memorable day, but in all honesty it can't count as our first Wainwright.

THE WAINWRIGHTS
April 2007

I can vouch for the fact that waiting does heighten expectation. After a gap of two and half years, we belatedly, but excitedly returned to the Lake District. I couldn't wait to see the mountains again, and Tania and I were looking forward to showing the boys some of our favourite places, both high and low.

This holiday was another house swap and we stayed in Kendal once again. The house was in a similar location to the previous one, close to the Brewery Arts Centre. It was an interesting house, spacious and full of old world charm, but not the cleanest place we have ever stayed in. In some places the dust was so thick it was taking on fell like proportions! We did however have the same delightful view over Kendal, towards the ruins of Kendal Castle.

We still had no fixed plans to complete all the Wainwrights, but decided that after the success of Wansfell Pike, we would tackle one of our favourite areas - the Langdale Pikes. We decided on two objectives, Pavey Ark and Harrison Stickle. Tania and I had both climbed these fells in the past, and in a variety of different weather conditions. I have climbed up Mill Gill in heavy rain and hail, I have climbed up whilst being blasted by freezing winds, and I've climbed up when there's been ice on the ground. Fortunately, the day we chose was a sunny and warm Easter Saturday.

Saturday 7th April 2007

1. Pavey Ark

Height: 2297 feet (700m)
Route: New Dungeon Ghyll Hotel via Mill Gill

The main face of Pavey Ark is over a quarter of a mile across and drops about four hundred feet. However, although Pavey Ark is the largest cliff in the Langdales, it faces east over Stickle Tarn and therefore appears less impressive from the Langdale valley. Towards the south-west it merges into the crags of Harrison Stickle, while the northern end descends into the valley of Bright Beck. We decided to climb Pavey Ark from the New Dungeon Ghyll Hotel. The sunny weather and the fact that it was Easter Saturday had brought out a lot of walkers. Whilst it is fantastic to be the only people climbing a particular fell, I think it is a little bit selfish to moan about large numbers of walkers out on a particular fell on a particular day. I love walking, but I'm not arrogant enough to think the Lake District should be set aside for my personal use. In my experience the vast majority of walkers are friendly and likeminded souls. We followed the crowds, and followed the route up Mill Gill to Stickle Tarn. Tom and I reached Stickle Tarn first; Tania and William were yet to find their walking legs. Stickle Tarn has been dammed to create some additional capacity. The stone faced dam is low enough not to spoil the character of the pool, and the water is used for public consumption in the hotels and homes below. The ridge of the dam also provided a lovely place to sit and relax after the exertions of the first climb of the day. Tom and I had a well earned drink at the Tarn, and looked at Jack's Rake on the precipitous edge of Pavey Ark.

Jack's Rake is perhaps the most famous way to ascend Pavey Ark. It is classified as a Grade 1 scramble, but it is said to be within the capability of many walkers; though it looks as if it requires a serious head for heights. I wouldn't like to attempt it in bad weather, who am I kidding? I'm not sure I would like to attempt it in any weather! The rake follows a natural groove in the cliff face and it can be clearly seen from Stickle Tarn. Wainwright wrote that for fellwalkers, Jack's Rake is "difficult and awkward", although there is "curiously little sense of exposure, for a comforting parapet of rock accompanies all the steeper parts of the ascent". Tom and I were not convinced! Eventually joined by Will and Tania, we walked to the very eastern end of the cliff, and then walked west over the top of the East Buttress. This path, following North Rake is a much less exposed and strenuous route, although it did involve some scrambling.

The summit, our first official Wainwright, provided a special moment for all of us. The boys were justifiably proud of themselves, and we were rewarded with some glorious views towards the Eastern and Southern fells. After a short rest and lunch with a view, we headed on towards Harrison Stickle, highest of the Langdale Pikes.

2. Harrison Stickle

Height: 2415 feet (736m)
Route: Ridge route from Pavey Ark – descent into Mickleden valley

The Langdales must be one of the most recognizable views in the whole of Lakeland, and it's the distinctive summit of Harrison Stickle that does much to give the Langdales their character. A clear path leads from the summit of Pavey Ark, roughly south-west to the Summit of Harrison Stickle. It took only a short time to reach our second summit, and what a summit, it is truly spectacular. We had glorious views to Stickle Tarn, the summit of Pike of Stickle, and all along the Langdale valley. After consulting Wainwright, we could also make out Bowfell and Crinkle Crags. The view from the summit is as good as the view of it, what a combination; Harrison Stickle really is a personal favourite.

After a fairly straightforward descent, I rewarded myself with a lovely pint at the New Dungeon Ghyll Hotel. I remember that marvellous feeling of total satisfaction brought about by a lovely walk, great weather, great company and good beer!

Wednesday 11th April 2007

3. Old Man of Coniston

Height: 2634 feet (803m)
Route: Walna road car park – descent via the slate mines

The next objective was another favourite; The Old Man of Coniston. This would be the boy's highest fell yet at two thousand, six hundred and thirty four feet. We wanted to challenge the boys a bit after Pavey Ark and Harrison Stickle, but at the same time we wanted a relatively easy climb. The Old Man fitted the bill perfectly, or so we thought! The Old Man of Coniston has always been considered to be the highest point on the Coniston Fells; that is until relatively recently. Wainwright certainly stakes the claim for the Old Man, but recent surveying would appear to favour its northern neighbour, Swirl How. If we accept Wainwright, and who are we not to? – Then the Old Man is the twelfth highest mountain in England.

The weather was good and we started the walk from Walna Road car park. In theory, the ascent should have been easy and clear cut, no chance of getting it wrong, 'going off' in the wrong direction or anything stupid like that. Now I admire Wainwright for describing so many different ascents of mountains, but we found a new route on the slopes of the Old Man. Everything started really well, and we were all in high spirits until I decided that it was time we actually started heading up the mountain. What appeared to look initially like a path, soon disappeared, and we were reduced to scrambling up some really steep slopes. Tania was a bit panicky, rightly so! I scouted ahead and attempted to keep everyone positive by basically lying about the upcoming continued difficulty of the climb, and the distance left to complete.

We do all love walking, but I would be lying now if I said that we didn't ever have family disagreements whilst walking. Unfortunately, almost all these brief occurrences are due to my poor navigational skills. I'm not sure what I would call this new ascent, perhaps the divorce court route, but I know I wouldn't do it again. We did reach the summit safely, and what a summit. I love the slate platform and distinctive cairn. The views from the summit were fantastic and all family disagreements were forgotten. The views took in much of the southern Lake District, Morecambe Bay, Blackpool Tower and the Isle of Man.

Thankfully, we returned by a different route, descending via the slate mines path – commonly referred to as the tourist route. Wainwright really doesn't rate this route, and whilst I can understand his view, I think that the old workings whilst not in any way beautiful add a sense of history and interest to the walk. The scars of mining are everywhere to be seen. The Coniston fells were mined for Copper in the middle of the nineteenth century. The veins of copper were hidden thousands of feet below the fells, and as a result the miners had to work in extremely hard and horrendous conditions. The mines went into decline in the late nineteenth century and were then abandoned. The machinery and buildings lie in a state of dereliction today, but I think they are an amazing feature of the landscape. It has also got to be remembered that Coniston owes its existence to the copper mines, not to walkers. These are real landscapes, with a very real history. We completed the walk with a really welcome drink at the lovely Sun Inn. All arguments were forgotten as we basked in the glory of a memorable day out.

This was the final summit of our 2007 holiday in Kendal. We had completed three Wainwrights, but we had also completed a number of low level walks – the most memorable of which was probably a walk from Kentmere to Troutbeck along the Garburn Pass. The Garburn Pass is a very old rocky road that has been closed to vehicles for a number of years. In places the Pass has been worn down to bed rock, it's extremely uneven and today is completely unsuitable for cars. Imagine our surprise, when we heard and then saw a Range Rover bumping along the Pass towards us. Initially I thought it must be a National Park vehicle of some description. The car was moving really slowly, and I noticed that walking next to the car was a lady in fluffy pink slippers. She didn't seem to be very happy with the driver and a fairly major altercation was taking place. The cause of the argument became quickly apparent, because the argument was so loud. The driver had just bought the car in Blackburn; he had decided to take his family for a spin, and his wife, thinking they were off for only a few minutes, jumped in the passenger seat complete with aforementioned slippers. Now in fear of the car toppling over on the Pass, she had decided to walk for it. They had two children with them;

they alternated between looking amused and terrified. The family drew a fairly large crowd in a short period of time. There was much discussion as to the relative merits of going forward or back, or staying put. I'm not sure how things were eventually resolved, but I presume all was well; it didn't make the local news anyway!

STANDING TALL
April 2008

House swaps are a great way to holiday, but you can't always find the right place to stay. We looked into the idea of another house swap for our Easter 2008 visit to the Lake District. We wanted to stay in or close to Keswick, but we had little success finding anywhere suitable. Forced into actually parting with some cash, we rented an apartment in Thornthwaite.

Situated just of the A66 to the south of Bassenthwaite, Thornthwaite offers the same fabulous, revelatory views towards Skiddaw, that I saw on my first ever visit to the Lakes. This visit, the view was if anything even more spectacular. Snow was lying above the two thousand foot contour and the mountain looked more majestic than ever. The apartment was fairly small, but absolutely lovely inside. We had already planned that our first walk would be Wainwright's favourite summit; Haystacks. Neither Tania nor I had ever climbed Haystacks before, and we were both really looking forward to the walk.

Saturday 13th April 2008

4. Haystacks

Height: 1959 feet (597m)
Route: Ascent from Gatesgarth via Warnscale and Innominate Tarn – descent via Scarth Gap

I went for a run in the morning before the walk, and only mention this because I had to climb Haystacks twice! Nice weather, overcast but dry, we started walking with all the energy and the enthusiasm of the first walk of a holiday. We reached Scarth Gap and stopped to take some pictures. It was at this point that Tom realized that he had left his camera at the foot of the mountain. This led to a hasty descent by me, and then an attempt to fell run back up the mountain. I soon realized that this was not an option. Tom and camera eventually reunited, we walked to Innominate Tarn; here we spent some time thinking about Wainwright's final resting place. Although Wainwright's favourite summit, he neglected to name the fell as a whole in his "best half-dozen", his reason – inferior height. But Wainwright does state that "for beauty variety and interesting detail, for sheer fascination and unique individuality, the summit of Haystacks is supreme. This is the best fell-top of all". Wainwright's ashes were scattered here by his wife Betty, near the shores of Innominate Tarn. We checked our boots carefully before we continued to the summit.

The summit sits on a short rocky spine; both ends of the spine have cairns, that at the northern end is the accepted summit. We agreed with Wainwright, a truly wonderful place to be. Tom, impressed with *Wainwright's Pictorial Guides*, spent some time sketching the view. The view is excellent and Tom had much to inspire him. We enjoyed fantastic views to Great Gable and down to Buttermere. The boys proved to be even better at descent than ascent; we genuinely could not keep up with them. They raced on ahead, laughing, joking, and generally chuffed to bits with themselves. We all met up by the shore at Buttermere, and rounded off the walk with an ice cream at Gatesgarth. Missed my pint!

We were overjoyed by the boys ability to walk and climb everything we had thrown at them so far, so we decided that it was time to tackle one of Lakeland's four peaks over three thousand feet. The fact that Skiddaw loomed large from the apartments sitting room window, combined with the fact that Skiddaw is the easiest of the four, three thousand footers to climb, made our second destination of the holiday an easy choice. Skiddaw rises to three thousand and thirty four feet; it is the fourth highest mountain in England. It dominates the skyline in the northern fells, but it features a relatively straightforward well-trodden tourist path from Gale road car park.

I had climbed the mountain before. On my thirtieth birthday I had set out armed with a bottle of bubbly in my rucksack. That day had been cold but bright, with a scattering of snow up high. We set out in similar weather conditions, although it was ominously a little more overcast. As soon as we stepped out of the car, you could feel the cold wind biting.

"It's freezing Dad" said Tom, William agreed, I should have listened.

We wrapped up as well as we could, complete with newly purchased snoods. The direct route from the car park is up the steep slopes of Jenkin Hill. It's hard going but you gain height quickly. Despite taking some short breaks to admire the scenery, we made good progress.

We soon saw the snow line approaching, and although a little cold, we were suitably attired and looked forward to sinking our boots into the pristine covering. At first we all thought the snow was great. I still, somewhat sadly perhaps, find it hard not to get excited about snow; we seem to see snow far less frequently than I remember from my childhood. As soon as the covering of snow grew thick enough, some idiot (me) started a snowball fight! Whilst lots of fun, the downside was that snow got into our jackets, gloves got wet and we all got a little colder.

We climbed onwards and upwards. As we approached Skiddaw Little Man, the sky became really black and the first snow of the day started falling. I know I should have been more responsible, but I don't like giving up on a walk and we were all wrapped up warmly, so we kept heading towards the summit. As we started our final climb, the snow picked up, the wind picked up, and we found ourselves in blizzard conditions. It got so bad at times that I had my first ever experience of a total white out. Now we were cold and finding navigation difficult. I hadn't thought for a single moment that we would face problems on Skiddaw, but we did. Tom got really cold, he didn't look at all happy. We made it to South Top, but it was all getting a bit too much. I tried (valiantly I think!) to cheer everyone up by forming some snow angels, but I just got colder, and the frowns just deepened. Only a few hundred feet from the true summit, we retreated back down the mountain.

Just as we descended below the point at which the snow had started on the way up, the snow stopped. From this point onwards the weather got warmer and brighter, and we had to stop to remove layers of clothing. When we reached the car park the summit was clear and bathed in sunshine. The weather really can change that quickly! Tania and I couldn't bring ourselves to tell William and Tom that they hadn't reached the true summit; they would have been devastated.

The day's failings made Tania and I all the more determined to complete another 'three thousand footer' before the end of the holiday. We were also determined to return and climb Skiddaw another day.

I should have listened to Tom!

Wednesday 16th April 2008

5. Scafell Pike

Height: 3210 feet (978m)
Route: Seathwaite via Stockley Bridge and Esk Hause – descent via the Corridor route and Sty Head Tarn

Frustrated by the walk on Skiddaw, we planned to climb Scafell Pike. Fully aware of the fact that we shouldn't make the same mistakes as we had on Skiddaw, we watched the weather forecasts carefully. We wanted to wait for perfect climbing conditions, but anyone who has ever walked anywhere, will be all too aware that perfect conditions never exist! Despite this fact, we planned optimistically. We also made sure of our route by using a GPS for the first time in conjunction with our trusted OS maps.

The first time I climbed the mountain, I walked from Seathwaite Farm via the corridor route to the summit. I returned hobbling (due to those boots!), via Esk Hause and Grains Gill. This time we decided to reverse the route, as Wainwright says this is the finest approach of all. We knew this would be a challenge for the boys, so realising that they were both a bit deflated after Skiddaw, we decided to give them an incentive. William and

Tom had spent a lot of time drooling over Swiss army knives in George Fishers, so a Swiss army knife each was to be their reward if they could climb to the highest point in England. A minor aside here, but George Fishers! What a delight. Situated in Keswick, along with Gaynors in Ambleside, these are definitely two of my favourite places to browse and shop. As a student I could spend hours looking through record shops, trying to find hidden gems by obscure bands. Nowadays I can spend hours looking at all the latest walking kit. Sad but true.

Scafell Pike is a long day's walk, so we set out early in the morning and parked close to Seathwaite Farm. Seathwaite is reputed to be the wettest place in England, receiving around one hundred and forty inches of rain per year. Between the 19th and the 20th of November 2009 – Seathwaite was to receive over twelve inches of rain in a twenty four hour period, a record for any place in the UK. The day we walked was cold but dry, it started brightly, but there was some cloud cover. We set off heading towards Stockley Bridge, full of excitement and resolve. Stockley Bridge is an old pack horse bridge, ancient and beautiful, an ideal photo opportunity. We continued walking along Grains Gill, towards the impressive cliffs of Great End. The cliffs dominate this line of approach. Snow lay on the ground above two thousand feet, and although the wind was growing in strength, we didn't suffer any of the problems that we had encountered on Skiddaw.

Our arrival at Esk Hause prompted some back slapping and self congratulation. Esk Hause is a mountain pass, where paths from Borrowdale, Eskdale, Langdale and Wasdale all meet. Here the gradient evens out, and for a while at least we could walk without puffing and panting. Relative rest however was only temporary, and we started to climb over the watershed towards Ill Crag. Bypassing the actual summit of Ill Crag, the route became uneven; the area being strewn with large boulders. Fortunately at this point the final summit came into view and provided a final incentive for our tired legs. In actual fact there was so much compressed snow between the boulders, that it made walking easier than I remembered. The only real negative about this approach is that as you bypass the summit of Broad Crag, you realize that you are going to have to descend before the final climb to the summit of Scafell Pike.

The final ascent looked really steep, Tania looked really worried. We took our time, kicking our boots into the snow, and despite some anxious moments, we successfully reached the summit. What a fantastic walk, and what a fantastic sense of achievement for all of us. William and Tom never moaned on the way up, and they were both really 'up' for the challenge. The boys were really excited to stand on the summit and be the highest people in England! (So was I). After taking our turn on the summit and admiring the extensive views, we found an area for lunch and then indulged in another snow ball fight. Before you think too badly of us, we made sure that we wouldn't be affecting anybody else. Some people do get overly sensitive about the mountains, you have to protect them and be aware of other walkers, but hey! You don't have to walk around in a permanent state of reverence!

Now it was time for the descent. I vaguely remembered some scary bits about this route, but I kept these memories to myself. I actually thought that they couldn't be as bad as I remembered. We scrambled down from the summit, heading towards Lingmell Col (where I think I met Wainwright). This part of the walk was fine, but then we set off along the corridor route. I haven't seen anybody else express any worries about this route, but with vertical drops and a couple of scrambles over vertical drops, it was testing enough for us. Tania is somewhat afraid of heights, so at a couple of points I didn't think she would be able to cope, but not wanting to stress out the boys, she coped magnificently. We stopped for a snack and a breather at the very picturesque Sty Head Tarn, and then made our way back to Stockley Bridge and the car at Seathwaite.

"So ends the greatest fell walk of them all" said Wainwright, we all agreed.

THE CHALLENGE
April 2009

After our successful conquest of Scafell Pike, we knew that the boys would be able to climb just about anything. It was at this point that we decided to try and complete all the Wainwrights. As mentioned previously, we thought that this would give us all a goal; we needed another source of inspiration after Scafell Pike, and we thought that the challenge would enable and encourage us to discover new areas of the Lakes.

The planning for this holiday had started on the way home from the previous one. We thought about all the walks we wanted to complete and where we would like to stay. After some deliberation, we decided to stay near Keswick again. We booked an apartment in the Old Swan Hotel at Thornthwaite, near Braithwaite. However, to maximize our time in the Lakes, we decided to come up a night early. We stopped in Penrith that first night, but despite all our careful planning we had neglected to plan a walk in the surrounding Eastern Fells. With little real knowledge of this area, we made a fairly uninformed decision to climb Gowbarrow Fell.

Saturday 11th April 2009

6. Gowbarrow Fell

Height: 1579 feet (481m)
Route: Path from Brow foot to Aira Force – descent via Green Hill back to Aira Force

Apparently, Gowbarrow is one of the best known of Lakelands lesser heights, but I had never heard of it. The popularity of the Fell, which we could see was never in doubt when we arrived at the busy National Trust car park, has much to do with Aira Force. Two waterfalls, High Force and Aira Force, see Aira Beck drop over two hundred feet. Aira Force has two stone bridges at the head and foot, making it one of the most photogenic sites in the Lake District. It was at Gowbarrow that Dorothy Wordsworth noticed daffodils growing, presumably she had seen some before, but this time she wrote in her journal – "When we were in the woods beyond Gowbarrow Park we saw a few daffodils close to the water side." It was a record that later inspired William Wordsworth to write one of his most famous poems.

We started walking from the National Trust car park, and we soon reached the very impressive falls. Taking numerous photos, we were pleased that our plan to climb all the Wainwrights had already brought us to a beautiful, previously unvisited part of the Lake District. We headed to the summit via Yew Crag. The climb was really wet underfoot, but the slightly drier top provided terrific views over Ullswater. We descended over Green Hill, this proved to be the boggiest ground yet encountered. Perhaps it was too boggy. Tom pushed me while I was off balance (honest!) and I became one with the bog!

Returning to the car, and sitting on newspaper, we headed onto to the newly named Swan House. We were delighted to discover that Swan House provided great views towards Skiddaw and Barf. The Bishop of Barf was clearly visible, but more about the Bishop later.

Sunday 12th April 2009 (Easter Sunday)

7. Grisedale Pike (The Coledale Round)

Height: 2593 feet (791m)
Route: Ascent from Braithwaite

We woke to clear skies and really warm weather. We had already decided that if the weather was good we would try to complete the Coledale Round. The one thing that we hadn't really done with the boys yet was a Round. The Plan was to climb not just Grisedale Pike, but Hopegill Head, Eel Crag, Sail, Outerside and Barrow.

We drove and parked in Braithwaite, and then started the relentless climb towards Grisedale Pike. The hard work starts almost at once, and it wasn't long before we all felt really hot. The amazing April weather meant that lots of people were out walking. One couple asked the boys if they would rather be at home eating Easter eggs. To their credit, they said they would rather be walking. A proud dad moment!

Grisedale Pike presents a striking appearance when viewed from Braithwaite, rising to a near perfect pyramidal peak. It has the nickname "The Matterhorn of Lakeland". That's probably why the final stretch to the summit is so steep, rocky and 'scrambly'. The clear skies meant that the views from the top were extensive and breathtaking; all the way to the coastal plain and the Solway Firth. We stopped long enough to catch our breath, cool down and appreciate the majestic scene, and then it was on towards Hopegill Head.

8. Hopegill Head

Height: 2525 feet (770m)
Route: Ridge from Grisedale Pike

We resumed walking and headed down an easy ridge to a slight depression, and then started a steady climb to our second summit of the day. The summit is an exhilarating place – a small pointed peak poised on the edge of Hobcarton Crag, giving wide ranging views. We thought we could make out the Isle of Man, the Scottish Border Hills and Helvellyn to the east. The summit was fairly busy; we stopped for a bite to eat and a lovely Border collie nearly made off with Will's cake! We then left the summit, descending, before climbing over Sand Hill; we idly thought that this could and should have been a separate fell. The great weather continued and I was struck by the fact that even on the summits the air was perfectly still. Walking weather doesn't get any better than this!

9. Eel Crag

Height: 2749 feet (839m)
Route: From Coledale Hause

After descending the other side of Sand Hill, which is so steep it's actually quite tricky; we climbed up a grassy slope towards the summit of Eel Crag. The summit bears an Ordnance Survey triangulation pillar, set on a stony plateau. It almost goes without saying that the views were fantastic; all of the major fell groups could be seen, with the Scafells being particularly fine. The only direction with limited views was west, with Grasmoor blocking the panorama a little. Tom was placed on the triangulation pillar and posed for a great photo. He got slightly miffed when I jokingly forgot to lift him down!

10. Sail

Height: 2530 feet (773m)
Route: Descending ridge from Eel Crag

From the summit cairn of Eel crag, an arête runs sharply down eastwards towards Sail. The descending ridge is steep, narrow and rocky. The route also has the added spice of sheer drops and scrambles. We were really careful with the boys, telling them to concentrate and to go slowly and carefully. Our advice wasn't helped by a completely 'out of control' boy behind us. He was very inadvisably running and jumping down the ridge, kicking loose rocks and stones towards us. His parents had no sense and no control. We cautiously let him pass and watched his continued progress with interest – we hoped he wouldn't fall off the mountain!

11. Outerside

Height: 1863 feet (568m)
Route: Via Sail Pass

The route from Sail follows an old cobalt mine route, the track was nice and easy after the ridge to Sail, and we were alone for the first time. Now, I like to meet other walkers, and on a glorious Easter Sunday you can hardly expect to have the Fells to yourself, but after the busy summits and the frankly 'mad boy', we were ready for some peace and quiet. The summit, though relatively lowly, was fantastic. We had amazing views of the route that we had walked, and we had the summit to ourselves. I remember thinking 'This is why I love walking' – the peace, the tranquility, being with my family. It was one of those special moments when everything seems just right. I still remember the summit, my feelings, everything, clearly to this day.

12. Barrow

Height: 1494 feet (455m)
Route: Ridge from Outerside

My positive mood continued as we walked towards Barrow. Following a pleasant path down to Low Moss and Barrow Door, we then followed a rising track towards the summit. Although again modest in height, we were blessed with terrific views; the vales of Keswick and Newlands provided a lovely spectacle. A small cairn on grass marks the summit. We could see the surrounding North Western Fells, together with the Helvellyn range across Derwentwater, and Skiddaw.

We all felt a real sense of achievement; this was after all, peak number six of the day. In total we had walked nine miles and we had climbed four thousand, six hundred feet of ascent. The boys had done remarkably well. We made the most of our last high place of the day, and then followed a winding route with great views back down towards Braithwaite. We stopped off to visit the Royal Oak, and I had one of the best pints I have ever had in my life – I had been dreaming about it for miles! We also enjoyed some perfect post walking food in the really friendly and lively pub – giant Yorkshire puddings filled with lamb and black pudding. We all felt shattered, but happily shattered. I remember thinking that this was the best day's walking I had ever had.

Monday 13th April 2009

13. Great Gable

Height: 2949 feet (899m)
Route: Honister slate mines – Moses Trod – Stone Cove – Beck Head – Summit – decent via Windy Gap to Green Gable

The weather was still good on Monday morning, but the forecast for the rest of the week was less than inspiring. Consequently, we decided to attempt another big walk, despite our tired legs. Great Gable lies at the very heart of the Lake District, appearing as a pyramid from Wasdale, and as a massive dome from most other directions. Great Gable looks like a real mountain should. All too often these days we say things are great for no obvious reason, but Great Gable lives up to its name. The distinctive summit is a real magnet for walkers and mountaineers; it commands the area and looks mighty impressive.

We decided to walk to Great Gable, but we also planned to visit Green Gable, Brandreth and Grey Knotts. In total an ascent of two thousand, three hundred and fifty feet, and a total distance of about six miles. We started the walk from the Honister Pass. The area around the car park is very industrial. We walked past the slate quarry and shop, and made a note to visit on the way back. The early easy path took us from Drum House along the western flanks of Grey Knotts, towards the Brandreth fence. There are glorious views to be had of Haystacks and High Stile, but due to poor map reading and poor mountain recognition (I thought the wrong summit was Great Gable) we got slightly confused, and we didn't really know what we were looking at. The path from Drum House was originally used to move slate by man-handled sledges, and is now referred to as Moses Trod. Moses was either an illegal whiskey producer, making whiskey from bog water, or an urban (should that be rural) myth. Moses Trod takes you on towards Great Gable, and when the true object of our walk became obvious, even to me, we really started to enjoy the approach.

As we walked under the huge cliffs of Gable Crag, we all wondered how we would ever be able to reach the summit. The route to the top from Beck Head was by no means clear. After unsuccessfully looking for an obvious path, we chose a route where we happened to see some walkers descend. Wainwright describes the route as 'a steep and stony track'; well if we were on the appropriate track, I think the description was accurate, but understated. The scramble became a climb, and in places it was frighteningly steep. At various times I thought it couldn't be the real route, far too dangerous, but descent by this stage looked to be worse than going on. I told Tania and the boys to think about three points of contact, and we made our way slowly, carefully and nervously to the summit. Things were not helped when some passing walkers said the route was too difficult for the boys. By then it was too late, and the walkers' comments only served to panic us. However, we did make it, the summit was achieved and what a real achievement it was.

The summit of Great Gable is strewn with boulders, and the highest point is marked by a rock outcrop complete with a cairn. We eat a well-earned lunch and then explored the summit. There is a plaque set on the summit rock, commemorating those members of the Fell and Rock Climbing Club who died in the First World War. An annual memorial service is held here every Remembrance Sunday – I hope the congregation doesn't use our route! The views from the summit were spectacular. Due to its central position within the Lake District, all of the main fell groups are laid out, filling the skyline.

14. Green Gable

Height: 2603 feet (801m)
Route: Descent from Great Gable via Windy gap

We left the summit of Great Gable, and the steep descent seemed easy after our earlier climb. Some people were obviously struggling as they went up this route, but we now felt that we could achieve anything. The route down was really windy, the weather had started to change and the cloud was beginning to build. The only part of the walk to Green Gable that wasn't windy was Windy Gap! A short climb up from Windy Gap brought us to our second summit of the day.

Green Gable offered great views in all directions, especially impressive was the sight of Gable Crag, and the view into the Buttermere Valley.

15. Brandreth

Height: 2344 feet (715m)
Route: Ridge from Green Gable

The route from Green Gable was straightforward, and we soon reached Brandeth. The top of Brandreth was stony and fairly featureless, but it was another summit we had to ourselves. It was a good place to be after the bulk of the walk had already been completed. We were still filled with a sense of achievement, and we were happy to be chatting, walking and anticipating the rest of our holiday.

16. Grey Knotts

Height: 2287 feet (697m)
Route: Ridge route from Brandreth

The summit of Brandreth is marked by a cairn at the intersection of three fences, one of which points the way to the summit of Grey Knotts. The summit of Grey Knotts looks like a tor on Dartmoor. The whole area is quite attractive, with a series of small tors and a few small tarns. We had a snack and a drink overlooking one of these small tarns, and then took a final look at all the captivating views. The walk back to the car should have been simple enough, but we lost the path and went cross country, or 'off road' as the boys like to put it. We eventually found our bearings, joined the Dubs Quarry path, and then returned to have a look around the Honister gift shop.

Tuesday 14th April 2009

17. Catbells

Height: 1481 feet (451m)
Route: Hawse End – Summit – Descent to Hawse Gate and Derwent Water

We were all really tired after two days of hard walking, but the weather still held so we thought we would keep going. We chose to complete an easier walk and then head into Keswick for a late lunch. We decided to climb Catbells, a low but popular fell. Catbells is situated on the western shore of Derwent Water, only about three miles from Keswick. It has a really distinctive shape, instantly recognizable. Wainwright acknowledged the popularity of Catbells among fellwalkers by saying: "It is one of the great favourites, a family fell where grandmothers and infants can climb the heights together". The fell's unusual name may well have come from a distortion of "Cat Bields", meaning shelter of the wild cat – although this is not certain. We didn't see any wild cats, they have long since disappeared from the Lakes. However, in the morning, I went for a run and saw a red squirrel. I had never seen one before so I was delighted. Smaller than the common grey squirrel, the reds are found in only a few areas of England. The grey basically 'out competes' the red squirrels, and it now appears to be policy in the Lakes to report sightings of grey squirrels so that they can be removed. How or where to? I don't really want to speculate.

We like most other people started to climb Catbells from Hawse End. We could tell it was going to be busy; it was difficult to park and as we approached the base of the fell we saw many others climbing up. We had been spoilt over the last few days, experiencing some summits by ourselves, and we all felt a little disappointed by the crowds. However, I suppose it's great that so many people want to go out walking. We followed the crowds, who followed an obvious route to the summit of Catbells. The route is fairly easy, but it does include some short scrambles over rocky areas. The summit is all rock, with many loose stones lying amid the small outcrops. The summit provided us with fine views down towards Derwentwater, the Newlands Valley, and along to Skiddaw. The descent was far less busy and much quieter than the ascent. We headed straight down to Derwentwater, and then enjoyed a lovely walk along the lakeside back to Hawse End.

We rounded off the walk by heading to the Dog and Gun in Keswick for lunch. The Dog and Gun is my number one favourite pub! The pub is small, attractive, old, and traditional. It has masses of charm, a great atmosphere, friendly staff, beer tasting (if you can't decide what to drink) and an amazing Hungarian Goulash – which allegedly has been bubbling away for years!

I love Keswick; it's my favourite town in the Lake District, and not just because of the Dog and Gun. I love the High street, the market that is held every Saturday, and the distinctive Moot Hall. I love the setting, shadowed by Skiddaw, and I love the atmosphere; the hustle and bustle, the mixture of walkers, climbers, locals and day trippers. Keswick is obviously geared up for tourism, but it feels less touristy than Ambleside or Grasmere. Anyway for some reason, maybe because I'm always on holiday when I'm here – I always feel good in Keswick.

Wednesday 15th April 2009

18. Barf

Height: 1536 feet (468m)
Route: Swan House up Beckstone Gill – Summit

Still feeling the cumulative effect of previous walks, we decided to find some more relatively low lying fells to climb. I didn't feel like driving, so we thought it would be a good time to tackle our nearest fell, Barf. We planned to combine this fell with Lord's Seat and Broom Fell. Every time we left our front door we could see the summit of Barf, and we could make out the 'Bishop.' The Bishop is a whitewashed rock, about seven hundred feet up the slopes of the fell. According to legend, in 1783, the newly appointed Bishop of Derry was on his way to Whitehaven, to take a boat to Ireland. He stopped for the night at the Swan Hotel, and after consuming several drinks, wagered that he could ride his pony to the top of Barf. Halfway up the pony stumbled at a large rock and fell, killing both horse and rider. The large rock known as the 'Bishop of Barf' is painted white in remembrance of his act, while at the foot of the slope is another white-painted rock known as the Clerk, where the bishop and his pony were buried. The 'Bishop' was whitewashed each year by staff at the Swan Hotel, until the Hotel was converted to apartments. The whitewashing is now carried out by members of Keswick Mountain Rescue. The Bishop is about seven feet high, while the Clerk is a much smaller stone.

Starting the walk from the front door of our apartment, we crossed the main road and then joined a path beside the Clerk. The ascent was made via Beckstone Gill. A short way up the beck, the path crossed to the left bank, and then climbed steeply until a small but awkward rockface was reached. We met a couple who had turned back from the rockface, saying that it was too difficult to cross. Emboldened by our experience on Great Gable, we managed to scramble over the obstacle, before moving onto easier ground. We continued to a forest road, and after a short distance crossed a stile onto the open fell. We followed the path as it crossed the beck again, and then wound its way to the summit of Barf. The summit is a small platform with a thin covering of grass, only a little way back from the eastern slope. The weather was a little overcast and the wind was really strong, we struggled to stay upright. The view eastward to Skiddaw over Bassenthwaite was excellent; we could also see our apartment and a collection of the Northern and Southern fells. However, our next objective, Lord's Seat, blocked out much of the view westward.

19. Lords Seat

Height: 1811 feet (552m)
Route: Westward path

Lords Seat could clearly be seen about three quarters of a mile away from the summit of Barf. The path was clear, but there were some muddy and boggy patches. We stopped to eat lunch as soon as we were slightly out of the wind, but it was still a pretty cold experience. As we walked to Lords Seat, views opened to the beautiful Wythop valley in the North. The summit of Lords Seat is a little less impressive than the name implies, it's bare and much like a moorland peak. It is said that the name derives from a throne like structure found in some rocks near to the north-west side of the summit. We were too cold to look for such a structure, so we made our way quickly on towards Broom Fell.

20. Broom Fell

Height: 1670 feet (511m)
Route: Ridge running North-west

We followed a fairly straightforward route over somewhat marshy ground to Broom Fell. The wind was if anything growing in strength, and it was a time for hats, gloves and extra layers. The summit sits on top of a grassy hill and is marked by a truly impressive cairn. The cairn looks to have been built from stones plundered from a nearby dry stone wall. Why this particular summit should be marked in such a distinctive style is a mystery. Return was by a direct route, allowing for detours around bogs, back to Beckstone Gill and Swan House.

Returning to the Clerk, Will, Tom and I decided to visit the Bishop. This route forms part of the direct ascent of Barf, described by Wainwright as "Not a walk. A very stiff scramble, suitable only for people overflowing with animal strength and vigour". I can honestly say that I have never been described as someone overflowing with animal strength or vigour! Whether this is a good or bad thing, I'm not sure! The slopes towards the Bishop are incredible steep; we were walking then scrambling on loose slate scree. It seemed that for every one step forward, we slid two steps back. I quickly decided that this wasn't such a good idea. We walked, we scrambled, we crawled, and we finally dragged ourselves upwards until we reached the Bishop. At the Bishop the boys and I found perches, and I took a picture to mark the occasion. Taking the picture meant I could no longer cling onto the mountain with both hands. Feeling less than safe or happy, we quickly decided to climb down again. Descent was for the most part carried out on our backsides, rather than our feet. Tania had probably made the right decision to stay on the path and observe our less than dignified progress from afar. However, later that evening as we looked out of our apartment, we had the satisfaction of knowing that we had climbed up to the Bishop.

Before we arrived in the Lakes, we had planned some walks that we definitely wanted to do if the weather was good. Other walks we half planned on the off chance that the weather stayed good, and yet others we plan the night before or even on the day. We aim to complete a mixture of high, low, long and short walks, and we try to find walks in different areas involving different types of scenery. The Coledale Round and Great Gable had been high on our agenda for the week, but the Newlands Round was one of those walks that we only planned to do if the weather stayed fine and we all felt OK. Fortunately, a belt of forecasted rain had still failed to arrive, so after a couple of low modest walks we decided to aim high again.

Tuesday 16th April 2009

21. Maiden Moor (The Newlands Round)

Height: 1887 feet (576m)
Route: Little Town – Hause Gate – Maiden Moor

We started walking from the hamlet of Little Town. However, we were faced with a slight dilemma. The usually unstoppable Tom was feeling a bit under the weather. Please don't think that we are insensitive, but we decided to continue with the walk anyway. Tom wasn't feeling too bad, and if the worst came to the worst, we knew that we could cut the walk down to two summits and walk back to the car after High Spy.

We walked along the edge of the road, and then on a steeply rising path to Hause Gate. From here we had hazy views to Catbells and Derwentwater; they must be spectacular on a clear day. After Hause Gate, we turned right aiming for the summit. A large cairn gives false hope of an early arrival at the summit, but it did provide us with some even better views. The climb was a bit of a slog, however the summit plateau provided easy walking over level ground. The only drawback was that it was practically impossible to find the actual summit. The top is all fairly level, with no point obviously higher than any other. After much debate, we opted for a position with a view that appeared to match Wainwright's sketch of the summit view to High Spy, our next objective.

22. High Spy

Height: 2143 feet (653m)
Route: Ridge from Maiden Moor

We started walking to High Spy along a path on the edge of Bull Crag. The drops were vertical and dramatic. Feeling a little unnerved, we retreated to a more obvious path away from the edge of the escarpment. After about a mile and a half we reached the summit of High Spy. The summit cairn was particularly impressive, towering above the boys heads. The most impressive view from the summit was the one of our next objective, Dale Head. Tom was feeling much better by this stage, so after a small family conference we decided to complete the whole of the walk.

23. Dale Head

Height: 2473 feet (753m)
Route: Descent to Dalehead Tarn – climb to summit path

The walk to Dale Head started with a long descent towards Dalehead Tarn. We stopped for lunch on the way down and faced our second dilemma of the day; finding a clear route to Dale Head. After lunch, and after a period of consultation with map and guide book, we decided to ignore the valley path coming out of Newlands (which can be used for a quick return to Little Town) and headed to the tarn. Here we ignored the direct climb to Dale Head, because it looked too steep. However, our alternative proved to be little better. After walking around the back of the tarn, we selected a route which we hoped would join the summit path. We ended up climbing an incredibly steep grassy slope, continually hoping that the summit path would arrive soon. As always, really wanting something to happen soon, makes time slow down. It seemed like an eternity until the slope flattened out and we reached a clear path. Our legs and calves were screaming, but we eventually made our weary way to the summit. Another tall, impressive cairn marked the top of Dale Head; this time perched right on the edge of a sheer drop. It is quite an interesting phenomenon that arriving at a summit seems to take away some of the tiredness, the aches and the pains – you seem to get a second wind. All this was true at Dale

Head. The views down into the Newlands valley and back towards High Spy and Maiden Moor were like water to a thirsty man. Unfortunately, the views towards Hindscarth and Scope End, although wonderful, reminded us that we still had a long way to go. I started to feel thirsty again!

24. Hindscarth

Height: 2385 feet (727m)
Route: Ridge from Dale Head – Descent via Scope End

We walked onto Hindscarth, the final summit of the day. The wind had picked up so we didn't stay long, but we did visit an interesting old cairn about two hundred yards from the summit. This cairn was hollowed out and provided temporary respite from the cold. The descent continued as we walked towards, and then along the narrow ridge of Scope End. This final part of the walk was fantastic; lovely views, thrilling drops (but not too scary) and the feeling that after a long days walk we were nearly home. It is quite often the case that it is only towards the end of a walk that you start taking everything in; savouring the final views of the day, whilst beginning to relax and enjoy the memories. We chatted all the way down.

The boys were impressed to hear that gold was once mined on Scope End, and they were keen to go prospecting. However, ignoring their pleas, we pressed on, passing the picturesque Newlands church and then returning to Little Town.

Today, we had walked nine miles and completed two thousand, seven hundred feet of ascent. We felt deeply satisfied, but suitably exhausted!

Friday 17th April 2009

25. Ling Fell

Height: 1224 feet (373m)
Route: Whythop Mill via Old School – along grass terrace to summit – Descent to Barthwaite

I mentioned previously that we planned to complete a variety of fells on our trips to the Lakes. Apart from differences in height and length of walk, we also wanted to ensure that we didn't complete all the better known, more famous fells first, and leave all the less known, perhaps more out of the ways fells until the end of our Wainwright challenge. With this aim in mind, our thoughts turned to the Wythop Valley. Wythop is a beautiful area; verdant, scenic, but somewhat remote from the normal tourist haunts. Consequently, Wythop is far quieter than the more popular parts of the Lake District. Ling Fell and Sale Fell are found in this part of the Lakes. Despite standing next to each other, the two fells have no real connection, being separated by Wythop Beck.

Ever since I had seen a red squirrel whilst out running, we had all kept our eyes open in case we could spot any more. As we set off for Wythop, I pointed out the spot where I had seen the aforementioned squirrel, and promptly nearly ran over another one. A squirrel ran straight in front of the car and I had to break sharply. Why did the squirrel cross the road? Possibly because of a death wish! We stopped the car and had a closer look as the unscathed squirrel bounded up a nearby tree.

Delighted by our encounter we made our way cheerfully to the village of Wythop Mill. Our first objective was Ling Fell; its name derives from the fact that it is largely covered in heather, also known as 'ling'. From the village we followed a road up to and then past the Old School. We then emerged on to a path, which initially contoured around the base of the fell, before heading directly to the summit. The summit is smooth and rounded, topped by a triangulation pillar. Not perhaps the most interesting walk, but it provided good views to Skiddaw and to Scotland. The rounded grassy slopes whilst perhaps not delivering on interest, did provide an ideal area to practice some fell running. Tom and William raced down from the summit, collapsing, laughing and exhausted at the foot of the fell.

26. Sale Fell

Height: 1170 feet (359m)
Route: Across Whythop Beck – Ascent by steep grassy slope, past Dodd Crag to summit – Descent to Kelswick Farm and Old Whythop Church

Sale Fell presents a more interesting profile. The Fell is an east-west ridge, about a mile long. The fell is clad primarily in grass and bracken, but the eastern end is heavily forested. We walked across Whythop Beck, and then climbed a steep grassy slope past Dodd Crag and onto the summit. This was an altogether more enjoyable walk, more like a mountain again. The wind was really strong on the summit, but we had good views to Lords Seat, and once again to Skiddaw. It was really satisfying to walk in a quiet area of the Lakes. Actually, I feel quite bad about writing about how beautiful and unspoilt the area is, for fear of attracting too many others. We only met one other couple out walking all day. Let us hope that there are always some areas of the Lake District where you can find beauty and solitude. We descended the fell by walking down towards Kelswick Farm, and on route we paid a visit to the interesting ruins of Old Whythop Church.

Our first week in the Lakes, since the decision to climb all the Wainwrights, had been a fantastic success. We had climbed more fells than we originally thought possible. The pound a peak for the boys was beginning to look like a bad idea. We had visited some magnificent, previously unknown to us areas, and the weather had stayed dry all week – a first in my experience of the Lake District. Unfortunately, we were now at that 'bittersweet' moment of any holiday. The time when you know you have had a great time, but you also know that the holiday is just about over. It was hard to believe that the week had gone past so quickly, but it was satisfying to think of all the things that we had done. Why is it that when you work, the days can go by so slowly, counting the hours, then the minutes, and in a bad week the seconds, until the weekend arrives? But when you are on holiday, time speeds up and the days fly by?

Reluctantly packing on our last night, we decided to make the most of our last day. We decided to drive back at night, thereby allowing ourselves the opportunity to climb a final fell and have a nice pub lunch. You may have picked up on the fact that I quite like my pubs – I do. The best pubs offer a combination of warmth, welcome and conviviality. In short, they are a perfect accompaniment to walking. Normally, because we are out walking, we carry lunch with us, but today we planned a walk with a stop for a pub lunch in the middle, bliss! The aim was to park at Grange, walk along the River Derwent, climb Castle Crag, walk to The Scafell Hotel at Borrowdale, and then return back along the river.

Saturday 18th April 2009

27. Castle Crag

Height: 985 feet (290m)
Route: Grange into the Jaws of Borrowdale - Summit - Descent to Rosthwaite - return to Grange along River Derwent

Castle Crag has an impressive appearance, a rugged height, seemingly blocking the valley of Borrowdale, which is squeezed between Castle Crag and Grange Fell. This narrow gap is known as the 'Jaws of Borrowdale'. Castle Crag is the only Wainwright included in the *Pictorial Guides* that is less than a thousand feet. Wainwright claims that the inclusion of the fell is based upon the fact that it "is so magnificently independent, so ruggedly individual, so aggressively unashamed of its lack of inches that less than justice would be done by relegating it to a paragraph in the High Spy chapter".

We loaded up the car, said goodbye to the apartment and headed for Grange. From Grange we walked along a road, and then joined a footpath running beside Dalt Wood. We eventually emerged beside the River Derwent. Wainwright describes this area, with the help of a hand drawn map, as "one mile of country containing no high mountains, no lake, no famous crag, no tarn, But in the author's humble submission, it encloses the loveliest square mile in Lakeland". The scenery is quite fantastic; the weather was also terrific, and once more we had to agree with Wainwright.

The path skirted the edge of the river, with plenty of river beaches at which to stop and stare at the beauty of it all. We then entered Low How woods, and started to climb the lower slopes of Castle Crag. The slopes have been extensively quarried and are full of caves. One such cave became the summer home of Millican Dalton, a self styled adventurer. Dalton was also a vegetarian, pacifist and teetotaller. Dalton lived in the cave from the 1920s until his death in 1947. He survived on an income earned as a mountain guide. He carved his own epitaph into the wall above where he slept. It reads: 'Don't Waste Words, Jump to Conclusions'. Unfortunately, we were unable to visit the cave; signs warned us that the entrance was blocked because of health and safety fears. I'm sure there is some irony here!

Continuing our walk, we headed up a steepening path, passing through a hole in a wall before emerging at the base of a massive slate spoil heap. The spoil heap has distinctive paths, almost carved into it; quite unique in my experience. Our path zig-zagged its way to a massive old quarry. The quarry was full of hundreds of slate 'sculptures', all of different shapes, sizes and designs. The 'sculptures' were quite surreal and gave the place an almost magical feel. We walked around looking at all the different designs, and then created our own. Satisfied with our creation, we left the quarry behind us and climbed the final short, sharp stretch to the summit. The summit area is thought to have been an ancient hill fort; it certainly looks as if it could have been one. The very highest point is a rock outcrop about eight feet high and twelve feet across. The boys scrambled to the top and assessed the defensive properties of the fell. The views, heightened by the sunny clear weather, were excellent in all directions. We had amazing views to Derwent Water, Skiddaw, Scafell and Great End. The summit is a truly beautiful spot and we felt privileged just to be there. Apart from enjoying the views and enjoying the moment, we took time to remember the men of Borrowdale. A memorial to the men of the area killed in The First world War is fixed to the rocky outcrop.

Eventually we left the summit and headed for Rosthwaite. The boys were in good spirits, until during a play fight Tom managed to 'attack' his own eye with a stick, and then lose his jumper in the panic that followed. Spirits were revived at the Scafell Hotel. We had a great lunch, sitting outside, enjoying the sunshine and warm temperatures. As the boys and I went into the bar to order some drinks, I noticed a plaque recording the winners of the Borrowdale Fell Race. I love running and have taken part in several races – albeit not very successfully. If anything the fact that I run makes me even more in awe of fell runners. The Borrowdale

Fell Race covers seventeen miles and includes six thousand, five hundred feet of ascent. It takes the runners to the summits of Bessy Boot, Scafell Pike, Great Gable and Dalehead. The record for the race is held by Billy Bland, he completed the race in a time of two hours, thirty four minutes and thirty eight seconds, that's just incredible. Billy Bland was born in Borrowdale, and he is one of the best long-distance fell runners of all time. Apart from the Borrowdale Fell Race record, Bland is the current holder of the record for the fastest time in the fell running challenge, The Bob Graham Round. The Bob Graham Round involves a circuit of forty two Lake District peaks, covering around sixty six miles. The round has to be completed in less than twenty four hours. Bland accomplished this in 1982 in a time of thirteen hours and fifty three minutes, that's just unbelievable! More about this race and fell running later.

Feeling that our own accomplishments might not be so impressive after all, we headed back to Grange along the beautiful banks of the River Derwent. The walk proved to be a fantastic end to a fantastic week - we even found Tom's jumper.

As we headed away from the Lakes we thought about our favourite moments of the holiday. Tania and Tom both loved getting to the top of Great Gable and seeing a red squirrel near Thornthwaite; William loved seeing the red squirrel and completing the Coledale Round; I loved the Coledale Round and the pint afterwards.

Eight days, twenty two fells and no rain, what a holiday!

Our challenge was well and truly under way.

THE RAINY SEASON
August 2009

Which is the best time of year to visit the lakes?

Well the Lakes are a year round destination. We have visited at Easter, when the days can be bright, clear and warm. The hillsides are covered in blossom and bluebells and daffodils begin to emerge in the woodlands and valleys. The weather can still have an icy chill, but if that's the case you can wrap up warm and enjoy the views of snow capped peaks. The autumn months provide the most marvellous colours, from green to gold, red, orange and yellow. The days begin to draw in, but you just have to get up a little earlier and enjoy the early morning views. In winter the days really shorten and some of the summits may be out of reach (to all but seasoned ice climbers), but the mountains often look at their best with a full covering of snow. If the sky is clear, the mountain reflections in the Lakes can be breathtaking. In summer the days are long; all manner of lengthy walks can be contemplated, and what's better on a balmy evening than a short walk or a lingering pint in a beer garden with a view.

Weather is often a key factor when deciding when to visit; people often say "there is no such thing as bad weather - only inappropriate clothing", to a certain extent I agree. You can wrap up warm, you can block out the rain and the wind, but don't tell me that walking in the driving rain with a gale blowing is as enjoyable as walking on a still, warm (but not too warm), dry day. The problem with the Lakes is that in my experience, wet and windy weather can occur in any season. The Lake District is England's wettest region. Typically the Lakes have two hundred wet days a year, twenty days of snow, and one hundred and forty five dry days. On average, gales blow on the summits for about a hundred days a year. In short, whenever you visit bring a waterproof.

What about temperature? The Lake District has comparatively moderate differences in temperature, although they might not feel moderate to the freezing cold walker. At sea level, average temperatures range from three degrees centigrade in January, to fifteen degrees centigrade in July. But remember, for every one hundred and fifty metres you climb, temperatures drop by about one degree centigrade – pack those extra layers if you are climbing high.

Whenever you visit the weather is going to be changeable. The secret is to use the forecasts and chose walks that are suitable for the conditions (must remember to take own advice).

In conclusion, all the seasons have positives and I don't think there is an answer to my initial question. There is no definitive best time of year, it's all about making the most of the time you have. Don't bemoan what you can't do, relish what you can.

Our first summer visit to the Lakes would take us to Chapel Stile. We wanted to stay in the Langdale valley, and Chapel Stile, a picturesque village on the River Brathay, fitted the bill perfectly. We rented a house for the week and once again we maximised our stay by travelling up early and spending one night in a hotel. This time we planned our first walk before we arrived, the objectives, Gibson Knott and Helm Crag.

Saturday 22nd August 2009

28. Gibson Knott

Height: 1376 feet (420m)
Route: Grasmere Village to Greenburn Bottom via Greenburn ridge route to Helm Crag.

We started the walk from Grasmere, probably The Lake District's most popular village – thanks to William Wordsworth. The village is almost totally given over to tourism, but it still looks idyllic. Most of the buildings date from the nineteenth Century, though the farms and Church are much older. William Wordsworth and his sister Dorothy moved into the village in 1799, living in Dove Cottage.They then moved to Allan Banks, a large house that William had condemned as an eyesore when it was being built. They lived here for two years with poet and friend Coleridge. They then moved to the Old Rectory, opposite St Oswald's Church, a cold and damp house where his two youngest children died. In 1813 they moved to Rydal Mount. In total William Wordsworth lived in Grasmere for fourteen years, he described it as "the loveliest spot that man hath ever found". William died in 1850, and he is buried along with many other members of his family in St Oswald's Church. We visited the Church and looked at the Wordsworth gravestones. I know it may be considered a little morbid, but there is something very moving and interesting about visiting graveyards. To quote another poet, Morrissey – "all those people, all those lives, where are they now? With the loves and hates and passions just like mine, they were born and then they lived and then they died." Sometimes it does us good to stop and think about the temporary nature of everything. It puts 'things' into perspective, and installs, in me at least, a need to live, love and experience, while I'm still here.

All this maudlin talk doesn't really do justice to our mood on the walk. We enjoyed Grasmere, told the boys all about Wordsworth, and quoting the one line we could remember from the great man (yes, that's the one) we strolled onwards, under bright, clear blue skies. We walked up to Greenburn Bottom; it was wet underfoot but there was much to keep us interested. We enjoyed the stunning views up to Helm Crag and the picturesque delights of a lovely waterfall. As we started to climb up towards the main ridge, I spotted some sundews and showed the boys. The carnivorous sundew plant, botanical name *Drosera*, is deadly to insects that fly too close. I remember being fascinated by carnivorous plants as a child, you can find sundews on Dartmoor and I had a Venus fly trap on my windowsill. The plant is called a sundew because of a sticky gel like substance on its tentacles. The gel makes the plants look as if they have morning dew on them all day long, especially when it glistens in the sun. Insects that get to close are 'caught' by the sundew and then slowly digested. After a short botanical, rather than the usual geographical lecture, we reached the ridge and turned towards Gibson Knott. Identifying the summit was not straightforward; there are a number of rocky outcrops of similar height. We asked a passing walker and he pointed us in a completely different direction, stating that we weren't even close to the summit. After taking his word for it and heading off in the wrong direction, we realized that we should start trusting ourselves a bit more. We retraced our footsteps and found the summit cairn on the westernmost outcrop.

29. Helm Crag

Height: 1299 feet (405m)
Route: Ridge from Gibson Knott – Descent to Grasmere via Easedale Beck

From the top of Gibson Knott, we followed a lovely ridge route to the distinctive summit of Helm Crag. Whilst not that high, Helm Crag looks really impressive from Grasmere, because it marks the end of the ridge. Tom fell in a bog on route; I thought it was poetic justice after the first walk of our last holiday, but Tom didn't see it that way. Helm Crag is one of the best known Lakeland Fells; it is renowned because of its distinctive summit. At either end of the highest ridge are two delightful rock outcrops. Only one can be seen from any point in the surrounding valleys, and both have a variety of names depending upon the profile seen from the particular vantage point. The northwestern outcrop is the true summit of the fell. It is variously called 'The Howitzer' 'the lion and the lamb' 'the old women playing the organ' or 'the lion couchant'. I favour 'The Howitzer'; it aptly describes the wall of rock that sadly we all failed to climb. After our failed attempt we visited the southern outcrop, prominent from Grasmere; this is the traditional 'Lion and the lamb'. Descent was straight down the steep, south-eastern face of the fell. We were in a rush to pick up the keys for our holiday home, and consequently missed the chance to have a nice cup of tea at the prettily located Lancrigg Hotel.

The house in Chapel Stile was in a great location; situated at the western end of the village and offering superb views towards Lingmoor Fell. After unpacking we walked to the very friendly local pub – 'Wainwrights'. Will and Tom noticed that a pub quiz was going to take place later on in the week; they were keen to take part (we might be back). We had all really enjoyed our first day and night in the lakes, and we looked forward to another long walk in the morning.

We planned to complete The Fairfield Horseshoe, a classic ridge route. Experience had taught us that it was a good idea to get a major walk out of the way at an early stage of the holiday, while we all still felt fit and fresh. The morning however brought rain, more rain and heavy rain. The forecast was bleak for the whole day, so feeling a little disappointed, we headed into Ambleside. You could accuse us of being fair-weather walkers, but the truth is we have been out in all manner of conditions. You do sometimes have to be sensible; driving rain, high winds and poor visibility, don't make for a particularly enjoyable or safe ridge walk.

Ambleside is situated at the head of Windermere, England's largest lake. Ambleside's history goes back to the Romans and the Vikings. The town was granted a market charter in 1650, and its Market Place became the commercial centre for agriculture and the wool trade. The situation of the town is stunning, to the west is Loughrigg Fell, to the north Red Screes and the Fairfield group, and to the east is Wansfell. Tania and I have a particular attachment to Ambleside, because as mentioned previously, we spent our honeymoon here (it rained all that week as well). We spent most of our morning in Ambleside, looking around the local shops. Ambleside, recently dubbed "Anorak Capital of the World", is home to a great variety of independent shops, so it made an interesting change from seeing the same old chain stores. The day was a total washout, but in the afternoon I ran from the house down into the Great Langdale Valley, and what a place to run. The views up to The Langdale Pikes, Crinkle Crags and Pike O' Blisco were truly spectacular.

Monday 24th August 2010

30. Low Pike (The Fairfield Horseshoe)

Height: 1657 feet (508m)
Route: Ascent from Ambleside and High Sweden Bridge

The weather was much better on Monday morning, so full of energy and the built up frustration of not walking the day before, we set out early to complete The Fairfield Horseshoe. The route is a high level circuit of the Rydal Valley. The walk is very popular and follows well defined paths, so in theory there should be little chance of getting lost. We followed Wainwright's advice and planned to complete the walk in an anti-clockwise direction. Wainwright sites easier gradients and the delight of an early morning approach to High Sweden Bridge. Once again Wainwright was spot on; the walk along Sweden Bridge Lane was delightful. We passed through woodland and then crossed Scandale Beck at High Sweden Bridge. Will and Tom said the area reminded them of the landscape in Tolkien's *Lord of the Rings*. Indeed it's hard to believe that he didn't get inspiration from The Lake District. After taking some obligatory photos at High Sweden Bridge, we climbed a rising path to the ridge, and then followed a substantial dry stone wall to the summit of Low Pike. This particular wall helps navigation along the Horseshoe for about six miles, although it does block out some of the views. The dry stone wall was about the only dry thing on this stretch of the walk. The ground was really boggy after the torrential rain of yesterday.

31. High Pike

Height: 2155 feet (656m)
Route: Ridge from Low Pike

We descended from Low Pike, and then following the dry stone wall climbed up the steep path to the summit of High Pike. The summit is flat and grassy; the cairn stands on the edge of crags overlooking Scandale.

32. Dove Crag

Height: 2603 feet (792m)
Route: Ridge route from High Pike along dry stone wall

A simple walk along a rising path from High Pike, still guided by the dry stone wall, brought us to the summit of Dove Crag. From the summit we enjoyed a great panorama of the major fells. Perhaps Dove Crag's major claim to fame is that it was the first chapter ever written by Wainwright for his *Pictorial Guides*. He wrote the Dove Crag chapter on the 9th of November 1952, as he started Book One. It would take Wainwright a further fourteen years to finish the complete series of seven books and 214 fells. I wondered how long it would take us to climb all the fells. At this stage of the walk the weather started turning cold (despite the season), so we had a quick lunch, sheltering in the lee of some rocks.

33. Hart Crag

Height: 2698 feet (822m)
Route: North-west ridge following dry stone wall

An easy but chilly walk from Dove Crag brought us to the rocky summit of Hart Crag. Once again we had really impressive views, this time to Helvellyn, with Striding Edge clearly to be seen. The view, spectacular and awe inspiring, unfortunately had a somewhat negative impact on the boys. They both expressed doubts about any future plans to cross the classic ridge route. Perhaps views can sometimes be a little bit too awe inspiring!

34. Fairfield

Height: 2863 feet (873m)
Route: Stony slope from Hart Crag

The path from Hart Crag brought us to the very large and impressive plateau of Fairfield. The top is flat but stony, and there are many cairns. We visited the summit and then retreated to the partial shelter of a windbreak. Fairfield is the highest fell on the Horseshoe, and we were rewarded with magnificent views in all directions. We used our *Wainwright* to pick out the names of the fell tops, and I tried to commit some of them to memory. We all felt a little tired at this stage, but we were pleased that we had completed over half the walk.

35. Great Rigg

Height: 2513 feet (766m)
Route: Descent from Fairfield

From the summit of Fairfield we headed south towards Great Rigg. We strode out over the 'springy grass' and bounced along fairly speedily. The views back towards Fairfield were particularly fine, and the views down towards Windermere were their equal.

36. Heron Pike

Height: 2003 feet (612m)
Route: Southerly descent from Great Rigg

On route to Heron pike we looked at the path to Stone Arthur, but decided that it was one fell too many. We had some problems identifying the actual summit of Heron Pike, there appeared to be two; one was as described by Wainwright – "a large outcrop of quartzite", but another more northerly top looked similar in height. We touched both to be on the safe side.

37. Nab Scar

Height: 1470 feet (440m)
Route: South-west descent from Heron Pike

The last stage of the Horseshoe was an easy descent to Nab Scar, once the favourite summit of the Lakeland Poets. On the shore of the lake below the fell is Nab Cottage, past home to several of the Lake Poets. They used to walk up to the summit to find 'inspiration'. Nab Scar was our eighth summit of the day and certainly inspired us. The high point is marked by a large pile of rocks, which Tom climbed and then promptly fell off. The summit is slightly unusual because it's not really a separate fell, but the end of the southern ridge of Fairfield. Descent was via a steep path to Rydal Hall, with lovely views of Windermere all the way down. Rydal Hall is an impressive early nineteenth century listed house, now used as a Christian Centre. We walked through the beautiful grounds of the Hall, unfortunately missing the path for Low Sweden Bridge, before tracking back to Ambleside. After the disappointment of yesterday (rain stopped play), we all felt really pleased with ourselves. We had walked eleven miles and climbed eight summits, with a total ascent of three thousand, four hundred and ninety feet. The Fairfield Horseshoe was our biggest 'family walk' to date.

Tuesday 25th August 2009

38. Blea Rigg

Height: 1776 feet (541m)
Route: New Dungeon Ghyll Hotel – Mill Gill – Stickle Tarn

I don't think you can come and stay close to the Langdales and not want to climb them, the temptation is just too much. We were all a bit tired after the Fairfield Horseshoe, but the forecast suggested that we were indeed in the rainy season, and today was likely to be the last dry day for the foreseeable future. Consequently, we decided to climb Pike O'Stickle and Loft Crag – thereby completing the Langdale Pikes. But we also wanted to add some additional fells. In the end Tania planned a walk that would take us to the summits of Blea Rigg, Sergeant Man, High Raise and Thunacar Knott, as well as Pike O' Stickle and Loft Crag. The first part of the walk was a repeat of our ascent of Pavey Ark. We parked at the New Dungeon Ghyll Hotel and climbed to Stickle Tarn by way of Mill Gill. The weather was excellent; some high cloud, but generally clear and warm enough for T-shirts and shorts. It was interesting to note that we made far easier work of the steep climb up Mill Gill this time. The boys were obviously a couple of years older and that much stronger, but we all seemed fitter. All this walking is obviously good for you. From Stickle Tarn we struck out eastward along a small track, squelching through some very boggy ground towards the summit of Blea Rigg. The summit wasn't the easiest to locate. There are a number of cairned outcrops and we had to use a GPS to eliminate our doubts and confirm our position. We all liked the summit; the views towards Fairfield and Helm Crag were particularly fine.

39. Sergeant Man

Height: 2414 feet (730m)
Route: Undulating North-west path from Blea Rigg

An easy path followed in a north-westerly direction brought us towards the easily identifiable summit of Sergeant Man. The walk was straightforward, but it was over very boggy ground again. We decided that after getting that 'sinking feeling' a couple of times, William should take over Tom's mantle as 'Bog monster'. Sergeant Man is really a secondary summit of High Raise, but it is prominent and impressive. The land falls away steeply to the south and it feels like a true summit. There were good all round views, apart from those obscured by High Raise.

40. High Raise

Height: 2500 feet (762m)
Route: North-west path from Sergeant Man

Another easy but boggy walk, north-west from Sergeant Man across a grassy plateau, brought us to the summit of High Raise. It is not one of the most spectacular mountains in the Lakes, however it is the highest point in the central fells of Lakeland. High Raise is also considered to be the most central point in the Lake District. The centrality of the fell provided a fine viewpoint from which we could admire the surrounding mountains. We could see Skiddaw, Helvellyn and the Scafells, along with just about every other major peak.

41. Thunacar Knott

Height: 2351 feet (723m)
Route: Southerly path from High Raise

After a short stop for a snack on High Raise, we headed south to Thunacar Knott. Thunacar Knott is apparently often by-passed by walkers because of its uninspiring appearance, being just a slight rise on the moorland between Harrison Stickle and High Raise. Indeed it was another fell that was difficult to locate. I raced Tom to the summit, only to find out that I had headed for the wrong summit (some geographer!). Many people do not regard Thunacar Knott as a separate fell, considering it to be just the outlying highest point of the Pavey Ark cliffs. Wainwright's comments on the fell are not positive, stating: "Thunacar Knott is completely unphotogenic ... this uninspiring characteristic extends to the whole fell, which is quite deficient in interest". The actual summit of the fell, which includes a small tarn, is the more southern of two contenders. It featured a smaller cairn than my race destination. Even though Thunacar Knott is quite insignificant, it is slightly higher than all the surrounding area, and therefore afforded good views, particularly to the west.

42. Pike O' Stickle

Height: 2323 feet (709m)
Route: Thunacarr Knott to Harrison Stickle path – Descent to path leading to Pike O' Stickle

We walked from the summit of Thunacar Knott to the path leading to Harrison Stickle, and then descended to the path leading up to Pike O' Stickle. Pike O' Stickle 'loomed' ahead – the mountains doomed shape is recognisable from virtually all angles. A 'stickle' is a hill with a steep prominent rocky top, while a 'pike' is a hill with a peaked summit. Pike O' Stickle is therefore given double emphasis, and rightly so. Tania expressed doubts about the final climb to the summit; she had climbed the peak before and not particularly enjoyed the experience. Indeed the final scramble was not as easy as Wainwright suggests – it provided some excitement and the odd scary moment. The summit is not one to wander about on; sheer drops and a narrow top awaited us. But the summit has to be one of my favourites. It provides a real sense of height and offers fantastic views to Bowfell and the Southern Fells.

Pike O' Stickle has another claim to fame, apart from its rugged beauty it is famous as the site of a Neolithic stone axe factory; it is one of the most important prehistoric axe factory sites in Europe. According to Wainwright a factory was set up here because of a vein of greenstone, a very hard volcanic rock, which comes to the surface around the head of the valley. Evidence of axe manufacture has been found in many areas of Great Langdale, but it is the screes of Pike of Stickle which have yielded the most discoveries. It is incredible to think that our ancestors were up here working in the mountains at such an early stage in human history.

43. Loft Crag

Height: 2270 feet (680m)
Route: Descent from Pike O' Stickle – rising path to summit of Loft Crag

From the top of Pike O' Stickle, the path to Loft Crag looked frighteningly steep and scarily daunting. We prepared ourselves for another tough scramble. However, our worries were unfounded; the actual route to the summit was an easy and pleasant stroll. After enjoying yet more wonderful views, we descended the Langdales by way of the main path below Loft Crag. We had enjoyed another great day, and we all really loved this walk; just less than seven miles, two thousand, eight hundred and seventy feet of ascent, and a fantastic variety of fell tops and scenery – well done Tania.

Walking back to the car the boys remembered the pub quiz at 'Wainwrights'. Consequently, we had an enjoyable evening demonstrating to our children (not for the first time) that in actual fact we are quite competitive, and we don't like losing.

Thursday 27th August 2009

44. Bowfell

Height: 2960 feet (902m)
Route: Old Dungeon Ghyll – The Band – The Bowfell

No walking yesterday, just torrential rain and a very wet run. We spent most of the day at the house and planned an assault on Bowfell. Bowfell was one of the first walks I didn't complete in the Lake District. I remember setting out in the rain and wind and being driven off the mountain about half way up. Ever since then I have been determined to complete the walk, and it was one that we had planned to do before arriving at Chapel Stile. Bowfell is the sixth highest mountain in the Lakes, and it is listed as one of Wainwright's top six best fells. I love the look of Bowfell, a huge pyramid of a mountain at the head of Great Langdale Valley. The east ridge of the mountain, The Band, divides Mickledon and Oxendale. We parked at The Old Dungeon Ghyll Hotel, walked past Stool End Farm and headed for the foot of The Band. The Band is a broad, grassy shoulder of Bowfell, which provides a direct path to the summit. We followed a well worn path, pausing often to catch our breath, and to turn and admire the stunning views behind us. The climb levels out at Three Tarns, before beginning again at a steep scree slope. Large sections of the route through the scree are by way of a stone staircase. Large blocks of stone have been embedded into the path to prevent further erosion. I'm not sure that I like the look of them, but they are a necessary evil. They help to prevent further erosion and protect the fells from walkers like us – so I really shouldn't complain. We passed some volunteer path makers on route, I certainly didn't complain to them.

Heading onwards, we took time to stop and take a look at the Great Slab; the large expanse of flat rock provided a stark contrast to the boulder strewn top of the fell. Picking our way through the stones and boulders, we finally reached the summit. We have been really lucky in terms of views from summits, but not today. The day had started brightly and fairly warmly, but cloud had been building and lowering, and eventually reached the summit shortly before we did. With no views to speak of, we didn't stay long. As we left the summit we met a couple who had completed all the Wainwrights. They asked the boys if they enjoyed climbing in the mountains – despite the poor weather they both said they loved it.

45. Esk Pike

Height: 2903 feet (885m)
Route: Path to Esk Pike via Ore Gap

After following the north ridge along the top of Bowfell, we descended to Ore Gap, and then climbed to the summit of Esk Pike. The summit is apparently noted for its colourful rocks, but by the time we reached Esk Pike, the cloud had completely descended and we couldn't see a thing. Descent was rather unnerving. We knew where we were heading, but we couldn't see what was surrounding us. Guided by compass (GPS proving temperamental), we were relieved to finally drop below the cloud as we reached Esk Hause.

46. Rossett Pike

Height: 2106 feet (650m)
Route: Esk Hause – Angle Tarn – Rosset Pike: Descent via Rosset Gill to Mickledon and Old Dungeon Ghyll Hotel

From Esk Hause we walked to Angle Tarn, stopping for a snack before climbing to the top of Rosset Pike. The summit is marked by a small cairn, and for the first time since Bowfell we had some fine views. We were below the cloud level, but the wind was really strong. Tania and I held on to the boys to prevent them from being blown off the mountain. Descent was via Rossett Gill. Wainwright was not a fan of this route "most certainly the least liked (foot-pass), due not to its steepness but its stoniness (a condition worsening year by year as swarming legions of booted pedestrians grind away the scanty vestiges of grass and soil". Things have obviously changed since Wainwright's time; the path is now easy and 'stepped', but we did face one minor disaster. Will and Tom had been taking lots of photographs throughout the holiday; they wanted to enter a competition. Unfortunately, Tom left his camera somewhere on Rossett Gill, and this time we couldn't find it again (let me know if you do). Losing the camera was a shame, especially as we passed some 'green' sheep towards the end of the walk. I think someone had got a little bit carried away with their sheep marker spray. From 'green' sheep I moved onto 'Black Sheep' – ale this time. We stopped off at the Old Dungeon Ghyll Hotel before heading back to the car. The Hotel has been providing food, drink and accommodation for over three hundred years. The Hikers Bar is a delight; traditional and friendly, serving good food and beer – in short, basic but brilliant.

So much for summer; the rainy season continued with no likelihood of ending before our holiday was over. Resigned to wet weather, we donned waterproofs and planned a walk that would take us from our house in Chapel Stile to Silver How, and then on towards Loughrigg Fell. We walked into the centre of the village and chose the direct route to Silver How, following Meg's Gill. The path, initially steep, passed beside some sheer drops, and although I got a bit worried on the boys behalf, they weren't worried at all. We made our way up to an impressive waterfall, crossed over the top of it, and then somehow managed to bypass the summit of Silver How as we headed towards Grasmere. I don't like to say "I told you so", but I did think we had gone the wrong way. We were using the GPS, but to cut a long story short, we had entered the wrong grid reference for the summit. Wandering from outcrop to outcrop, but with the benefit of hindsight obviously dwarfed by the actual summit of Silver How, Tania and I got frustrated, and more than a bit fed up. Our moods weren't enlivened when the rain became torrential, and then turned to hail. After eating some very soggy sandwiches and thinking things couldn't get any worse, a flash of lightning split the sky, quickly followed by a clap of thunder.

We walked quickly to Spedding Crag, and then decided to head back to Chapel Stile. We sought refuge from the rain in Holy Trinity Church. The village church stands below cliffs and is built from the local distinctive green slate. The building dates from 1857 and is beautiful inside and out. Tania and I came here for the Christmas Day service in 1993; I remember walking to the church through deep snow, and enjoying an idyllic festive morning.

Saturday 29th August 2009

47. Lingmoor Fell

Height: 1530 feet (469m)
Route: Ascent from Little Langdale

This was the final day of our holiday, and despite the poor forecast we were determined to complete some more fells. The plan was to park at Little Langdale, walk to the top of Lingmoor Fell, return to Little Langdale for lunch, and then climb Holme Fell. Lingmoor Fell divides the valleys of Great Langdale and Little Langdale, and is a separate and distinctive summit. Just like Ling Fell, Lingmoor Fell derives its name from the Old Norse word for heather. The ascent was straightforward; we followed an old quarry track for much of the way. The heather clad summit was very windy, so we sheltered behind a dry stone wall after taking in the views. From the summit, the view to The Langdale Pikes was particularly impressive, but we probably got more excited about being able to see the house that we had been staying in. Descent was ascent in reverse, and then it was lunch at an old favourite, the 'Three Shires' in Little Langdale

48. Holme Fell

Height: 1040 feet (317m)
Route: Ascent from Little Langdale

Energised by food and drink, we stared out on what proved to be a lovely walk from Little Langdale to Holme Fell. I have mentioned before, but it's worth mentioning again, that some of the lower walks offer the best views, the biggest variety of scenery, and some interesting features. On route we passed a massive disused green slate quarry. The quarry, which closed just before the start of the Second World War, has flooded chambers and tunnels, which are now used by cave divers for sport. But, it is a dangerous location and several divers have died over the years, they have become lost in the murky waters of the tunnels. The quarry is also used by rock climbers and we saw some in action. They may have been climbing the extreme routes of "First Night Nerves" or "Wicked Willie".

When we arrived at Holme Fell, we were delighted to discover that the summit was simply stunning – a rock outcrop surrounded by a beautiful expanse of purple heather, with terrific views to the north and south-east. We enjoyed the views, spent some time reminiscing about our holiday, and then headed back to Little Langdale.

Just in case we had forgotten that it was the 'rainy season', we were accompanied by some of the heaviest rain of the holiday – high land, hard rain.

REGRET IS FOREVER
April 2010

Our first two family holidays to the Lake District had seen us staying in other people's houses. You may remember me singing the praises of house swapping; unfortunately it was proving to be ever more difficult to arrange any swaps in the Lakes. The problem was twofold; firstly, we had more definite ideas about locations we wanted to stay in, those that would provide a good base from which we could climb a range of fells, and secondly there appears to be a shortage of people willing to swap houses in the Lakes. Consequently, Easter 2010 saw us heading back to the Old Swan Hotel in Thornthwaite; albeit in an attached cottage this time. Following the usual routine, we headed up the night before and planned a walk from Grasmere to the summit of Stone Arthur.

Saturday 10th April 2010

49. Stone Arthur

Height: 1652 feet (500m)
Route: Grasmere Car Park - Greenhead Gill - Summit

We nearly climbed Stone Arthur when we completed the Fairfield Horseshoe, but at the time had rightly judged it to be a fell too far. We thought that this would be a nice, easy, first climb of the holiday, will we never learn? Stone Arthur is fairly low, really just part of the south-western ridge of Great Rigg. It has Wainwright to thank for its elevation to separate fell status. Although not high, the ascent from The Swan Hotel (Grasmere) was really steep and very hard work. I think our discomfort resulted from a combination of factors; the gradient, early holiday lack of fitness and the extremely hot weather. This was the sort of weather that I thought we would face on our last visit; too hot to walk comfortably. The 'pay off' however, was fantastic views over Grasmere and Easedale Tarn. The climb had been difficult and finding the summit was almost as difficult, but after some careful deliberation, we finally satisfied ourselves that we had reached the true top.

Sunday 11th April 2010

50. Dodd

Height: 1612 feet (502m)
Route: Applethwaite Farm - Dodd

Ever since our failure to reach the true summit of Skiddaw, Tania and I had been determined to return and conquer Lakelands fourth highest peak. We decided not to simply return and march up Jenkin Hill, but to complete a Skiddaw round. The plan was to climb Dodd, Carl Side, Long Side, Ullock Pike, Skiddaw, Skiddaw Little Man, Lonscale Fell and Latrigg.

The route was quite ambitious, but we set out in positive and determined style. We parked the car at Applethwaite and headed towards Dodd. Shortly after starting the walk, Will and Tom suddenly shouted

"Kangeroos!" Checking to see that it was indeed a few days after April the first, I told the boys that it was early, but not early enough to catch me out. They maintained their cries of surprise and it turned out that they had located a field of Wallabies. An interesting example of farm diversification and an interesting sight on the slopes of a Lakeland fell.

We walked on; Dodd is really a separate fell, not linked with the others, with the benefit of hindsight it might have been more sensible to complete it on its own. Dodd lies on Forestry Commission land, and for many years conifers were planted right up to the summit. The top of the fell has now been cleared, but the lower slopes are still densely forested. The trees were to provide an awkward obstacle. The main route to the summit had been closed to protect some nesting Ospreys, and it was difficult to plot a new path. Dodd is home to the only pair of nesting Ospreys in Northern England, we were to find out more about them when we visited the Whinlatter Centre. Forced to choose an alternative route, we went for the direct ascent through the trees. This is not a route to be recommended. An initial narrow path disappeared and we ended up climbing through some really vicious vegetation. The prickly pine ripped my arms and legs to shreds, and didn't do much for my spirit either. Tania and the boys were largely unscathed; they must be made of sterner stuff. Not in the best of moods, we finally emerged on a clear path to the summit, a clear path that we could easily have picked up further down - hindsight is a wonderful thing.

The final ascent was steep, but free of trees, so I wasn't complaining. The summit is marked by a slate memorial pillar, 'In memory of John Lole and Ian Sandelands, Ist Seaton Scout Group.' The views from the top were excellent; we could make out Scafell Pike, Great Gable, Bowfell, the whole of Bassenthwaite Lake, Derwent Water, and our cottage. We didn't stay on Dodd for that long, but George Smith did. Known as the Skiddaw hermit, Smith lived in a make shift home of branches, on a ledge, on the fell in the 1860s. Nice views, but he must have preferred trees to people.

51. Carl Side

Height: 2448 feet (746m)
Route: Descent to Col – Ascent via White Stones

We walked down a clear path from the summit, the path that we should have used on the way up to avoid the vicious 'veg'. Then it was a steep climb towards Carl Side via White Stones. We stopped for lunch on the summit path when we reached the first patches of snow. Tom was struggling a bit, so at this stage we had a few doubts about whether we would be able to complete the whole walk. We decided however, that we would climb to the summit of Carl Side and then make a decision about the rest of the walk. Tania and I were fairly determined that we would not let Skiddaw beat us this time, and Tom is often revived by an intake of calories. The summit is a predominantly grassy plateau, smoothly sloping away on all sides, except to the north where some shattered crags look down upon Southerndale. A small cairn marks the highest point. The view southward down towards Derwentwater was excellent, but I tried to distract Tom from the view towards Skiddaw. The mountain's mighty gray flanks and the extremely steep path that we might have to climb later, looked impressive, but they might have sent Tom into further decline. Instead we looked along the ridge towards Long Side.

52. Long Side

Height: 2408 feet (734m)
Route: Ridge from Carl Side

We followed a simply beautiful ridge route from Carl Side to Long Side. Long Side marks the mid-point of the north-western ridge of Skiddaw, and the views in all directions, all along the ridge were stunning.

53. Ullock Pike

Height: 2408 feet (680m)
Route: Ridge from Long Side

The walk from Carl Side to Long Side had been lovely, but the walk from Long Side to Ullock Pike was even better. Skirting the rim of Longside Edge, with steep descents on either side of the ridge, the walk provided a real sense of height and excitement with no real danger. The top of the fell is a small neat spot carpeted with heather, with fine all round views. The fells name is another that derives from Old Norse. The boys were interested to hear that it translates as "The peak where the wolves play." Interested that is until I started talking about werewolves, and they got a bit 'freaked'. Time to return to Carl Side; sometimes it is a bit depressing to retrace your footsteps on an 'out and back' walk, but the fact that we had to retrace our footsteps on this ridge just doubled the pleasure.

54. Skiddaw

Height: 3054 feet (931m)
Route: Return along ridge to Carl Side – North-east ascent via scree slopes

As we returned to Carl Side, we persuaded a slightly reluctant Tom to aim for the summit of Skiddaw. I don't want people to think that we are really 'pushy' parents, or worse uncaring, but Tom was just a little out of sorts and I knew that he would be more upset if he didn't complete the climb. I remembered a standard running mantra, 'pain is temporary, regret is forever'. I'm not sure if this worked on Tom, but I have always found it quite useful. I started thinking about running, and thinking about how you overcome difficult periods in a race. The secret is to distance 'yourself' from reality. As soon as you focus on your aching legs and screaming lungs, as soon as you think about the distance you still have to run, you might as well give up. You need to concentrate on something which will take your mind off your current situation – If running, watch out for cars at this point. Tom is a great story teller, so at the base of the climb I asked him to tell me about his then, favourite series of books (*How to train your Dragon* by Cressida Cowell). The plan worked. Tom talked nonstop, recounting almost every detail from the stories; suitably distracted he got to the summit more quickly than anyone else, and he was back to his usual self. Tom did well, so did Will and Tania – the climb up the scree was really hard work. We reached South Top first and then enjoyed a beautiful stroll over snow to reach the true summit. On route we explained to the boys that we had not reached the true top on our last visit. Will picked up on this fact and pointed out that they should therefore get another pound this time, we couldn't fault his logic.

This was the boy's second 'three thousand footer', an impressive achievement and a lovely place to be. We spent a few minutes by the triangulation pillar that marks the summit, taking in all the views. The colours were fantastic; the bright clear sky allowed the sun to reflect off the snow and made for a wonderful scene. Whilst at the summit cairn, staring into the distance but dazzled by the sun, a fell runner appeared as if out of nowhere. He told me that he had run up from the Gale Road car park in just fifty five minutes; feeling exhausted by the mere thought of his achievement, we went and had another rest at a wind shelter. Some summits you don't feel like lingering on, but I was enjoying every minute of my time on Skiddaw, we all were. The weather was such a contrast to our last visit, I think we all thought we should make the most of our time here. Content and feeling very satisfied with ourselves, blessed by great weather and glorious views, we did linger, perhaps for too long, until we reluctantly decided it was time to move on. Our exuberant moods continued as we strolled across the summit plateau, heading towards our next objective, Skiddaw Little Man. I had the feeling that this was going to be one of those fantastic walks that you remember for a life time.

55. Skiddaw Little Man

Height: 2832 feet (865m)
Route: Southerly path from Skiddaw

The walk from Skiddaw was superb; feeling full of energy and inspired by our meeting at the triangulation pillar, Will, Tom and I, ran down the grassy slopes of Skiddaw, and then ran ever more slowly up the grassy slopes towards Skiddaw Little Man. Eventually running became walking, and then exhausted, we ground to a complete stop. We lay on the grass; laughing, joking and contemplating our future prospects as fell runners. Little Man by name, but not by nature; It is a distinctive fell, with a lofty summit. The cairn matched Wainwright's sketch with rusty metal sticking out of the stones at all angles. If anything the views were even better than from Skiddaw. We took in the wonderful panorama and then made our way to the Jenkin Hill track by way of Skiddaw Lesser Man.

56. Lonscale Fell

Height: 2346 feet (715m)
Route: Across Jenkin Hill

As we approached the flat top of Jenkin Hill, our legs began to feel really tired; it's quite extraordinary how quickly you can change from feeling full of energy to full of weariness – too much fell running perhaps. We debated missing out Lonscale Fell and returning to the car, but recognising that it was a difficult fell to complete on its own, we ignored our aching legs and we went for it anyway. The walk was a bit of a trudge and not particularly interesting, but we were pleased that we had decided to complete it. The highest point bears a small cairn and has fine views to Thirlmere and Derwentwater.

We descended via Whit Beck and the Jenkin Hill track. As we reached the Gale Road car park we decided to leave Latrigg for another day, we thought it was another fell too far. We were growing increasingly tired, the day was getting late (too much lingering on Skiddaw), and we didn't realise just how close the summit of Latrigg was. However, it was probably the right decision. The walk along the road to Applethwaite seemed endless, it got to the stage where each footstep was an effort – still after twelve miles and four thousand and ninety five feet of ascent it wasn't surprising. Tiredness aside, my thoughts on the top of Skiddaw had been spot on; the walk had been fantastic, one to remember. We drove straight to the Coledale Inn in Braithwaite, for a well earned meal (and a pint).

I woke up early the next morning after a deep and restful sleep, but before I really knew what I was doing, or had a chance to think better of it, I went out for a run. My protesting legs were a bit stiff from yesterdays walk, but after a couple of miles they actually felt a bit better. When I returned to the cottage one of the neighbours was waiting to speak to me, he wanted to know if it was OK to paint the back of our holiday home. Initially I thought it would be a bit of a pain, but exhausted and sweating profusely, I was too tired to put up any objections. After I had recovered the powers of speech, we chatted about the work he had to complete and then got round to talking about running. This was when he mentioned that he had once completed the Bob Graham Round.

Now, I think fell runners are a breed apart, but completing the Bob Graham Round puts you into a different category all together. Only about fifteen hundred people have ever completed this arduous ultra-running event; you need to be mentally tough, resilient, and incredibly fit. I mentioned the race previously when I was talking about Billy Bland, but at this stage I feel I need to say a little more about this massive challenge.

The Bob Graham Round is a circuit of forty two fells, including Skiddaw, Helvellyn, Scafell and Scafell Pike. Bob Graham, a guest house owner from Keswick, created the round in 1932, when he set the record for the highest number of fells reached in a twenty four hour period. Just to make the feat seem even more incredible, Bob Graham completed his round wearing tennis shoes, long shorts and a pyjama jacket; whilst fueled by bread, butter and a lightly boiled egg. Despite many attempts, the feat was not repeated until 1960, when Alan Heaton covered forty two fells in a slightly quicker time. Today, any contender who covers the forty two fells within twenty four hours is eligible for membership of the prestigious Bob Graham Club. The length of the route, starting and finishing at the Moot Hall, Keswick, is about sixty six miles and includes approximately twenty six thousand feet of ascent (Mount Everest stands at 29029 feet). As mentioned previously, Billy Bland stills holds the record for the fastest completion of the round, but others have tried to increase the number of fells covered in twenty four hours. In 1975 Joss Naylor visited seventy two peaks, covering over one hundred miles and climbing thirty seven thousand feet in twenty three hours and twenty minutes. In 1997 Mark Hartell, managed seventy seven peaks in twenty three hours and forty seven minutes. These records are just incredible, they are superhuman achievements. Another record held by Joss Naylor, a sheep farmer from

Wasdale Head and probably the most famous fell runner of all time, put our family challenge into perspective. Joss holds the record for the fastest ever completion of the Wainwrights - all 214 peaks in just seven days. This was achieved in 1986, when Joss was fifty. Thinking that we had better get on with our challenge, I went to get ready for the day ahead. Despite my decision to go for a run, the reality was that climbing Skiddaw and its neighbouring fells had left us all feeling tired, so the order of the day was a less challenging walk.

Monday 12th April 2010

57. Walla Crag

Height: 1234 feet (379m)
Route: Keswick Theatre - Rakefoot - Summit - Descent via Cat Gill - Landing Stage - Return by ferry

We decided to climb Walla Crag, a low but very popular fell, said to give superb views over Derwentwater. Tania planned a walk which unusually for us wouldn't be circular, although the whole trip would be. The plan was to walk from Keswick to the summit, descend via Cat Gill, and then to return in style on a ferry across Derwentwater. We parked close to the Theatre by the Lake, and headed towards the landing stages on Derwentwater. The landing stages present a wonderful image and are quite iconic; used in many a poster and calendar shot of the Lake District. From here we followed a track through Cockshot Wood, exiting onto a fenced lane which led across fields to the Borrowdale road. Crossing the road and climbing some stone steps, we entered Castlehead Wood. Another short climb brought us to the fine viewpoint of Castle Head. Crossing over a bridge by Springs Farm, we headed towards Rakefoot. Crossing another footbridge over a stream, we then crossed a stile and emerged onto the open fell. Climbing steeply, we eventually reached a path following the edge of the Crag, which finally took us to the summit. From the top we had fantastic views of Derwentwater and yesterdays walk. The boys and I were pleased that we could name all the fells of the Skiddaw Massif. Descent was via the very steep, but beautiful Cat Gill. The final section of the walk took longer than we expected, but the river, the waterfalls and the woodland, made it an enchanting excursion. When we reached Derwentwater, we found that our embarkation point was another beautiful landing stage. Sitting, dangling our feet over the water, while soaking up the warm sunshine and admiring the spectacular views, we all decided that this was another of those perfect moments. The ferry trip back to Keswick was equally as enjoyable; Will and Tom were pleased to be doing something 'touristy', and together we enjoyed a delightfully relaxing afternoon.

Tuesday 13th April 2010

58. Great Cockup

Height: 1726 feet (526m)
Route: Orthwaite Village - Burntrod Gill - Summit

You can imagine the boys' reaction when we told them we were going to climb Great Cockup; after a few minutes of laughter, smirking and worryingly innuendo, I pointed out in an annoyingly knowing way, that we were off to climb a large fell, in a secluded valley, that was home to many woodcocks. Not quite so interested now, they went off to pack their rucksacks. The idea today was to complete a 'Back of Skiddaw Round', taking in Meal Fell, Great Sca Fell, Brae Fell and Longlands Fell, as well as Great Cockup. We started the walk close to Orthwaite village, and as soon I stepped out of the car I immediately regretted my decision to wear shorts. The weather had changed significantly from yesterday, now it was overcast and decidedly chilly. We walked along a road, before following a gently rising bridleway, and then we completed a final steep 'yomp' up through some heather. The heather was another reminder that shorts were not such a good idea. Legs only recently recovered from 'prickly pine' attack, were scratched to bits again. I also remembered a story from last night's news about ticks. So scratched, cold and now paranoid, I made my way wearily to the summit.

59. Meal Fell

Height: 1804 feet (550m)
Route: From Great Cockup via Trusmadoor

From the summit of Great Cockup, we descended to the pass of Trusmadoor, here we stopped for what turned out to be a very cold lunch. Keen to get walking again in an attempt to warm ourselves up, we set forth quickly and completed the short but steep climb up to Meal Fell. The summit was really interesting and quite useful. A large circular shelter, possibly an old grouse butt, provided temporary respite from the biting wind.

60. Great Scafell

Height: 2136 feet (651m)
Route: Rising grass slope from Meal Fell

From the summit of Meal Fell, we followed a clear route, ascending a steep grassy slope to reach the summit of Great Sca Fell. The summit is a broad plateau on which the highest point is marked by a small cairn. Although still cold and overcast, the views towards the Solway Firth and the Scottish Borders were excellent. As we celebrated another Wainwright, we met a walker who told us that he had completed all the Wainwrights three times. He asked us where we were going to next, and when we said Brae Fell, he pointed out the way; but he was pointing in completely the wrong direction (Perhaps he had stood on the wrong summit three times). Saying nothing, but trusting ourselves this time, we headed off in the right direction.

61. Brae Fell

Height: 1923 feet (586m)
Route: Northward leading bridleway

At last the weather started improving, the wind dropped and the sun made an attempt to come out. At long last I began to thaw out, and I started feeling a little happier with life in general, and walking in particular. It's strange, but after the euphoria of the last few days, I struggled today, and began to have doubts for the first time ever, about our plan to complete all the Wainwrights. I think it was a combination of getting far too cold far too quickly, being over tired (another morning run wasn't a good idea), and not being overly impressed with the smooth, hilly and grassy Udale Fells. It's difficult to always be upbeat and positive when completing a challenge over a long period of time. I think it's inevitable that you are going to experience 'off days', when negative thoughts get in the way and you doubt the wisdom of your decisions. Fortunately, as I warmed up (still regretting shorts), I started to cheer up, and I remembered how lucky I was to be out walking with the people I love most in the world. I also remembered the message of my words to Tom on Skiddaw; giving up is easy but regret is forever. The summit of Brae Fell marked the end of my dark mood, fairly ironically it turns out. Wainwright comments that "if all hills were like Brae Fell, there would be far fewer fell walkers". The top was marked by an impressive large cairn, and it provided more great views towards the Scottish Uplands and towards our final fell of the day.

62. Longlands Fell

Height: 1585 feet (483m)
Route: Across Charleton Ravine – Summit – Return via Old Cumbria Way

We could see the summit of Longlands Fell from Brae Fell, but we could also see a deep ravine that made any direct approach problematic. However we were too tired for detours, and consequently walked straight towards the ravine. When we arrived, Tania and Will skirted the edge to find an easier passage, whilst Tom and I continued with the direct route; sliding down one side on our backsides, and scrambling up the other side on all fours. After this point all was plain sailing, a gentle easy stroll across a grassy slope brought us to the summit of Longlands Fell. The cairned top offered more great views to the north and also towards Skiddaw in the south. The walk back to the car was a lengthy one, but an enjoyable one. Will and Tom loved fell running down the grassy slopes from the summit, and the final walk along the Old Cumbria Way took us past fields full of gamboling lambs; all very idyllic – think I'll skip the lamb casserole tonight.

Wednesday 14th April 2010

63. High Crag (The High Stile Range)

Height: 2441 feet (744m)
Route: Buttermere – Scarth Gap – Gamlin End – Summit

Fantastic weather today, so the plan was to complete the High Stile Range. I first completed this walk over twenty years ago, and ever since then I have remembered it as one of my favourite Lakeland walks. I remember the breathtaking views into the valleys of Ennerdale and Buttermere, afforded by the spectacular high level ridge from High Crag to Red Pike. Some people complain about the plantations in Ennerdale, rightly claiming they are not natural, but the reality is that the vast majority of the landscape of the Lakes isn't natural. The traditional fell sides that we all know and love, are all managed; without constant sheep grazing they would be covered in deciduous forest. I'll accept the argument that the plantations are full of non native species, but to my mind they still present a glorious view. My only worries about returning to the High Stile Range, were doubts that the walk could possibly live up to last time and doubts that Tania, Will and Tom, could possibly enjoy the walk as much as I had – I thought that I might have built it up a little too much.

We parked at Buttermere and crossed to the other side of the lake. Here we followed a charming path beside the lake, until detouring to follow a path climbing towards Scarth Gap. The route presented us with lovely views down to Buttermere, and impressive views up to the precipice of High Crag. I was delighted to be back in the high mountains after the moorland hills of yesterday, and the weather was perfect for walking; bright, clear, and just the right temperature. Everything was going well and I was enjoying the walk as much as last time, unfortunately, just like last time, I couldn't see a direct path to Gamlin End, so we followed a direct line instead. The route was incredibly steep, looking down induced vertigo, and scrambling on all fours was required for much of the way. I can't say it was a particularly enjoyable section of the walk, but when we reached the line of the ridge, the hard work heightened the satisfaction of our achievement. From the ridge we climbed up a steep scree slope (this time following a path) and reached our first summit of the day. The views were tremendous, particularly fine were those towards the Scafell group and Great Gable. I needn't have worried about Tania and the boys, they were really enjoying the walk and it was only going to get better.

64. High Stile

Height: 2648 feet (807m)
Route: Ridge route from High Crag

After a short descent from High Crag, we followed a path skirting the edge of the ridge. The views were simply fantastic, just about all the major fells could be made out, and the valleys of Ennerdale and Buttermere were as beautiful as I remembered. The only thing breaking the dream like quality of it all was a fighter plane putting on an impressive display of low flying. This was to be the last day that anything flew for a few weeks; all planes being grounded as a result of a volcanic dust cloud emanating from Iceland. The delightful ridge route led directly to the highest point on our walk, the summit of High Stile. Several cairns looked like contenders for the highest point, so we touched them all, just to be on the safe side. The views were simply fantastic, and we took some time out, just to take them all in. The highlights were probably the North Western Fells, Buttermere, Ennerdale and Crummock Water.

65. Red Pike

Height: 2477 feet (755m)
Route: Ridge route from High Stile - descent via Bleaberry Tarn

The path to Red Stile is an obvious one, and the summit is even more obvious - very red! The ridge continued to delight, but poor Will suffered from sore feet as his newly purchased and hideously expensive boots started to rub. We slowed our pace accordingly, but soon reached the top. The summit is sheer on three sides, and the views continued to impress; this time highlights included views to Crummock Water, Buttermere, Ennerdale Water, Pillar and Grasmoor. Whilst the walk so far had been fantastic, and Tania, Will and Tom were in agreement with my views on the subject of the High Stile Range, the descent was to prove less popular. The initial descent was down loose red scree. It was impossible to stand up and we all quickly developed very red backsides. After the scree, boulders and stones had been laid to form a rough path, but the path seemed to go on forever. Tania considered it to be the worst descent she had ever made. We did however spend a few delightful minutes at Bleaberry Tarn, and the view of Fleetwith Pike, reflected in the clear and still waters of Buttermere, was more than adequate compensation for the difficulties encountered. Extra compensation if required was to be found in a beer glass whilst soaking up the evening sun at the Bridge Hotel.

Thursday 15th April 2010

66. Binsey

Height: 1466 feet (447m)
Route: Binsey Lodge - Summit

The decision today was to try and complete a couple of the 'easier' fells. Our first objective was going to be the isolated fell of Binsey, which logic dictated could be climbed on its own, and our second objective was to climb Latrigg, the one summit we missed out of our Skiddaw Round. Binsey is situated in an otherwise low lying watershed. It has a distinctly rounded, 'pudding basin' shape when viewed from most directions. The walk did prove to be easy; the ascent only took twenty five minutes. We parked on the roadside, close to Binsey Lodge, and quickly scampered up a clear track to the summit. The relative isolation of Binsey provided fine panoramic views. To the north the Solway Firth and Scotland could be clearly seen, and to the south the Coniston Fells. The top of the fell was quite interesting; a tumulus marks the top, and some of the stones have been used to produce circular wind shelters. Although I was prepared this time (many layers and trousers), we did use the shelter to get some respite from the very chilly northerly wind. However, not wishing to allow the cold any chance to take hold, we soon decided to walk back down the fell. Will and Tom decided to run down, and with the wind behind them they reached the foot of the fell in only ten minutes.

67. Latrigg

Height: 1203 feet (368m)
Route: Gale road car park - Summit

Our next destination was Latrigg; we drove to the Gale road car park and completed a very short and easy walk. Possibly too short - it felt a bit like cheating. We decided to complete the walk from where we would have started from if we hadn't previously given Latrigg up as being a fell too far. Latrigg is one of the lowest fells in the Lake District, but we didn't even really climb it. Latrigg is the most easily accessible Wainwright and a recently constructed pathway allows disabled access to the summit. Partly following this route, our walk from the car park was a simple ten minute stroll. Latrigg is a popular fell, not just because of ease of access, but also because of its fine views. Northward are Skiddaw and Blencathra, while to the south are Keswick, Derwentwater, Borrowdale and the high fells of Central Lakeland. Wainwright delighted in the view, describing "a panorama of crowded detail, all of it of great beauty: indeed this scene is one of the gems of the district". We completed both walks in the morning, so we had time to go into Keswick for a pub lunch at the Oddfellow Arms - even though we hadn't earnt it. It's a nice pub, full of horse racing memorabilia, cheap, cheerful and excellent taste in music (non-stop Smiths).

Friday 16th April 2010

68. Great Crag

Height: 1476 feet (440m)
Route: Watendlath – Great Crag Summit

Today we planned to walk from Watendlath and climb two fells – Great Crag and Grange Fell. The drive from the Borrowdale road to Watendlath was an experience in itself; beautiful scenery, but a long, winding and very narrow road. I'm used to the country lanes of Devon, but felt anxious at several stages on the drive today – nearly running out of petrol didn't help. The road crosses Ashness Bridge, one of the most picturesque and consequently one of the most photographed spots in the Lake District. The view down from the bridge towards Derwentwater, must be a contender for one of the best views in Lakeland. Eventually, feeling slightly stressed, but relieved to have arrived, we parked in Watendlath. Watendlath is a small hamlet owned by the National Trust. The location of the hamlet is stunning; sitting high between the Borrowdale and Thirlmere valleys, next to an attractive tarn and surrounded by fells. Leaving Watendlath, we experienced a few directional problems as we walked towards, or more accurately away from Great Crag; Tania was following directions from a walking guide, but the main path had been diverted to avoid the worst of the boggy terrain, consequently we overshot the summit. I have previously drawn attention to my sometimes poor lack of direction, but this time I had correctly located the summit using map and compass, but my thoughts had been summarily dismissed. Annoyed at having gone the wrong way, I was also secretly pleased that I had been proved right for once. Back on track, we wandered through bogs, and then climbed through heather to reach the rocky tops of Great Crag. I say 'tops', Great Crag has two similar high spots, both identified by cairns; we visited both and thought to ourselves (not for the first time), that we really should buy a new GPS.

69. Grange Fell

Height: 1363 feet (410m)
Route: Rosthwaite Path – Grange Fell Summit – return to Watendlath

We took a bearing from the top of Great Crag, to ensure that we stayed on course for Grange Fell. We didn't get lost, but the route was really boggy, comparable to some of the mires on Dartmoor. The fell has three main summits, Brund Fell (the highest), King's How (a memorial to King Edward Vll), and Esther Knott. The boys enjoyed scrambling and climbing over the rocky tops, after which we returned to Watendlath for a nice cup of tea. We weren't quite ready to end our last full day in the Lakes, so we headed to Derwentwater and hired a motor boat; great fun and great views of the fells.

Saturday 17th April 2010

70. Whinlatter

Height: 1610 feet (525m)
Route: Whinlatter Visitors Centre – Ascent through forest footpaths

After packing and saying farewell to the Old Swan Hotel, we headed to the Whinlatter Visitors Centre. The weather was still good, so we had decided to visit another two fells before heading home. The plan was to climb Whinlatter, and then to drive towards Rydal Water and climb Loughrigg. The Visitors Centre at Whinlatter is situated in England's only mountain forest. Planted just after the First World War in an attempt to combat a timber shortage, the forest has now become a major recreational area. If you have a head for heights you can 'Go Ape'; swinging from ropes and zip sliding some forty feet in the air. The Centre also includes a large purpose built mountain bike trail and numerous walking trails; one of which was to lead us to the top of Whinlatter. Before starting our walk we looked around the centre, and spent an interesting few minutes learning all about Ospreys. The nest which had caused our re-routing on Dodd can be observed via CCTV from the centre. The volunteers staffing the area were interesting and informative; their knowledge was impressive and their enthusiasm was infectious. Ospreys are spectacular fish-eating birds of prey, with a wingspan of nearly five feet. They have incredibly sharp eyesight, and they can be seen (although not by us) hovering above Bassenthwaite Lake, looking out for their next meal. The Ospreys' relatively recent return to the Lake District, was a result of several years of hard work, and required the construction of purpose built nesting sites. I think it was well worth it, and if I ever spot them in flight, I might even forgive them the 'prickly pine' detour. The walk to Whinlatter itself was nice and easy. After initially climbing up through forest paths (looking out for red squirrels), we then followed the forest fence, before climbing onto the open fell to reach the summit. We looked towards Hopegill Head and Grisedale Pike, pleased with the fact that we could name an increasing number of fells.

71. Loughrigg

Height: 1099 feet (335m)
Route: White Moss car park – Loughrigg Terrace – Summit

We drove to White Moss car park, and joined the crowds appearing to be making their way towards Loughrigg summit. We walked through woods before leaving Rydal Water behind and joining Loughrigg Terrace. This path has apparently been a favourite viewpoint since Wordsworth's time, and it's easy to see why. The path delivers excellent views over Grasmere towards the Helvellyn Range, Dunmail Raise and the Easedale fells. At the far end of the terrace we turned sharp left and started climbing up the path to the summit. It was at this point that the crowds disappeared. We were certainly not alone, but it was evident that the majority of walkers appeared to have some kind of phobia towards slopes. As we neared the summit I decided to challenge the boys to a race. Feeling confident I gave them a headstart, a headstart that I never made up – I obviously must have been carrying an injury. The summit was marked by a triangulation pillar, and I was marked by the realization that the boys were getting faster and I was getting slower. Interestingly, when we returned to the car, we noticed that it was covered in a layer of what could only have been volcanic ash. It was only at this point that we realized we hadn't seen any planes flying since climbing the High Stile Range.

Another fantastic holiday was sadly over; another eight days and this time twenty three Wainwrights. We had all loved completing the Skiddaw Round and going for the meal afterwards; Tania and I particularly enjoyed the High Stile ridge, and Will, Tom and I thoroughly enjoyed the motor boat on Derwentwater. Whilst discussing the highlights of our holiday on the journey home, we made an easy and a unanimous family decision to return to the Lakes in August – surely it wouldn't be the 'rainy' season again!

PHILOSOPHICAL WANDERINGS
August 2010

I really enjoy all the planning and preparation that proceeds a holiday in the Lake District; thinking about likely walks, planning routes and even sorting out all the walking kit. What I also love is thinking about which books to take with me. I love reading, fiction mainly, but also history, travel, and well, just about anything and everything. While I'm working I find it difficult to read, time doesn't always allow me the luxury of being able to get fully immersed in a novel. On numerous occasions I have nodded off whilst still holding a book in my hands, waking up slightly confused moments later, and consequently having to read the same page over and over again. Often I will deliberately leave an eagerly anticipated novel until the next holiday comes along, and I have time to savour every word. "There's more to life than books you know. But not much more" sang the Smiths, I know what they mean; some of my books are amongst my most treasured possessions. In the event of a house fire, once the family are safe, I'll be going back in for them.

The best books stay with you, make you think and perhaps influence some aspect of your life. For evidence of such influence, you have probably already spotted that the opening lines of this book were inspired by one of my favourite classics; if you didn't, swallow your pride, put your prejudice to one side, and go back and have another look. I had read and thoroughly enjoyed a number of books since our last trip to the Lakes, two of them proved to have an influence on our holiday this time.

Firstly, *Born to Run* by Christopher McDougall; nothing to do with Bruce Springstein, but a book about a hidden tribe, ultra running and ultra runners. The hidden tribe in question are the Tarahumara, famed as long distance runners. Living in the Copper Canyon area of Mexico, the Tarahumara live in widely dispersed settlements and have developed a tradition of long distance running to link the separate communities together. Their endurance is legendary, their prowess as runners belies the mantra of 'no pain, no gain'. They cover vast distances and run for days, but they run in a relaxed style and they use the 'toe strike' method favoured by barefoot runners. 'Toe strike', involves bouncing along on the balls of your feet, rather than striking the ground with your heels; this in theory puts far less pressure on the joints, prevents injury, reduces effort levels, and thus allows huge distances to be covered. It is now widely believed that our ancient ancestors used this method to hunt prey. Humans are literally 'born to run'. No other animals have our endurance. We may not be the fastest creatures over a short distance, but over time humans can track and chase to exhaustion just about any other animal on the planet. Today, many ultra-runners use this technique to increase performance. I thought I would give it a go. I imagined myself gliding effortlessly to lots of new personal best times, what I actually achieved was a torn Achilles. I'm sure that running like a Tarahumara is a good idea for most, but trying to change my running style at an advanced age, and far too quickly, left me unable walk for a few days and unable to run for a couple of months. I arrived in the Lakes with a still sore Achilles, fairly unfit and anxious about my ability to complete any steep or arduous walks.

The second book which had an influence on my holiday was *What I talk about when I talk about running* by Haruki Murakami. The book is essentially a personal memoir that links Murakami's philosophy of life to his philosophy of running. He states that the qualities he needs for writing are those he learnt from running. Murakami, a successful Japanese writer; believes that challenge and discipline are essential to success on all levels. He makes the following statement 'Pain is inevitable. Suffering is optional' and uses this as a mantra for life. I found the book fascinating, and I do believe that challenge is essential to fulfilment. It's important to have goals - Wainwright thought that "life without ambition is, well, aimless wandering". Thinking about all these philosophical wanderings, I looked forward to resuming our family challenge.

Saturday 21st August 2010

72. Raven Crag

Height: 1520 feet (461m)
Route: Thirlmere Reservoir car park - Summit

The first walk of our August holiday started from Thirlmere Dam, but my ability to complete the climb without difficulty had been sealed earlier in the day. My Achilles wasn't great, but the real problem was an all too tasty breakfast in Ambleside. I loved my 'full English' at the time, but it proved to be poor sustenance for walking. The main face of the fell rises above the dam and appears as a five hundred foot crag. Our climb followed a steep path, rising through forest before emerging at the top. Feeling far too full and far too thirsty, I made slow progress as Tania and the boys raced ahead. I was relieved to eventually reach the summit, however one difficulty was replaced by another as we were surrounded by very hungry midges (they obviously hadn't had a cooked breakfast). Not wanting to linger on the summit for too long, we took in the views to the reservoir and then headed down. Descent was back the way we had come, and my Achilles didn't like it at all; silently cursing 'toe strike' running, cooked breakfasts and midges, I walked slowly, carefully and a little miserably back to the car.

Sunday 22nd August 2010

73. Souther Fell (A Blencathra Round)

Height: 1680 feet (522m)
Route: Mungrisdale Village – Summit

My negative mood of yesterday hadn't lasted for too long. A trip to Keswick put my on the road to recovery, and a trip to the 'Dog and Gun' raised my spirits further. What finally completed my renaissance was seeing our apartment (another situated in the old Swan Hotel), it was absolutely beautiful, a real home from home. My only worry today was a nagging doubt about my Achilles, but remembering the words of Murakami, I was determined to ignore the pain. The plan today was to complete a Blencathra Round; starting from Mungrisdale village we wanted to reach the summits of Souther Fell, Blencathra, Mungrisdale Common, Bannerdale Crags and Bowscale Fell.

The day was bright and clear, if a little breezy, and we were all looking forward to our first major walk of the holiday. This was one of those walks that we had thought about and planned in advance, so we knew that we would have few navigational problems. Full of confidence we left the car armed with a new GPS, OS map, additional route notes and confidence; minutes later we were completely confused and unable to find the start of the walk. For once I don't think we were to blame. The landscape tied up with the map, we could clearly identify where we had parked, but a road and a bridge that existed on the map, didn't exist in the landscape; was the OS map wrong? I know it's hard to believe, but after a delay of some thirty minutes, walking up and down the road, scrutinising the map and countryside, we concluded that it must be. Good moods evaporating and frustration taking over, we took off our boots and forded the river at the point where we judged the bridge should have been (a long disused road did lead to the river at this point). The bed of the river was very rocky and very slippery, but we managed to cross without anyone having to swim. Finally able to start the walk, after drying our feet, we picked up a clear path which traversed and then climbed the slopes of the grassy fell.

The highest point of Souther Fell was difficult to locate, the top is a wide ridge, but this time our GPS came to the rescue and we identified the fairly indistinct summit. Tania told Will and Tom about the "ghost army" of Souther Fell. On the evening of Midsummers Day 1745, a line of marching troops and cavalry were seen travelling along the summit ridge. The ground over which they appeared to move was known to be too steep for such manoeuvers, but the procession continued for some hours until night fell, constantly appearing at one end of the ridge and disappearing at the other. Many sober and respected witnesses were assembled to view the proceedings and later testified on oath to what they had seen. The next day Souther Fell was climbed and not a footprint was found on the soft ground of the ridge. The only scientific explanation ever offered was that this was some bizarre mirage or reflection of the army of Bonnie Prince Charlie, who were exercising on the west coast of Scotland.

I began to think that the missing bridge from the beginning of our walk might have been some spectral imagining; perhaps the OS map makers had come to Mungrisdale on a Midsummers day. The boys listened attentively, gripped by the story; I wouldn't dream of suggesting that they were scared, but they were keen to leave the ghostly Souther Fell behind them.

74. Blencathra

Height: 2847 feet (868m)
Route: Scales Fell – Summit

Souther Fell is a ridge of Blencathra, so our route was straightforward; the only question in our minds was whether to approach the summit via Sharp Edge or Scales Fell. Tania had already decided her chosen route and it didn't include Sharp Edge. Wainwright notes that Sharp Edge is the highlight of any ascent of the mountain, its former name was Razor Edge, and both names aptly describe the narrow ridge with its sheer drops on either side. Shorter in distance than Striding Edge, it is supposedly more awkward to cross. On a previous visit to the Lakes I climbed Blencathra alone and then descended to Sharp Edge, but the ridge was covered in ice and I decided to leave it for another day. Unfortunately in attempting to retrace my steps back up the mountain, I tracked too far to my left and ended up having to climb out of Tarn Crags. I have never, before or since, been so scared in the mountains; the experience was not one I ever wish to repeat. At one stage I completely froze and couldn't contemplate climbing up or down, fortunately I pulled myself together and pulled myself up the mountain. I think you know where this entire preamble is going. As we got closer to the point of no return, I decided that today was not 'another' day; consequently I headed up Scales Fell with Tania, William and Tom, and with cries of 'wimp' ringing in my ears (cheers boys). From our route we could see a number of 'braver' individuals picking their way carefully across Sharp Edge; perhaps I should have gone for it after all.

As we reached the summit, we made our way through the crowds (and kite flyers!) towards a large cairn, supposedly marking the highest point of the fell. The cairn however, didn't appear to be constructed on the highest point of the mountain, checking with the GPS and finding our suspicions to be true, Tom started to construct a new cairn on the 'real' summit. The views from both summits were excellent. To the west we could see Skiddaw, and from the west round to the north-east, the Back O'Skiddaw Fells, backed by the mountains of The Southern Uplands. The Pennines formed the horizon from the north-east to the south-east, and to the south we could see Helvellyn. From the south to the south-west many major Lakeland peaks could be seen, many of these we had already climbed; Scafell Pike, Grisedale Pike and Great Gable, to name but a few. We spent a few quiet minutes taking in the whole panorama, and then plotted a course for Mungrisdale Common. It was at this point that I remembered my Achilles; it wasn't that I was ignoring the pain; it was that my Achilles hadn't hurt all day. I realized that yesterdays walking must have acted as a very effective form of physiotherapy.

75. Mungrisdale Common

Height: 2068 feet (633m)
Route: Blencathra Summit - North - Mungrisdale Common

With the GPS leading the way, we descended over some very boggy ground heading towards Mungrisdale Common. The whole area is a rather featureless plateau and was allegedly Wainwright's least favourite fell, but we rather enjoyed it. Wainwright commented that it "has no more pretension to elegance than a pudding that has been sat on". He also stated that "Any one of a thousand tufts of tough bent and cotton-grass might lay claim to crowning the highest point...A thousand tufts, yet not one can be comfortably reclined upon, this being a summit that holds indefinitely all the water that falls upon it". Fortunately, since Wainwright's time some enterprising soul has constructed a small cairn, and we were happy to accept this as the true summit; unfortunately, the summit still holds all the water that falls upon it. The cairn was in the centre the boggiest ground yet encountered, and someone (they shall remain nameless) splashed Tom whilst he posed for a summit photo (Tom wasn't happy).

76. Bannerdale Crags

Height: 2330 feet (683m)
Route: South-east walk across bog from Mungrisdale Common

We headed south-east from Mungrisdale Common, walking back across the bog and skirting around the base of Foule Crag, until we climbed up to the summit of Bannerdale Crags. The route wasn't that long, but it seemed much longer; the energy sapping bogs had been taking their toll on our already tired legs. The top of the fell was smooth and grassy, the summit, slightly set back from the crags was marked by a small cairn of flat stones. The summit provided more lovely views to the Coniston Fells and to Sharp Edge – perhaps I did make the right decision.

77. Bowscale Fell

Height: 2306 feet (702m)
Route: North and then NNE to Summit

We walked back along the ridge of Bannerdale Crags to the summit of Bowscale Fell. The ridge provided stunning views, and the summit complete with a wind shelter on the highest point provided some more. We returned to Mungrisdale Village via the East Ridge. The route included a steep descent, but had much to recommend it; especially the section by the Glenderamackin River. We had walked eleven miles and completed three thousand feet of ascent; we all agreed that it had been another fantastic walk.

Monday 23rd August 2010

78. High Seat

Height: 1995 feet (608m)
Route: Ashness Gill - South-west to Summit

One of the reasons why I like running is that it gives me time to think, I sometimes like to muse and contemplate ideas and issues. Whilst running this morning I began to think about the key ideas discussed in the two books mentioned at the beginning of this chapter, and whether they applied to us as a family. Firstly endurance; many people have said to us that the boy's can't possibly complete this walk or that walk, but we have never doubted the boy's abilities to walk long distances, and consequently they have never doubted themselves. The reality is that we are all capable of far more than we think we are. Secondly, what about pain and suffering? As mentioned previously 'suffering' can be alleviated or at least diminished with a little positive thinking, when we walk we do always try and keep positive, it is sometimes all too easy to give up and to give in to difficulties. Completing my run I realized that a lot of the 'stuff' I think about is rubbish. I did however think that we would have to keep positive today, the forecast was for rain and low cloud, followed by heavy rain.

Covering ourselves from head to foot in waterproofs, we decided to walk from Ashness Bridge to High Seat and Bleaberry Fell. We left the car and walked alongside Ashness Gill. The walk is wet underfoot in normal conditions; today the whole route was waterlogged. Despite some slippery rocks and large bogs, the walk was really enjoyable. At one stage we heard and then saw a lovely waterfall, it suddenly appeared as if out of nowhere, emerging through the swirling cloud and mist. When we left Ashness Gill to make our way to the summit, the route became more difficult to follow and the GPS came in to its own. When we thought it couldn't get any wetter, we encountered some extremely boggy areas and the fell appeared to be surrounded by its own defensive moat. We were relieved when we finally set foot on the small, dry, stone platform that marks the summit. No views to speak of, but we did catch glimpses of our next destination.

79. Bleaberry Fell

Height: 1932 feet (590m)
Route: North from High Seat

The route to Bleaberry Fell took bog stomping to a new level. The ground was completely waterlogged and our boots sank up to ankle level; unfortunately Tom's boots were not waterproof. Wainwright states that "This is a walk to wish on one's worst enemy" and he recommends it "only as a penance for sins", perversely we enjoyed the walk. We were all dry under our waterproofs (apart from Tom's feet), the weather was so bad it was truly impressive, and we weren't suffering. The summit was marked by a small cairn and a shelter (unfortunately no roof), the views are alleged to be impressive, but we could only see each other (still fairly impressive). The rain somehow managed to increase in intensity, so with our heads literally in the clouds, we headed off the fells. Our GPS guided us to the car and our stomachs guided us to the Dog and Gun in Keswick; beer and goulash proved to be a warm and winning combination

Tuesday 24th August 2010

80. Great Mell Fell

Height: 1760 feet (537m)
Route: Ascent from Brownrigg

Today we decided to focus on the Eastern fells; the objectives, Great Mell Fell and its twin, Little Mell Fell. Great Mell Fell, was yet another fell that should have been easy to climb, but once again we succeeded in making hard work of it. We brought two guide books with us today and they recommended different routes (sometimes choice is a dangerous thing). Both books started the walk from Brownrigg Farm, but the first guide book wanted us to cross the first stile encountered, and the second guide book the second stile. We took the first option and then followed a path that skirted the base of the fell. As we walked, we looked for a path that would take us through the trees to the top of the fell. The lower slopes of Great Mell Fell are densely forested, and remembering Dodd, we didn't want to endanger life and limb by forcing are way through. After what seemed like an age, and after appearing to have walked around the entire fell with no sign of an upward leading path, we decided to head up anyway.

The climb was steep, awkward and relentless; every time I thought the summit was in sight, it turned out to be that little bit further away. Tania and Tom didn't like this walk, I didn't either, but I kept up a positive attitude (remember, suffering is optional), Will loved the walk, and it was he who smiling broadly, conquered the fell first. The summit is believed to have been a Bronze Age burial mound, and when Tania and Tom arrived it looked like another funeral might have to be arranged. At the summit we noticed, perhaps unsurprisingly, an obvious, clear path leading downwards, downwards all the way to the second stile – if only.

81. Little Mell Fell

Height: 1657 feet (505m)
Route: Direct ascent from The Hause

We drove to The Hause, and as suggested by Wainwright planned a straightforward up and down route. Little Mell Fell is actually not much 'littler' than Great Mell Fell, but this time the walk did prove to be much easier. A fifteen minute steep climb up the isolated fell brought us to an OS triangulation column which marked the summit. Wainwright describes the fell as "an uninspiring, unattractive, bare and rounded hump", but we all quite enjoyed the climb and the resulting panorama. The views towards Ullswater, The Eastern and The Far Eastern Fells, were impressive, to say the least.

Wednesday 25th August 2010

82. Whiteside (Grasmoor Round)

Height: 2317 feet (707m)
Route: Rannerdale car park – Lanthwaite Green – Whiteside via Whin Ben

Not all great walks have to be great all the way, but I think they have to end well. A bad start can be forgiven and forgotten, but a bad ending stays with you; perhaps it's a little bit like life! The plan today was to complete a Grasmoor Round, climbing Whiteside, Hopegill Head, Grasmoor, Wandope, Whiteless Pike and Rannerdale Knotts. The only downside of this route was that however we planned it we knew that we would have to include a long section, walking along the B5289. Correctly anticipating that this wouldn't be a particularly enjoyable section, we decided to get it out of the way first. The road is quite busy by Lake District standards, and has many blind corners; consequently we had to keep our eyes down, looking out for cars, rather than being able to look up at the stunning mountain scenery. The real walk started from Lanthwaite Green. After crossing Liza Beck, we headed up a steep path, scrambling our way towards the subsidiary top of Whin Ben. After reaching this point, the path levels out, providing a little relief before the final climb to the summit. This final section was very steep, more scramble than walk and in places more of a climb than a scramble. The route follows the edge of the crags overlooking Gasgale Gill; with sheer drops and awkward steps, some sections were genuinely scary. Tania coped by not looking down, I coped by hanging on for dear life, and the boys, they weren't fazed at all. The sense of achievement involved in reaching a summit is often proportional to the degree of difficulty involved; it's fair to say that Tania and I felt very pleased with ourselves. We enjoyed an early lunch on the top of Whiteside, but so did the midges; somewhat more quickly than anticipated, we set off towards Hopegill Head.

The ridge walk from Whiteside to Hopegill Head was described by Wainwright as "An exhilarating high-level traverse with a grand finish", he wasn't wrong. The walk was stunning; combining great views with the excitement of an exposed, but perfectly safe route. Arriving at Hopegill Head for the second time (we had first visited the fell as part of our

Coledale Round) put pay to the theory that things are 'never as good as the first time'. The rocky summit and the views were as good as we remembered.

83. Grasmoor

Height: 2791 feet (852m)
Route: Sand Hill – Coledale Hause – Summit

Leaving Hopegill Head behind us, we climbed over Sand Hill before descending to Coledale Hause. Climbing up from here was hard work, and we all slowed down as our energy levels evaporated in the warm weather; all that is apart from Tom. The final ascent of the fell saw Tom striding out in front, quickly climbing the grassy slopes and putting the rest of us to shame. The top of the fell is an extensive grass covered plateau, and many think that the abundant turf gives the fell its name, but Grasmoor is derived from the Old Norse word *Grise* – meaning wild boar – fortunately wild boar were not abundant. The summit, the highest in the north-western fells, is marked by a large stone cairn. The cairn is divided into compartments, each providing shelter and spectacular views; particularly memorable were those towards Scotland, the Isle of Man and the High Stile range.

84. Wandope

Height: 2533 feet (772m)
Route: Descent to Coledale Hause – West to Summit

From the summit of Grasmoor we retraced our footsteps to reach Coledale Hause, and then headed west to reach the top of Wandope. We were all in high spirits; the weather was clear and bright, the walk had provided a great variety of interest, and the vast majority of the ascent had been completed. The summit was marked by a small cairn, resting on a gentle grassy dome. The origin of the cairn stones must remain a mystery as the area was bereft of any other rocks. Fantastic views extended in all directions, with the Scafells being particularly impressive. The only negative was the return of the midges.

85. Whiteless Pike

Height: 2159 feet (660m)
Route: West and then South-west to Summit

From a distance, the walk to Whitless Pike looked like it was going to be perilous. As we got closer we realised that it was a beautiful, but thankfully easy ridge walk. Passing over Saddle Gate we reached the small peaked summit, and were rewarded by both breathtaking views and solitude – if you don't include the midges.

86. Rannerdale Knotts

Height: 1160 feet (355m)
Route: South then WNW to Summit

Today's walk had started with a bit of a trudge along the B5289, but it was finishing in style. Leaving Whiteless Pike we descended over Whititeless Breast, and enjoyed constant, glorious views towards Buttermere. Turning right at a small cairn, we followed Low Bank heading towards the top of Rannerdale Knotts. The path runs above the side valley of Rannerdale, said to be the site of a battle. In the eleventh century, invading Normans marching from Cockermouth, were stopped in their tracks by local warriors under the command of Earl Boether. Historical evidence as to the truth of this tale may be a bit thin on the ground, but it does look like the perfect spot for an ambush. Whatever the truth of the tale, the fell is a real mountain, a mountain in miniature maybe, but perfectly formed. The summit is preceded by a series of rocky outcrops, and Will and Tom led the way. Tania and I couldn't keep pace with the boys, we shouted ahead telling them to wait – they did for a while and then they bounded off enthusiastically. Today's walk was rapidly becoming one of my favourites; it had it all – scrambles, ridge walks, impressive summits and lovely views. The final summit of the day didn't disappoint either. It was late in the day, we had the fell to ourselves, and we were provided with a simply enchanting view of Buttermere. The summit provided a great end to a great walk.

Pride comes before a fall. Congratulating ourselves on completing the long road section of the route first, we descended directly to the car and drove into Buttermere for some much needed food and drink; someone had forgotten to pack the extra water bottles this morning, and consequently we were all very thirsty. Downing my pint rapidly, rather than savouring every mouthful, I thought the beer didn't taste quite as it should. Unfortunately by the time I confirmed my suspicions that the beer had definitely passed its prime, my glass was empty, and the damage had been done. Philosophy is all very well, but some suffering is not optional.

Thursday 26th August 2010

87 Fellbarrow

Height: 1363 feet (416m)
Route: Ascent from Thackthwaite via Drovers road

I went to bed feeling grim and woke up feeling worse. I felt annoyed with myself for drinking something that I knew didn't taste right. I felt bloated, nauseous, and I was definitely suffering. Looking back, I think we have been lucky that illness has never stopped us from completing a walk; looking forward, I was determined not to let myself or anyone else down. I said I would be fine, and we planned a small walk over two fairly low fells. Shortly after everyone else had had breakfast, we headed for Fellbarrow in the Western Fells. We planned to start the walk from Thackthwaite, and it should only have been a short drive, but the bridge at Lorton had been washed away in the 2009 floods. Consequently, our journey involved a large detour, taking us via Loweswater to reach our starting point. I can't say I particularly enjoyed the prolonged trip, but thinking that the fresh air would make me feel a little better, I was happy to arrive in the sleepy hamlet of Thackthwaite.

We left the car and followed a drove road, which gradually gained in height. I gained in height more gradually than everyone else; I had no energy and each footstep was a struggle. I was trying hard to be positive, but I felt pretty miserable. Eventually we reached the top of the drove road, and from here we made a direct approach to the top of the fell. I'm sure the ascent wasn't that steep, but feeling increasingly light headed, it could have been vertical. We crossed a fence to reach the summit; a gently curving grassy dome. I made sure that I touched the cairn, before collapsing in an exhausted heap. Apparently the views to the Irish Sea and the Solway Firth were great, but they were wasted on me. I should mention, least you think otherwise, that the rest of the family had realised that I wasn't feeling very well, and had been suitably sympathetic. Tania suggested returning to the car at this point, but we worked out that walking to Low Fell wouldn't actually involve much more total distance. I also presumed that Low Fell wouldn't be that high, it would certainly be easier than Fellbarrow.

88. Low Fell

Height: 1388 feet (428m)
Route: Across the watershed from Fellbarrow – Descent via Drovers road

The walk would have been lovely if I had felt fine, but after resting and reviving slightly at Fellbarrow, I started feeling worse than ever. The final ascent of Low Fell, felt like the last mile of a marathon. I was totally exhausted and much to my horror, the final climb to the summit looked to be even steeper and higher than Fellbarrow; surely it couldn't be? Wainwright had had to estimate the height of Low Fell, and considered it (albeit doubtfully) to be the lower fell, but recent Ordnance Survey mapping reveals the opposite to be true. Staggering to the summit, I could appreciate the magnificent views to Grasmoor, Crummock Water, and Buttermere, but I couldn't appreciate much else. I was a spent force and could happily have fallen asleep on the grassy slopes. Eventually persuaded that my bed might be more comfortable, we all headed home, and I headed off for a long sleep.

Friday 27th August 2010

89. High Tove

Height: 1665 feet (515m)
Route: Watendlath - Ascent via Raise Gill - Summit

After about fifteen hours of uninterrupted sleep, I felt like a new man; Tania said she felt like a new man as well! Despite such a harsh comment I was pleased to be feeling much better, and relieved that we would be able to complete another walk. I felt fine, but just to be on the safe side, we planned a short 'up and down' walk, which would take us from Watendlath to High Tove and Armboth Fell. Despite Wainwright's lack of enthusiasm for High Tove, he said that "It is hard to imagine that anybody feels any affection for High Tove, apart from the sheep whose natural heaf it is", we were looking forward to the walk. Our positive expectations were quickly reinforced; the drive to Watendlath didn't seem to be quite as bad as we remembered, and Watendlath itself was as lovely as we remembered. Our walk involved an initial steep climb beside Raise Gill, followed by a gentler climb over boggy ground towards the summit. When I say boggy, I mean that the ground was completely saturated. It does appear to be the case that Wainwright wasn't overly keen on such conditions, but helped by waterproof boots (apart from Tom), we all quite enjoy a bit of 'bog stomping'. The summit is marked by a large cairn standing above the surrounding heather, and in the words of Wainwright it "offers a seat to travellers who wish to pour the water out of their boots". We took up the offer of a dry seat, but kept our boots on as we plotted a route to our next destination.

90 Armboth Fell

Height: 1570 feet (479m)
Route: South-east direct route

The direct approach to Armboth Fell is not recommended by Wainwright (too wet), but we went for it anyway. The route was very boggy and the going was slow, but we stayed reasonably dry, even after crossing a completely waterlogged area of ground close to the top of the fell. A rocky outcrop forms the summit, and from the cairn there were fine views towards Hellvelyn and down towards Thirlmere. In the past you would have been able to see the village of Armboth, but in 1894 the village was drowned when Thirlmere reservoir was created. Two smaller lakes were dammed to form the reservoir, the function of which was to supply water to the growing city of Manchester. John Ruskin, poet, artist and conservationist, thought that "Manchester should be put at the bottom of Thirlmere". Mindful that we didn't want to drown, we searched for and eventually found a slightly drier path that took us back to the top of High Tove. We then retraced our footsteps to Watendlath.

The plan was to walk on Saturday, but we woke to the return of the 'rainy season'. Hoping for at least a small break in the weather, we dressed in all our finest walking gear, but the clouds got lower and the rain got heavier. It's all very well getting soaking wet when you know you can go home and have a warm shower, but the thought of being wet and stuck in the car for six hours, curbed our enthusiasm to climb a final fell. We visited the Armitt Ambleside museum instead, learning a little bit more about Wordsworth, Ruskin, Beatrix Potter and many other famous Lakeland characters. The lack of a final fell was disappointing, but we had enjoyed another fantastic week in the Lakes, and we were comforted by the fact that we would be returning in October. The highlight for all of us had been the Grasmoor round; personal highlights for me were, no more problems with my Achilles, and that eagerly anticipated novel – *Stone's Fall* by Ian Pears.

MILESTONES
October 2010

Driving up to the Lake District, I was even more excited than normal. I had that usual feeling of euphoria that coincides with the start of a holiday, and I always look forward to seeing the mountains, but this holiday I was also excited about the prospect of completing our one hundredth, and one hundredth and seventh fells. One hundred, a century of fells, seemed like an obvious milestone, and one hundred and seven, half of all the Wainwrights completed, seemed like another.

The excitement even survived the nightmare of the journey; our worst yet. All started well, but from just south of Birmingham to just north of Manchester, the motorways resembled little more than car parks. Sometimes we were able to crawl forward, but for most of the time we were essentially parked. I know it was a Friday and that the school holidays had just started, but surely traveling shouldn't be this difficult. Just as the roads cleared a little and we were able to move out of second gear, the heavens opened and a rain storm of biblical proportions ensured that our rate of progress didn't dramatically increase. We finally arrived in the Lakes, a day later (well, just after midnight), we were greeted by thunder, lightning, high winds and flooded roads; the outlook for walking looked a little bleak.

Saturday 23rd October 2010

91. Black Fell

Height: 1056 feet (323m)
Route: Coniston road – Park Fell – Black Fell

The journey had been horrendous, but waking up in Chapel Stile and taking in the lovely view towards Lingmoor Fell, we quickly realized that the journey had been worth it. Our spirits were also enlivened by the clearing skies and the prospect of another week in the Lake District. Keen to get walking, but having to get some provisions in Ambleside, we decided on a short walk to climb Black Fell. Black Fell is isolated from other high ground in an area bounded by Windermere, Langdale and Coniston. Parking the car on the Ambleside to Coniston road, we picked up a clear path which initially headed in the right direction for the summit. The path revealed superb views towards The Langdales, but then started to take us away from our destination. Wainwright mentions that none of the paths continue directly to the summit, but states that "a simple walk across grass…soon brings it underfoot". We chose a direct route, then another and then another, but every time we attempted to head to the summit our progress was blocked by a maze of dry stone walls. Eventually, we had to resort to climbing and nearly destroying one such wall (please accept our apologies) before we were finally able to reach the impressive rocky top.

The highest point of the fell is marked by a triangulation column, emblazoned with a metallic National Trust symbol, stating that this spot is known as Black Crag. Despite the fact that the high fells were hidden in cloud, the views were impressive and we could see a large number of lakes and tarns; Windermere, Blelham Tarn, Barngates Tarn, Priest Pot, Esthwaite Water, Tarn Hows and Coniston Water. Taking our time to fully appreciate the views, I started to tell the boys about Donald Campbell.

Campbell was the holder of world land and water speed records. He died in Coniston Water on January 4, 1967, while trying to break his own record. Possibly striking a log, or hitting his own wake, his jet powered boat Bluebird disintegrated at around three hundred miles an hour. He is said to have wanted to emulate his father Sir Malcolm Campbell, in setting speed records on land and on water. He had broken the world water speed record seven times in ten years when the accident happened. Having hit two hundred and two miles per hour on Ullswater in July 1955, he bettered it on December 31, 1964, at Dumbleyung Lake, Australia, when he reached two hundred and seventy six miles an hour. Returning to the Lake District for a final record breaking attempt, his last reported words heard over the intercom were – "She's going, she's going". Bluebird was recovered from the lake in 2001 and some artifacts are now housed in the Ruskin Museum. Campbell's body was also recovered in 2001, and he was laid to rest in Coniston cemetery. We took a last solemn look at Coniston Water, descended to the car, and then drove home slowly.

Sunday 24th October 2010

92. Wetherlam

Height: 2502 feet (762m)
Route: Ascent from Coniston via Red Dell valley

Part of the reason for staying in Chapel Stile, was to be within striking distance of the Coniston Fells. The Old Man of Coniston was one of the first fells that we climbed with the boys, and now that they were older, the plan was to return and complete a Coniston Round. Our ambitious plan was to climb Wetherlam, Swirl How, Great Carrs, Grey Friar, Brim Fell and Dow Crag. We knew that we needed to start the walk early, but even the best laid plans are not always fully realized. Wetherlam is the most northerly of the Coniston fells, standing apart from the main north-south spine, the connection being made along the east ridge of Swirl How. We started the walk (later than anticipated) from the Sun Inn, following a path and then an unsurfaced road into Coppermines Valley. In the past Wetherlam was extensively exploited for its mineral resources. Wainwright states that "this fine hill...is too vast and sturdy to be disfigured and weakened by man's feeble scratchings" – I think he was right. Disused copper mines and abandoned slate quarries abound, but far from taking anything away from the majesty of the area, I think they add something. I have mentioned before that I think the old workings are fascinating, adding interest and a sense of history. According to Wainwright they give Wetherlam its "one great claim" (too fame, presumably). Wainwright dedicates a map to Wetherlam's 'hundred holes', and we passed many old caves, shafts and quarries as we headed to the top of the mountain by way of Red Dell valley.

The weather today was ideal; clear blue skies, and warm but cool enough for walking (if that makes any sense). We really enjoyed the ascent, even the final climb up a steep grass terrace. The steepness provided an excuse to stop and take in the breathtaking views. I love the Lakes at any time of year, but the autumnal colours made the landscape look even more beautiful than usual. This year the colours appeared to be even more spectacular than usual – a veritable sunburst of shades, topped off with burnished gold. Apparently this was a particularly spectacular autumn. The long drought of the spring, and the wet and cool of the late summer that followed combined to produce an outstanding autumn leaf display. The sharp climatic shift between the two seasons intensified the process of leaf ageing and dying, producing a fantastic show of colour. The autumn colours are produced when chlorophyll, the bright green pigment which plants use for photosynthesis, ceases to be dominant at the end of the growing season, and other natural pigments present in the leaves begin to show themselves. These produce the yellows, oranges and browns of the autumn leaves. Another set of pigments, compounds known as anthocyanins, are manufactured at the end of the summer, and these produce the deeper colours, the fiery red, the bronzes and the purples. The combination of all these colours provided a spectacle to be admired and remembered; allegedly the best display in over eighty years. The summit of Wetherlam is a broad, gentle dome – surprisingly rocky after the grassy slopes. The highest point is marked by a large cairn, and we enjoyed more fine views, before indulging in an early lunch.

93. Swirl How

Height: 2630 feet (802m)
Route: South-west from Wetherlam

Descending a stony slope from Wetherlam, we crossed Red Dell Head and then climbed to the summit of Swirl How. I mentioned previously that there is some debate as to which is the highest of the Coniston Fells. Wainwright advocates the Old Man of Coniston, but the British Mountaineering Council states that Swirl How is the higher fell. I have used Wainwright figures, but accept that for Swirl How they may be inaccurate. Whatever the arguments over height, there is no doubting that Swirl How is the geographical centre of the Coniston group. The top of the stony summit is marked by a cairn, located at the Greenburn edge of a long and level plateau. The great weather continued and as a result, we continued to enjoy clear views in all directions.

94. Great Carrs

Height: 2575 feet (780m)
Route: West and then North from Swirl How

We left the top of Swirl How and headed northward along a ridge leading to Great Carrs. The ridge is named Top of Broad Slack. Broad Slack is a frighteningly steep grassy slope, climbing out of the Greenburn valley. The ridge is a grassy plateau, and bears a sad memorial to the crew of a Halifax bomber that crashed here in 1944. The plane ran into thick cloud and descended to get a visual fix on the landscape. Descending too low, the plane crashed into the ridge, killing all on board. When rescuers arrived on the scene the Halifax was almost entirely intact, but because it couldn't be moved, it was cut up and pushed into Broad Slack. What was particularly sad about the memorial was the age of the crew; apart from the pilot and navigator, they were all under twenty one. The boys were very moved by the memorial and showed empathy beyond their years. We paid our respects and then moved somewhat solemnly towards the top of Great Carrs. The summit is marked by a small cairn, sitting on the edge of a precipice. The views to the north were particularly impressive, but we couldn't stop thinking about the crew of Halifax LL505.

95. Grey Friar

Height: 2536 feet (770m)
Route: South-west to Summit

After taking our leave from Great Carrs, we headed south-west towards Grey Friar. The fell forms the eastern wall of the Duddon Valley, and although part of our Coniston Round, all drainage from Grey Friar goes to the Duddon Valley and not to Coniston Water. We were accompanied on this section of the walk by a very friendly and very talkative Liverpuddlian. It's usually interesting to meet fellow walkers and hear different views and opinions, and this man certainly had a number of interesting views and a lot of opinions. The summit of the fell is stony and has two cairned rock outcrops. After much deliberation and discussion with our new traveling companion, we decided that the south-easterly summit was the higher, but the north-westerly offered the better view. Increasingly worried however (somewhat uncharitably) that we might be subjected to more monologues on the state of the nation, I was happy to wave a cheerful goodbye to our companion as he headed back towards Great Carrs and Swirl How.

96. Brim Fell

Height: 2611 feet (796m)
Route: via Fairfields path

The walk from Grey Friar along the Fairfields path provided us with lovely views down towards Seathwaite Tarn. The Tarn is a good example of a man made structure that looks fantastic in its natural setting. A small existing tarn was enlarged in 1904 to provide water for Barrow in Furness. The walk was an easy stroll for the most part, but as we started to climb towards the summit of the 'whalebacked' ridge, the stroll became a bit of a slog. We kept spotting cairns on the horizon, and each time we did, we thought we had the summit in our sights. Unfortunately, the summit was always one more cairn away. Reduced to an increasingly slow pace and frequently stopping for water, we thought the top would never arrive. After what seemed like a lifetime, we spotted a large, fabulous slate cairn, and were relieved to discover that we had finally conquered Brim Fell. I know my description seems like an overstatement, an exaggeration of the degree of difficulty involved, but after a long days walking, we all felt very tired. With this thought in mind and the fact that daylight would soon be disappearing, we made the decision to miss out Dow Crag. The revised plan was to take the shortest route and walk back to Coniston via the Old Man. It was a frustrating decision because we would have to return and complete Dow Crag on its own. However, I'm sure that it was the right decision. Walking back from Dow Crag in complete darkness wouldn't have been much fun. Decision made, we started to relax and enjoyed the fantastic view to the south – the distinctive summit of the Old Man of Coniston.

A simple short stroll from Brim Fell, took us to the summit of the Old Man of Coniston. The boys remembered the fell and were more than happy to return. This time, probably because it was late in the day, we had the fell to ourselves. We enjoyed the views, and after taking numerous photographs we started the steep descent towards Low Water. The tarn looked spectacular; the sun was low in the sky and the twilight shades combined with the colours of autumn to produce a truly memorable scene. Reluctantly leaving Low Water in a race to beat the setting sun, we continued down the much berated slate mine path. Wainwright states that the only thing that this route has its favour is that "the route is absolutely safe". Well I'm not usually one to argue with Wainwright, but in the fading light I was nearly decapitated by a steel cable hanging over the 'safe' path. Head fortunately intact, I still believe that this route has much in its favour. Despite having to shorten our route, the day had been a memorable one. As the last rays of the sun disappeared and darkness descended, the Sun Inn appeared. After walking eleven miles and climbing a total of four thousand feet; a pint of Lakelands finest provided a perfect ending to a perfect day.

Monday 25th October 2010

97. Pike O' Blisco

Height: 2304 feet (705m)
Route: Old Dungeon Ghyll - Wall End - Summit

The plan today was to climb Pike O' Blisco, Cold Pike and Crinkle Crags. We didn't want to have to rush the end of the walk, so we rose early in an attempt to make the most of the daylight. The early morning view towards Lingmoor Fell, normally stunning, was even more beautiful than usual. The sun was out, the sky was a clear blue, and a hoar frost provided the 'icing on the cake'. For once we managed to combine waking up early, with actually getting out of the house early. We drove to the Old Dungeon Ghyll Hotel to start our walk. Although it was a fantastic day for walking, as we stepped out of the car we experienced the bitter cold which was the unavoidable consequence of the clear skies. The summit of Pike O' Blisco was clearly visible and the steep climb looked daunting. Daunted but excited, we followed a path straight up the slope of Side Pike, and then followed a track above Redacre Gill. The walk was straightforward, but we did have to watch our step because ice was an almost constant companion. As the walk got steeper, we had to take occasional breathers. We used the opportunities proved by these breaks to gaze towards the Langdales. A stone staircase assisted progress, leading the way onwards and upwards. We passed the cliffs of Kettle Crag and emerged onto a big sloping platform of rock. The final approach to the summit involved some interesting scrambles, and we had to think carefully about our route. Tom led the short climbs, and for a while at least, we felt like real mountaineers. The summit was an impressive place; the cairn is situated on a platform of rock. The platform provided excellent views in all directions. At this stage of the walk the skies were still mostly clear, but the wind had picked up and cirrus clouds announced a forthcoming change in the weather.

98. Cold Pike

Height: 2259 feet (701m)
Route: Descent to Red Tarn – Ascent – West then south to summit

Feeling hungry, but keen to avoid the worst of the biting wind, we descended towards Red Tarn. It is always a little depressing to have to lose height when you know you will have to gain it again, but the wind did abate. We found a nice sheltered spot overlooking the tarn, and enjoyed a brief lunch stop. Wainwright describes Red Tarn as "an unattractive sheet of water", but we quite enjoyed our view. Red Tarn is a walker's crossroads, and after descending to the tarn itself, we picked up the Crinkle Crags path. The climb up from the tarn was fairly steep, and became even steeper when we detoured from the main path. The grassy slopes leading the way towards Cold Pike were not particularly attractive, and this section of the walk was definitely a bit of a slog. The top was the best part of the fell, grass gave way to rock and the summit consisted of three outcrops. Each outcrop is marked by a cairn, and like a small scale Crinkle Crags, they descend in altitude from north-west to south-east. The highest point provided an excellent position from which to survey our next destination, but we didn't stay for too long. Cloud now filled the sky and with no sun to provide even a modicum of warmth, Cold Pike really did live up to its name.

99. Crinkle Crags

Height: 2816 feet (859m)
Route: North-west from Cold Pike

Descending from Cold Pike, we rejoined the path to Crinkle Crags. The route provided some amazing, if somewhat frightening views. Five 'crinkles' make up the summit ridge, and Wainwright describes the ridge thus – "a fell walkers delight. A constantly changing scene, beautiful and dramatic views, fine situations and an interesting course throughout make this a walk to remember". The serrated skyline of Crinkle Crags, so impressive from Great Langdale, has always intrigued me. I eagerly anticipated the walk, and I was looking forward to completing the 'Bad Step'. The main path leads directly to the first crinkle, and provided a dramatic view to the second and third crinkles. The first crinkle is crossed by way of a rocky and rough ridge, and as we climbed we lost sight of the other crinkles. The wind threatened to tear us from the mountain and we trusted in cairns to keep us on track. The reappearance of the massive rocky dome of the second crinkle provided clear proof that they had. We descended the first crinkle and arrived at a grassy depression; from here a scree gully leads upwards to the top of the second crinkle. However, the gully is blocked by two chockstones, forming a vertical wall ten feet high – this is the Bad Step. As we approached, a large group of walkers were trying to descend the Bad Step. An orderly queue had formed, but their progress was understandably slow. After waiting for some considerable time, we decided we would have to move on and find an alternative route to the top of crinkle number two. I made myself a promise to return, and then we headed left before climbing a steep path to the summit. This is the highest point on the ridge and it provided fine views to Great Langdale, Eskdale and Scafell Pike. As we paused to look at the views, it became obvious that the weather was deteriorating. The clouds were lowering, rain threatened, and the wind continued to grow in strength. We decided that we shouldn't stay on the mountain for too long. Once again we would have to rush the last stages of a walk, but at least today it wouldn't be because of a late start.

The third crinkle rises like a pyramid, but we quickly scrambled to the top. Possibly too quickly, Will made his own 'bad step' and bashed his knee quite badly. Still conscious of the weather, but wanting to avoid any more accidents, we preceded a little more cautiously. Crinkles four and five are lower in height and easily accessed from the main path, both gave fantastic views of Great Langdale. From the fifth crinkle we descended to Three Tarns, another grassy depression. We relaxed in the knowledge that from here on, the weather could do its worst, but we would be perfectly safe. We checked out Will – his knee was bashed and bruised, but nothing was broken. Three Tarns is another walker's crossroads, but it is also a beautiful spot. We rested for a short while and made the most of the photo opportunities offered by the location. Leaving Three Tarns, we descended via The Band.

Although a long descent, the fabulous spectacle of Great Langdale distracted us from our aching feet (aching knee in Will's case). Blessed with beautiful views, we also managed to keep a few steps ahead of the approaching storm. As the first raindrops arrived, we arrived at the Old Dungeon Ghyll Hotel. I have already talked about the post walking benefits of this fantastic pub, and it didn't disappoint today. After some ideal walking, or should I say 'post walking' food, we decided that Crinkle Crags had been a walk to remember.

Wednesday 27th October 2010

100. Steel Fell

Height: 1814 feet (553m)
Route: Gill Foot - Ash Crags - Summit

We had been fortunate to keep ahead of the rain on our descent from Crinkle Crags; our departure from the Old Dungeon Ghyll was greeted by another biblical rainstorm. This time the rain continued for the about thirty six hours, and consequently we didn't walk on Tuesday. We had all been looking forward to completing our one hundredth fell, so we anxiously awaited the forecast for Wednesday. Wednesday was also the day that we had arranged to meet up and walk with some friends, so we had another reason to hope for an improvement in conditions.

The forecast did look more promising, and Wednesday, although overcast and windy, was dry. The plan was to complete a Greenburn Round; climbing Steel Fell, Calf Crag, Gibson Knott and Helm Crag. We had already completed the last two fells, but we thought it would be an enjoyable walk and it would allow us another opportunity to try and climb the 'Howitzer'. After meeting up with our friends in Grasmere, we drove to our starting point at Gill Foot; here the lane from Grasmere crosses Green Burn. We had used the same starting point when we climbed Gibson Knott the first time. This time, instead of heading to Greenburn Bottom, we climbed directly up the south-eastern ridge of Steel Fell. The ascent was a steep slog from bottom to top. However, distracted by pleasant conversation and interesting views of the summit of Helm Crag, we seemed to arrive at the summit of Steel Fell in no time at all. Several small cairns lie close to the top, but the highest point on the fell is marked by a rough stone cairn standing alongside the old county boundary fence. We posed for photos and celebrated our one hundredth Wainwright.

I realize that I haven't praised Will and Tom for their efforts for a while. I think it's because they never fuss and they never complain, consequently (much to our shame), Tania and I probably take their achievements for granted. The reality is that Will and Tom have achieved an amazing amount, and we are incredibly proud of them.

101. Calf Crag

Height: 1762 feet (537m)
Route: South-west from Steel Fell

Leaving fell one hundred behind us, we headed west, following the boundary fence towards Calf Crag. Wainwright states that "He who reaches Calf Crag with dry feet has cause to be satisfied with his boots". The route is very marshy and we had to include some detours to keep our feet dry. The summit is small and rocky, but it offers a lovely view towards the Vale of Grasmere. From Calf Crag we headed east, walking along a ridge which led us directly to the summit of Gibson Knott (thereby avoiding the confusion of our last visit). After a pause to admire the views, we continued along the ridge to reach the summit of Helm Crag. Surely I would be able to climb the 'Howitzer' this time. Tania and I, Will and Tom, our friends Ian, Karina, and their boys Alex and Eliott, all looked at the pinnacle of rock and searched for the best route to the top. We all had slightly different ideas and set off scrambling and climbing in different direction. Unfortunately, all routes proved to be problematic and no one was successful, but I did get tantalizing close this time. We will have to return again; hopefully it will be 'third time lucky'. We left the summit, initially walking back on ourselves and then walking down a very steep and slippery slope towards Gill Foot. This was the first, and as it would turn out only time that we would complete some Wainwrights with friends; it had been nice to have lots of company, and it had been great to complete our hundredth Wainwright.

Thursday 28th October 2010

102. Sour Howes

Height: 1585 feet (483m)
Route: Troutbeck Church – Summit

The weather forecast for the last two days of our holiday was grim, but we planned optimistically. The intention was to complete six fells over the last two days, and thereby reach the half way stage in terms of Wainwrights completed. The plan today was to head to the far eastern fell and climb Sour Howes, Sallows and Troutbeck Tongue. We didn't have particularly high expectations for the walk; low cloud was abundant, persistent rain was due to arrive by late morning, and Wainwright states that "Sour Howes is a fell with no obvious appeal to walkers".

We parked close to Troutbeck Church, walked to the main road, crossed a bridge and then turned left onto the Garburn road. Just before a pine plantation, we crossed into a field, and then crossed over Dubbs road before picking up a ridge that led us to the summit. As the ridge took us higher, the wind kept getting stronger, and by the time we reached the top a gale was blowing. The highest point on the fell is small grassy ridge; here we experimented with the potential for human flight. We lined up on the ridge, opened out our jackets like wings, and jumped high to see if the wind would blow us backwards. The results of our experiment are still a source of family debate, but there was no debate about the quality of the view towards Windermere.

103. Sallows

Height: 1693 feet (516m)
Route: North then East to Summit

Leaving the summit of Sour Howes, we were literally blown towards our next destination. We headed north, and with the wind behind us we made rapid progress. The walk was along an easy ridge, with no discernible gain or loss in height. Turning off the main path before Garburn Nook, we soon reached the summit of Sallows. The top is grassy and the highest point is occupied by a curving ridge of shale. Low cloud obscured most of the views from the summit cairn, and somewhat unbelievably the wind continued to gain in strength. We decided to descend towards the Garburn Road. We searched for somewhere to eat lunch, somewhere that would offer a little shelter from the wind. Just as we found such a location, the heavens opened and it was 'soggy' sandwiches once again.

The forecast rain had arrived, and it looked like it was going to stay around for quite some time. Wet and windblown, we decided that we had walked far enough for today, and we abandoned our plan to climb Troutbeck Tongue.

Initially reluctant to abandon our plan, I thought back to our original reasons for attempting to complete all the Wainwrights. We wanted to explore new areas and we thought quite rightly that it would be a great achievement. The intention was never to complete the Wainwrights in a rush, or even in a certain time frame; we just wanted to enjoy the experience. Part of enjoyment is knowing when to quit; understanding that sometimes more will result in less. Part of my initial reluctance to abandon Troutbeck Tongue was the realization that we probably wouldn't reach our one hundredth and seventh fell on this visit, but I soon realized that it didn't matter. If we didn't climb any more fells this holiday, we still would have had a fantastic holiday. What's more, we would have a major milestone to look forward to on our next visit.

We didn't climb any more fells. Friday brought more persistent rain and low cloud. We headed back to Devon, not disappointed, but excited about that next milestone.

HALFWAY
February 2011

"The Lakes in February, you must be mad!" Such was the standard response to our holiday plans. Needless to say I was relishing the prospect. I was looking forward to the sight of snowcapped peaks, and I was looking forward to the sound of my boots crunching into fresh snow. In preparation I investigated the possibility of buying or hiring crampons, and the family purchased a range of highly flattering thermal wear. Freezing temperatures, ice, snow and the prospect of reaching the halfway point in our challenge; I was as excited as a young child on Christmas Eve.

Saturday 19th February 2011

104. High Rigg

Height: 1171 feet (354m)
Route: Ascent from Dale Bottom

We headed up to the Lakes after a hard day at work. We all felt tired, but we were happy about being on holiday, and we were excited by the prospect of seeing the Northern Lights. A giant solar flare had been unleashed by the sun. The electrically charged particles thus emitted, collide with atoms in the earth's atmosphere, causing those atoms to emit the characteristic red or green light of the *aurora borealis.* I have always wanted to witness the Northern lights, the possibility of doing so without having to leave the UK was thrilling. Excited shouts emanated from the back of the car (and the front), at any and every bright spot of light that appeared in the darkening sky. Unfortunately, the Northern Lights were to prove to be elusive. Cloud rolled in from the west, extinguishing the stars and any prospect of a spectacular light show. The Northern Lights may not have heralded our arrival in the Lakes, but snow did.

When pressed, meteorologists will admit to the fact that weather forecasting in the Lake District is a fairly imprecise science. The varied landscape gives rise to a wide range of micro climates, and consequently weather conditions are highly localised. Nothing served to illustrate this more than the first morning of our holiday. It was still snowing and our car was blanketed. Snow lay on the ground, and as we headed west from Penrith, we could see that the dual carriageway way had been reduced to a single lane. We thought about the first walk of our holiday, and after taking the weather conditions into consideration, we decided to climb a modest fell. We felt sure that we would be climbing up through snow and ice.

However, after driving only a short distance, all evidence of overnight snow disappeared and we could see that the snow line in the central and western fells was at about eighteen hundred feet. I say we 'thought' about our first walk, rather than planned our first walk. Planning was problematic. All maps and guide books (including my beloved Wainwrights) were buried deep in the boot of the car (Buried deep in a suitcase of Titanic proportions). Usually when we stop on route, we transfer relevant books and maps to an overnight case, but in our rush to pack, plans had gone awry.

How do you plan a walk without any maps? Well, our solution was to fill up with petrol, and whilst paying, scan the guide books in the garage. We had a quick flick through the somewhat understandably limited selection, and we spotted a short walk from Dale Bottom to High Rigg. The walk looked like an ideal way to start our holiday. We memorised the directions and headed off to our starting point. I parked the car and checked my rucksack. One of the golden rules of hill walking is to always walk with a map; so it felt strange to be setting out without one. I am still amazed that some people walk in the hills without map or compass. We have been asked on several occasions to offer directions, or help fix a location for walkers without even the most basic map. You only have to look at the annual reports of the various mountain rescue groups to see where a lack of preparation can lead. I usually make sure that we have an OS map, compass, GPS, First Aid kit, whistle, torch, spare batteries, water, food, survival sack, waterproofs and extra clothing. It sounds like a lot of kit, but it really isn't, and it could save your life.

High Rigg is surrounded on all sides by higher fells, but is isolated from them. A modest fell, but it has it all; crags, tarns and intermediate summits. We climbed a steep slope directly from the roadside, and then crossed the short distance to the rocky summit. We were rewarded with good views in all directions. Skiddaw and Blencathra dominated the view to the north, and Clough Head and the Helvellyn range the view east. Thirlmere was visible to the south and Bleaberry Fell to the west.

Perhaps we hadn't really earned it, but after returning to the car we headed into Keswick for lunch at the Dog and Gun. Despite not walking far enough to justify building up an appetite, I felt ravenous. I attacked a defenseless goulash with the sort of violence which if witnessed would have had me arrested for GBH.

Revived and fortunately still free, we headed off to find some walking and climbing shops. Despite the season I was determined to spend some time in the high mountains. I wanted to make the most of the conditions and I wanted to get above the snow line. Prior research had led me to believe that hiring crampons wouldn't be a problem, but I had underestimated our litigious society. Apparently shops don't hire crampons or ice axes anymore, because of the real fear of litigation. Some individuals have blamed accidents, not on chance or poor use of the aforesaid equipment, but on faulty instructions on how to use the equipment. Not surprisingly, shops no longer want to take the risk. It's great that we all have a far greater understanding of our rights today, but what a shame that some people don't understand the concept of responsibility.

Sunday 20th February 2011

105. Stybarrow Dodd

Height: 2766 feet (843m)
Route: Ascent from Stanah via Sticks Pass

Statistics show that winter mountaineering accidents are most commonly caused by simple slips, and advice suggests when snow becomes too steep or hard for step kicking, crampons should be worn. I still wanted to venture into the snow, but without crampons we would have to plan carefully. The idea was to find a high fell with a relatively gentle approach. We settled on Stybarrow Dodd; its characteristic wide grassy slopes and its absence of outcropping rock appeared to fit the bill. We also planned to visit Stybarrow's northerly neighbours; Watson Dodd and Great Dodd.

Completing the 'Dodds' would mean that we would finally reach halfway in our Wainwright odyssey. The weather was cold but the forecast was good; early morning low cloud was predicted to clear by mid morning, leaving clear skies. We parked at Stanah and began climbing up beside Stanah Gill. The initial going was steep but straightforward. Taking a break we rested at a conveniently located sheepfold and enjoyed the views down to Thirlemere. We reached snow at about eighteen hundred feet, and we were embraced by cloud shortly afterwards. As we climbed higher the snow cover grew progressively thicker and the main path became difficult to follow. At times the path was still obvious, but then it would completely disappear. We placed our trust in bearings and following footprints in the snow.

Visibility continued to deteriorate, but we were close to Sticks Pass, and therefore close to the summit. Sticks Pass climbs to a height of two thousand, four hundred and forty five feet. This makes it the highest pass in the Lake District crossed by a regular bridleway. Now of use purely to walkers, it once provided the only connection between the communities on either side of the Helvellyns. The name is believed to be taken from the guideposts originally used to mark the route.

When we reached Sticks Pass our route became clear. Thankful for our thermal wear and fortunately not slipping or sliding, we decided to head to the summit. Despite the lack of visibility, we enjoyed the initial stages of our final push. The boys launched themselves into the snow, attempting to find the deepest drifts, and Tania and I chatted contentedly. We were all in high spirits, but how quickly things can change. As we climbed higher, the wind got stronger. Wind chill and freezing temperatures combined with low cloud to produce an interesting, but uncomfortable phenomenon. Cloud droplets can remain liquid, even when the air temperature surrounding the suspended liquid is below freezing. This occurs because the liquid needs a surface to freeze upon. Unfortunately, we provided that surface. We were all quickly coated in a film of ice crystals. Our thermals kept us warm, but any exposed skin was quickly chilled. At first we were all amazed by the unique patterns and shapes created by the freezing fog, then we realised that we were getting cold. Just to add to our problems, we walked past and then away from the summit. We realised our mistake and tracked back to the small summit cairn, but conditions were becoming decidedly unpleasant. After some muted celebrations we abandoned plans to visit the other 'Dodds'. We beat a hasty retreat; our sole aim now was to get lower and warmer as quickly as possible.

It's surprising how quickly your body temperature can change, fortunately today this worked to our advantage. After feeling decidedly chilly at the summit, we quickly warmed up. Descent took us out of the wind and the snow, and we were soon shedding layers of clothing. Once again we stopped at the sheepfold, and for the first time in what seemed like ages we had some views to enjoy. It was evident that most areas apart from the 'Dodds' were free of cloud.

Monday 21st February 2011

106. Graystones

Height: 1477 feet (456m)
Route: Ascent from Scawgill Bridge

We woke to the sound of heavy and persistent rain. The forecast suggested conditions would improve, so we spent the morning in our apartment and planned to go walking in the afternoon. We were staying once again at the

Old Swan Hotel, and consequently we were able to enjoy fantastic views from the comfort of the lounge; but we were keen to get out and about. The weather finally broke in the late afternoon, I say broke; the persistent rain had stopped, but now it was snowing. We decided to set out anyway and headed towards Graystones. We parked at Scawgill Bridge, wrapped up warmly and started to climb. Wainwright describes the ascent thus – "Short, direct and fool-proof in any conditions of weather, but it lacks excitement and is hardly worth the effort". Hardly a glowing endorsement! The climb was a bit of a trudge; a short steep climb, beside a fence, next to a wall. But, it was great to be out and about again and we did catch occasional glimpses of Coledale Hause. The highest point of the fell is marked by a cairn, situated on a slight upthurst of rock. We enjoyed the moment and we decided that it had been worth the effort (just about).

The weather on Tuesday morning was terrific, perfect walking conditions. Forecasts predicted that today was indeed the day; conditions would deteriorate for the rest of the week. Tania and I planned a walk in the far eastern fells, and I couldn't wait to get started. Unfortunately Tom wasn't feeling well, and much to my shame, I wasn't that sympathetic. Eventually we decided to abandon 'bagging' any fells for the day, but we did think that if Tom perked up we would head out for short walk and some fresh air later on. Tom felt better by mid morning, so we strolled over to the Whinlatter Visitors Centre. I started the walk feeling and acting a bit like a sulky teenager – I was desperate to climb fell one hundred and seven. But, the weather was crisp and bright, the smell of pine was in the air, and I have to admit that the walk along the forest paths was delightful.

Wednesday 23rd February 2011

107. Hallin Fell

Height: 1273 feet (388m)
Route: Ascent from St Peters, Martindale

I had begun to feel that we were fated. In my paranoid state I felt that everything was conspiring against us, and that we would never reach the halfway point in our quest. Recognising the signs of an imminent breakdown, Tania provided the words of comfort I required. "Today we will climb Hallin Fell, come wind or rain".

We parked by St Peter's Church in the Martindale valley, and you could feel the car being buffeted by wind and rain. In the somewhat cramped confines of the car (well Hallin is regarded as the motorists' fell) we struggled into our waterproofs. Emerging into the inclement conditions, we headed straight up the grassy slopes. Wainwright states that the fell can be "ascended comfortably in bare feet"; however, being in no hurry to develop frostbite, I kept my boots on. Shortly after we started climbing the rain ceased and the sky began to brighten, but the wind continued to grow in strength and was ferocious on the summit.The highest point is marked by an imposing cairn; the sturdy stonework provided some shelter from which to admire the fantastic views. Despite Hallin's somewhat lowly stature, we could see High Street, Helvyllen, Blencathra and almost the whole of Ullswater. Wainwright considered the views to be "out of all proportion to the slight effort of ascent". We all agreed.

It was intensely satisfying to know that we had completed half of all the Wainwrights. We were all suitably delighted. I thought about all the wonderful places that we had visited and all the precious moments that we had shared as a family. However, somewhat sadly, I realized that part of me never wanted this challenge to end.

A great day was rounded off by a great night at the Theatre. We went to see *Private Peaceful* by Michael Morpurgo. The play was performed at The Theatre by the Lake in Keswick. The theatre has a beautiful location; situated beside Derwentwater, with views across Borrowdale and the Western Fells. The play is about a soldier called Thomas "Tommo" Peaceful. He looks back on his life as he awaits execution at the hands of a firing squad. It may not sound like the most uplifting of stories, but the tragic tale, underlining the senselessness of war, was excellent.

Thursday 24th February 2011

108. Burnbank Fell

Height: - 1558 feet (475m)
Route: Maggie's Bridge - Holme Wood - Burnbank Fell

We may well have reached the halfway stage, but so far on this holiday we had failed to climb more than one fell on any one day. Today we planned to rectify the situation. The aim was to climb Burnbank Fell, Blake Fell and Gavel Fell. Wainwright describes Burnbank as "a dull fell". The weather was certainly dull. An encouraging forecast promised "a day of spring like sunshine"; but once again we walked in the shade. We appeared to be walking in the only area of the Lakes covered in cloud. We thought and hoped that the cloud would break, but it stubbornly refused to do so. The walk started with a pleasant, but steep stroll through Holme wood. Initially we had some views, but they disappeared at about eleven hundred feet. Leaving the wood, we crossed Holme Beck, and climbed a very steep, heather covered slope. We were quickly reduced to an exhausted state; the springy heather sapped our energy. The higher we climbed the more tired we became. As our strength diminished the wind became stronger and visibility continued to deteriorate. It got to the stage where we could see little more than each other. Fortunately, just before we became completely disorientated, we stumbled upon a small cairn next to an old fence post. We had reached the summit, but we could have been anywhere.

109. Blake Fell

Height: 1880 feet (573m)
Route: South along a ridge from Burnbank Fell

Conditions on the summit were miserable. We stopped for a bite to eat, but with nowhere to shelter it was a fairly unpleasant experience. We contemplated our situation - visibility had been reduced to a few feet, but we weren't in any real danger of getting lost - we could follow a fence all the way from Burnbank to Blake Fell. We decided to press on.

However, the walk quickly became more of a chore than a pleasure. With no views, strong winds, and little to enjoy; conversation dried up and we became lost in our own thoughts. I know my thoughts turned to warmth, food and shelter. At least the summit, when it finally arrived, offered some protection from the elements; never was a wind shelter more welcome. We huddled down low and gained some temporary respite from the howling gale. Blake Fell is the highest of the Loweswater Fells, and Wainwright states that "The view inland, comprising a splendid array of mountains, is excellent; seaward it extends uninterrupted..." Our view was completely interrupted; Lakeland scenery was becoming an all too distant memory.

110. Gavel fell

Height: 1726 feet (526m)
Route: SSE from Blake Fell

Our next destination was Gavel Fell, the centremost of the Lowswater fells. Thankfully, we were able to follow a fence again; considering the conditions this was a relief. We walked for about a mile, descending and then climbing through the mist. The highest point is marked by a large cairn; we could see little else. I think we were more pleased by the fact that the walk was nearly over than we were about reaching the summit, we were all disappointed with the weather. Disappointment turned to frustration as we descended towards High Nook Farm. Finally emerging from the cloud, we could see that the rest of Lakeland was blessed with clear skies. Even the mighty summit of Grasmoor was bathed in sunshine. My thoughts were now dominated by the lyrics of a song by Travis – *Why does it always rain on me?*

Friday 25th February 2011

111. Bakestall

Height: 2208 feet (673m)
Route: Peters House Farm – Cumbria Way – Birkett Edge

We all felt a little downcast yesterday and I apologise for our negativity. We had made the wrong decision in our choice of fells, but we all agreed that even a disappointing walk in the Lakes is better than no walk at all. Feeling more positive today, we planned to climb Bakestall. Strictly speaking Bakestall is not a separate fell, being just an insignificant rise on Skiddaw's northern slopes. But Wainwright rewarded Bakestall with its own chapter in his *Pictorial Guide to the Lakeland Fells*, for two reasons – Dead Crags and Dash Falls.

After a lengthy walk along the Cumbria Way, we were rewarded by the sight of Dead Crags. Composed of Skiddaw slate, the Crags drop five hundred feet down into a corrie on the northern side of the fell. The crags provided an impressive jagged contrast to the surrounding smooth and rounded hills. Shortly afterwards, we heard and then saw the equally as impressive Dash Falls. The falls were quite stunning; they must be amongst the finest in the Lake District.

Finally taking our leave of the Cumbria Way, we headed towards the summit of Bakestall. We approached by way of Birkett Edge. The climb is straightforward, but a bit of a slog. The steep approach did however provide a suitable excuse to stop and admire the views. The summit of the Fell is located at a turn in a fence, but views were restricted at this point. We walked north to another larger cairn; this provided fine views to the Solway Firth and the Scottish Border hills.

Saturday 26th Februry 2011

112. Wansfell

Height: 1597 feet (487m)
Route: Ambleside – Stock Ghyll – Wansfell Pike – Wansfell

It may have taken us nearly seven years, but at last we could make up for our 'false start'. The plan was to have lunch in Ambleside and then climb Wansfell. Our last attempt to climb the fell had led us to Wansfell Pike – a major achievement at the time and a wonderful summit, but not a Wainwright. Feeling slightly too full, we followed a road leaving the town centre, walked past Stockghyll Force and then followed a restored footpath to the summit of Wansfell Pike. We were back where it had all started. We attempted to restage Will and Tom's first summit photo, and I thought about all the summits we had visited in the intervening years. I also reflected on the passage of time, and wondered where all those intervening years had gone. I probably should have been reflecting on the present. The day was rapidly disappearing and Tania was anxious about the time remaining to complete today's walk. After a quick confab, we decided that we couldn't let Wansfell elude us for a second time, so we headed north-east. The route follows a ridge for about a mile, however the walk took us longer than we expected – many small ascents and descents slowed our progress. The summit is a small grassy hummock, only a little higher than the land around it. We agreed with Wainwright; Wansfell isn't as impressive as Wansfell Pike, but we were delighted to have finally climbed the fell.

By now the light was beginning to fade. We retraced our footsteps (literally at some points) and made our way back to Ambleside. The final descent from Wansfell Pike provided some fantastic views. Ambleside and Windermere both looked stunning. Twilight illuminated and enhanced the landscape, providing a glorious finish to another wonderful week.

What was the Highlight of our week? – Well, climbing Hallin Fell of course!

HIGH DAYS AND HOLIDAYS
April 2011

There is no denying the fact that we teachers have long holidays, but believe me we earn them and much of the time is often dedicated to school work. There is no denying either that teachers like to complain – usually justifiably. My one complaint about the holidays is inflexibility. How nice it would be to take a Friday or a Monday off, and spend a long weekend somewhere, anywhere! How nice it would be to spend your birthday somewhere other than at work.

This year I was fortunate; a late Easter meant that for once I could celebrate my advancing years on holiday, and in the Lake District.

Shortly before setting off north once again, Tania and I sat at home and gazed at a large map of the Lakes. The map was satisfyingly covered in a large number of red dots; all of which signified summits climbed so far. Satisfying and also illuminating. Whilst we had now climbed a large number of peaks in many areas, other areas had barely been visited. The Far Eastern Fells were a case in point – sadly lacking in the red dot department. A decision was made to stay in Kendal for a couple of nights and visit this largely unexplored (by us at least) area, we would then move on to Thornthwaite for the rest of our holiday. I looked at the map again and tried to think of a suitably inspiring mountain to climb on my

Wansfell Pike Photo by Tania Grigg
Sunset over Windermere Photo by Andy Grigg

The Old Man of Coniston Photo by Tania Grigg
Grisdale Pike Photo by Tania Grigg

Derwent Water after descent from Catbells Photo by Andy Grigg
Buttermere Photo by Tania Grigg

Skiddaw Summit Plateau Photo by Tania Grigg
Skiddaw Photo by Tania Grigg

Grange Fell Photo by Andy Grigg
Great Langdale from Crinkle Crags Photo by Tania Grigg

Striding Edge Photo by Tania Grigg
Tarn Crag Photo by Tania Grigg

Wasdale Head Photo by Andy Grigg

Brothers Water Photo by Andy Grigg

The Men In Black Photo by Tania Grigg
Catstycam – our final fell Photo by unknown walker

birthday; maybe Helvellyn, maybe a triumphant return to the Dodds, possibly Scafell. So many mountains, such little time!

Somewhat unfortunately, the start of our holiday coincided with the start of a family cold. We considered delaying our departure, but more in hope than the expectation of being healthy enough to walk anywhere, we headed to Kendal. It was obvious on the first morning after our arrival that a big walk wasn't really an option; we abandoned plans to visit the Far Eastern Fells and decided to explore Kendal instead.

Our first destination was Kendal Castle. Kendal Castle, probably constructed in the late twelfth Century, is now a ruin, but it was well worth a visit. The Castle was built as the home of the barons of Kendal. The Parr family is the best known of the baronial families, the most famous member being Katherine Parr, the sixth and last Queen of Henry VIII (although it's unlikely that she ever lived at the castle). Most of the castle walls survive, along with one of the towers and part of the manor hall. We explored the castle and enjoyed the fantastic views of Kendal provided by the ramparts. After a picnic lunch on Castle Hill we headed to our next destination, Kendal Museum.

As a family we usually tend to enjoy the same things, but Kendal Museum was to bring out some contradictory emotions. Tania, William and I loved the place, but Tom will probably never return. The Museum of Natural History and Archaeology, founded in 1796, is one of the oldest museums in the country, housing outstanding displays of natural history and archaeology, both local and global. We all enjoyed looking at the artefacts from the Galva Roman Fort at Ambleside, and the Natural History Gallery, which provides glimpses of many Lakeland habitats. We loved the Wainwright Gallery, which included original text and drawings from the great man, along with a recreation of his office and even a pair of his walking boots. Controversy however was created by The World Wildlife Gallery, which houses a collection of animals from different continents. All the animals were long since deceased and suitably 'stuffed'. Some of the animals were rare, some extinct. I was particularly interested to see a Tasmanian tiger or *Thylacine*. These fantastic creatures were probably driven to extinction by European settlers in Australia in the 1930s. I say probably, because unconfirmed sightings still occur. I was interested, Tom was horrified! He was dismayed that the animals had been hunted and shot in the first place, and outraged that they now had to suffer the indignity of perpetual display. He considered the museum to be complicit in the murder of the aforesaid creatures. To some extent I can see his point of view, but what should we do? Hide the animals away and forget that such events took place, or keep them on display to study and to remind ourselves of how barbaric we humans can be? The debate lingered on!

After ruining Tom's day we returned to the hotel. Differences were eventually reconciled over some plates of pasta.

Saturday 16th April 2011

113. Silver How

Height: 1292 feet (394m)
Route: Grasmere Car park – Kelbarrow Path – Summit – Wray Gill – Grasmere

Our previous attempt to climb Silver How had resulted in a disappointing error of navigation, and a missed summit. This time we walked from Grasmere, armed with prior knowledge, map and GPS. We walked through the village and up the road to the Kelbarrow path. Wainwright states that this approach is a "delight to the eye…for the intermingling of crag and conifer, juniper and bracken, is landscape artistry at its best". The approach was delightful and we enjoyed the scenery as we skirted the base of Silver How. The final approach to the summit was by way of the same steep scree gully we had climbed on our last attempt. This time however, we successfully navigated our way from the top of the gully to the top of the fell. The actual summit is marked by a large tumbled cairn sitting directly above Grasmere. A fell race was taking place at the time and Silver How was being used as a check point. We watched for a while, provided some snacks for some of the competitors and then decided to head down by a different route. We descended, steeply at first, down the northern side of the summit heading towards Wray Gill; then we walked past the woods of Allan Bank (once the home of William Wordsworth), before heading back to Grasmere.

Sunday 17th April 2011

114. Watson Dodd

Height: 2584 feet (789m)
Route: Stanah Gill – Summit

Continuing the theme of revisiting the site of previous failures, we decided to return to the Dodds. Our last excursion to the Lakes had seen us climb Stybarrow Dodd, but then retreat in the face of the extremely cold conditions. Today we decided to complete the round. Once again we would have to climb Stybarrow Dodd, but then we would hopefully continue and visit Watson Dodd, Great Dodd, and because we were feeling optimistic, Clough Head. Once again we parked at Stanah, and we began our approach with a steep climb beside the Gill. The route may have been the same, but the weather conditions could hardly have been more different. Today was warm and bright, so we walked in T-shirts and shorts. It was hard to believe that a mere six weeks ago the weather had been freezing and everything above eighteen hundred feet had been covered in snow.

Whenever you repeat a walk, in the lakes or anywhere else, it results in a unique experience. It was reassuring to think that if we did eventually manage to climb all the Wainwrights, we could return and climb the same fells, perhaps by the same routes, and still have a fantastic time.

The views today were fantastic; extensive and impressive, providing another marked contrast to our previous experience. We could even see the ski tow on the slopes of Raise. The conditions meant that it was easy to follow the clear path to the summit, a path which had previously been almost impossible to locate. Determined to enjoy Stybarrow Dodd this time, we eat a fairly leisurely lunch whilst enjoying the luxuriating warmth and the stunning views.

Eventually and somewhat grudgingly, we decided that it was time to move on. We headed north-west, our enthusiasm quickly rekindled by the fine views on offer. We strolled towards Watson Dodd in near perfect walking conditions. The highest point of the fell is marked by a small cairn, situated at the western end of the grassy, triangular top. Only one hundred fells to go!

115. Great Dodd

Height: 2807 feet (857m)
Route: North-west from Watson Dodd

Leaving Watson Dodd we headed north-east towards Great Dodd. The summit area of Great Dodd is a short ridge, with the highest point at the north-west end marked by a small cairn. A larger wind shelter lay to the south-east, and we could see another cairn part way down the western slope on the path to Clough Head; this marks the minor top of Little Dodd. The views were fantastic; we could see most of the Lake District and a section of the northern Pennines.

116. Clough Head

Height: 2381 feet (726m)
Route: West and then North-east

Clough Head is the lowest and the northern most top of the Helvellyn range. The plan was to approach Clough Head by way of Calfhow Pike, then return to Calfhow Pike and descend to Beckthornes. Wainwright describes the walk as a "dull trudge"; it was a bit of a trek, but we enjoyed the experience - our pleasure enhanced by the continuing fine weather and glorious views. The summit was marked by a triangulation column and a cairn cum-windbreak. To the north, Blencathra looked magnificent. Wainwright must have agreed! He drew himself reclining on Clough Head and admiring the same view.

We tracked back to Calfhow Pike and headed east to pick up the path descending to Beckthorns. Despite careful scrutiny the path proved to be elusive. As we reached a line of ominous crags we realized that we must have overshot our destination. Forced to track uphill, moods changed quickly from quiet enjoyment to sullen despair; we had walked too far to the south. We did eventually find the missing path, and to be fair to our navigational abilities, the path was overgrown and indistinct. The path was fortunately spotted by the eagle eyed Will. This route up and down the mountainside is obviously rarely used, and we found out why as we slipped and slid down a steep scree gulley towards Beckthorns.

Monday 18th April 2011

117. Bonscale Pike

Height: 1718 feet (524m)
Route: Howtown - Bonscale Pike

A long drive beckoned today. Despite being based in Thornthwaite, we decided to head for the Far Eastern Fells. The plan was to complete a round of five summits; Bonscale Pike, Arthur's Pike, Loadpot Hill, Wether Hill and Steel Knotts. We had originally planned to complete this walk on our last visit, but Tom had felt unwell. The drive, although long, did bestow on us the privilege of driving past the shores of Ullswater. Ullswater is the second largest lake in the Lake District, and is regarded by many as the most beautiful of the English lakes; it has been compared to Lake Lucerne in Switzerland. It is a typical long narrow 'Ribbon Lake' - formed after the last ice age when glaciers eroded the valley floor. When the glaciers retreated the deepened sections were filled with meltwater, thus forming the lake. For much of its length Ullswater forms the border between the ancient counties of Cumberland and Westmorland. Apart from its obvious natural beauty, Ullswater's biggest claim to fame is probably the Ullswater 'Steamers'. These boats offer trips around the lake, calling at Pooley Bridge, Glenridding and Howtown. The 'Steamers' operate all year round and were originally working boats. The boats were used to move mail, workers and goods, to and from the Greenside lead mine at Glenridding.

We drove past the eastern shores of the lake, parking close to the little hamlet of Howtown. The craggy western face of Bonscale Pike rises steeply behind the hamlet. Wainwright recommends two routes to the top - we had difficulty locating either of them. After much deliberation we headed up the very steep breast of the grassy fell, and then followed a path leading up through the higher crags. The climb was relentless, the gradient was severe. Shattered and breathless, we eventually arrived at the summit; a small cairn on a grassy mound. The views were hazy, but we had the summit to ourselves and we had stopped climbing, so we weren't complaining.

118. Arthur's Pike

Height: 1747 feet (532m)
Route: South-east, North-east and then North from Bonscale Pike

Beginning to feel a little hungry, we headed south-east towards Swarthbeck Gill. A sheepfold appeared to present a perfect lunch spot, but others had got there first. Taking care to keep our feet dry and our stomachs under control, we climbed up from the Gill and made our way to the summit. The small summit, set back from the crags on a grassy plateau, provided us with superb views across Ullswater. It also provided a delightful picnic spot; who wants to eat in a sheep fold anyway?

119. Loadpot Hill

Height: 2201 feet (671m)
Route: South along the Old High Street

After refueling, we headed south, crossed one path and then joined the old High Street. Indistinct in places, this Roman road was built to link Brocavum (Brougham) and Glannaventa (Ravenglass). The Roman surveyors decided to avoid the valleys of Lakeland; dense forest and marshes made such areas susceptible to ambush. The boys, interested in all things historical, were thrilled to be walking along a Roman road. Will kept a keen eye out for artifacts, and we all wondered what it must have been like for soldiers, far from home, marching across such a desolate area. We followed the old High Street for about a mile until it began to head south-west, skirting the base of Loadpot Hill. We climbed the northern face of the fell, heading directly for the summit. The broad top, adorned with a massive triangulation pillar and summit cairn, provided extensive views to the west.

120. Wether Hill

Height: 2210 feet (670m)
Route: South from Loadpot Hill

Just to the south of Loadpot Hill, we passed the remains of Lowther House. Even more of a ruin than in Wainwright's day, the old shooting lodge is now nothing more than a pile of stones. Continuing south for about a mile, we soon reached Wether Hill. According to Wainwright; "Two rounded grassy mounds of similar altitude, separated by a slight depression, form the summit". Confusingly, we spotted several grassy mounds, but none of them matched Wainwright's description. To banish any doubt, we marched across the whole top and used a GPS to find the highest point.

121. Steel Knotts

Height: 1414 feet (432m)
Route: Descent to Fusedale Beck - Summit

Shortly after leaving Wether Hill, we headed down a steep grassy slope towards Fusedale Beck. From the delightful but marshy beck, a clear path rises to the summit ridge of Steel Knotts. The ridge, sometimes called Martindale edge, runs for about two miles. Impressive and exhilarating (but not life threatening), affording excellent views in all directions, the ridge provided a memorable finish to our walk.

Tuesday 19th April 2011

122. Rosthwaite Fell (Bessyboots)

Height: 1807 feet (550m)
Route: Rosthwaite to Stonethwaite via the Cumbria Way - Summit via Stanger Gill - Descent to Comb Gill - return to Rosthwaite

I may have experienced quite a few birthdays, but I still look forward to them. Waking a year older, but feeling both optimistic and celebratory, I thought about the day ahead. Initially I had considered tackling a major mountain, possibly Helvellyn, but decided on a short walk instead. I wanted to have enough time to open presents, linger over a tasty breakfast, walk and have a late lunch at the Dog and Gun. The short walk chosen was Rosthwaite Fell, and after being spoilt rotten by Tania, Will and Tom, we headed out.

We parked at the Scafell Hotel and then walked along the Cumbria Way towards Stonethwaite. The weather was fantastic; clear, bright and warm. The walk was delightful; sunlight reflected of babbling brooks, glorious views were to be seen in all directions, and I had the best of company.

Unfortunately, our perfect start to a perfect day was briefly interrupted by our first sight of Rosthwite Fell. It was difficult to see how we would reach the summit – the cliffs looked daunting and forbidding. But, trusting in Wainwright's assessment that such a climb was possible, we walked south-east from Stonethwaite and looked out for his route – "the path leading into the wood, just after crossing the second of two streams, close together". We counted the streams, but we couldn't see a route. Contented happiness interrupted for a second time, we suppressed a rising sense of panic and continued heading south-east. Fortunately we discovered a clear, stepped path, leading up beside Stanger Gill. This was one of those occasions when an updated copy of Wainwright's guides might have been useful. The path was unrelentingly steep, but quite beautiful. We climbed up between the trees, with dappled sunlight guiding our way. The views back down towards Borrowdale were spectacular, if a little unnerving. We decided that this was definitely a route to ascend, rather than descend.

Bypassing Bull Crag, we realized that most of the hard climbing was over. Pinpointing the summit, we headed over marshy ground towards Bessyboot. The first thing that hits you, when reach the summit is that Bessyboot is not the highest point in the surrounding area. To the south, Rosthwaite Cam is clearly higher. Wainwright chose Bessyboot as his summit, because he claims it is "the most distinctive summit in the northern half of the fell". Wainwright might well have chosen fells in a slightly idiosyncratic way, but he usually chooses well. Bessyboot was a lovely summit; interesting, rocky, and an ideal platform for some fine views.

Still enjoying a fantastic day, things got even better when Tania and the boy's produced a birthday cake, complete with candles. Slightly worried however that the intense heat and light created by the flames might cause beacons to be lit on surrounding fell tops – I quickly made a wish. For once it came true – nothing changed!

Descent saw us heading towards the Tarn at Leaves, before heading down the western slopes of the fell. The final return to Rosthwaite took us through fields full of gamboling lambs, and still the sun continued to shine. Driving back to Keswick via Borrowdale, we saw a red squirrel, and then I settled down for Goulash and a pint at the Dog and Gun.

Birthdays don't get better than this!

Wednesday 20th April 2011

123. Robinson

Height: 2417 feet (737m)
Route: Ascent from Newlands Hause

Today was another day, when we contemplated rather than climbed Helvellyn. We woke late and consequently set our sights on a lesser prize – Robinson. Our route would take us from Newlands Hause to the summit (a bit of a cheat I know). Starting from this point means that most of the climb is completed by car, rather than by foot. The short, but steep ascent saw us climb to the right of Moss Force, before walking across the Moss itself. Buttermere Moss, in Wainwright's words is "a wide marshy depression from which water cannot escape except by being carried away in the boots of pedestrians".

Feet remarkably dry, we soon reached the impressive summit; hardly a lesser prize. The top is rounded and mainly grassy, but there are two low outcrops of rock with loose stones between them. The more westerly of these is the summit and bears a cairn. The weather continued to smile on us; bright, clear blue skies, afforded fantastic views in most directions.

The boy's decided to run back down the fell and across Buttermere Moss, but we hadn't been forewarned. They ran more quickly than I thought possible, and were soon out of hearing. With visions of them both plummeting over the cliffs, down to Newlands Hause, I set off in pursuit.

Frantic shouting and waving eventually grabbed the boy's attention, but also the attention of several other walkers on the fell. I'm surprised I didn't create a massive panic, or instigate a mountain rescue call out. Boys suitable admonished, we returned to the car.

Thursday 21st April 2011

124. Helvellyn

Height: 3118 feet (950m)
Route: Glenridding – Glenridding Beck – Mires Beck – Striding Edge – Summit – Nethermost Pike – Dollywagon Pike; Descent via Grisedale Tarn and Valley

Well, we couldn't put it off any longer; we had run out of excuses. After two days of modest exertion, we awoke to near perfect walking conditions. Bright, clear, windless skies meant that there would be no better time to climb Helvellyn; the third highest and one of the most popular fells in Lakeland.

Helvellyn lies at the centre of a massive range that forms a natural barrier between the valleys of Thirlmere and Ullswater. Other fells in this range include Dollywaggon Pike, Nethermost Pike, Catstycam, Lower Man, White Side, Raise, and The Dodds.

Wainwright points out how different the Helvellyn range is on its gentler western slopes, compared to the mountainous crags and sheer edges on its eastern side. He writes "the smooth slopes curving up from the west break abruptly along the ridge, where, in complete contrast, a shattered cliff of crag and scree falls away precipitously eastwards: here are the most dramatic scenes Helvellyn has to offer".

Striding Edge is one of the dramatic scenes referred to by Wainwright. He describes this ridge linking Birkhouse Moor to Helvellyn Plateau as – "all bare rock, a succession of jagged fangs ending in a black tower". Despite this description, Tania and I were determined that we would climb Helvellyn via Striding Edge. We planned an approach from Patterdale, and our challenging itinerary also included the summits of Nethermost Pike and Dollywagon Pike.

Tania and I were excited; however, the boys appeared less than enthusiastic about the prospect. I think the problem was that despite our best intentions, we had over emphasized the risks associated with Helvellyn. We told the boys about the dangers of Striding Edge, but instead of instilling a sense of respect and caution, we instilled a sense of fear and dread.

We started walking from a large pay and display car park in the centre of Glenridding. We headed west along Greenside Road, before walking up a track to the campsite at Gillside Farm. Keeping the campsite on our left, we headed towards Rattlebeck Bridge. From here we continued heading uphill; crossing a ladder stile and then picking up a rising path beside Mires Beck. The walk was enjoyable, but it was incredibly hot and we soon felt dehydrated. We made frequent stops to take on more water as we headed towards the 'Hole in the wall'. Wainwright states that "The gap (hole) in the wall…is always reached with thankfulness". We were certainly thankful; the gradient evened out, a refreshing breeze cooled us down, and the delightful aspect of Red Tarn came into view.

Enclosed by the arms of Striding Edge and Swirral Edge, Red Tarn is one of the highest and most beautiful tarns in the Lake District. The tarn was formed when the glacier that carved out the eastern side of Helvellyn melted.

We enjoyed the view and then headed south-west, but I would be lying if I said we headed off confidently. Tania was determined to conquer her fears, but looked nervous; Tom looked very nervous.

Fortunately, the initial part of Striding Edge is relatively rounded and has a good path running along the right hand side; unfortunately our sense of relative safety was short lived. As we emerged onto the top of the ridge it became apparent that the sheer drops and sense of exposure were too much for Tania and Tom. Fear was replaced by panic, so we descended to a side path running just below the ridge. I have to say that I think the side path gives the illusion of safety, rather than being safer in any real sense. It's narrow, crumbling in places, and more difficult to walk over than the ridge itself, but no one was listening to me.

Tania and Tom were happier, but happy is probably the wrong word to use. We slowly inched our way along the path. Will encouraged Tania, and I tried to assist a traumatized Tom.

Hindsight is a wonderful thing. Whilst this route was well within Tom's capabilities, his fear today was increasing the risk; safety was becoming a real issue. In an attempt to encourage and calm Tom, I ended up completing large sections of the route walking backwards – I wonder if this has ever been done before?

The right hand side path continues until near the end of the ridge, at this point we had to climb to the very top of Striding Edge again. From here Tania and Will took the direct approach, climbing up How Spying How, whilst Tom and I switched over to a side path to the south. We reunited at a col between Striding Edge and Helvellyn. Tom began to regain his composure, and we all began our final ascent – scrambling up the loose rocky slope towards the summit of Helvellyn.

Striding Edge is a notorious accident spot and has to be respected. One of the first things we came across on the summit plateau was a memorial to Charles Gough. In 1805 he slipped and perished. The story of Goughs faithful dog, which stayed with his body for three months until his body was discovered, has inspired many poems, including those of *Fidelity* by William Wordsworth, and *Helvellyn* by Sir Walter Scott. Whether it was fidelity or hunger that encouraged the dog to stay beside his master is open to conjecture.

The highest point on Helvellyn is marked by a cairn; to the north is an Ordnance Survey triangulation point, a little lower than the summit at three thousand, one hundred and eleven feet. We took in the views and then retreated to a large stone cross shaped shelter. Tania was elated; Will was justifiably proud of himself; Tom said he was going to ring Childline!

Fortunately, Tom was unable to get a mobile signal.

After a short rest and a snack, we headed south, exploring the summit plateau on the way. The top of Helvellyn is broad and largely flat; this fact encouraged John Leeming and Bert Hinkler to land a plane on the summit, thereby becoming the first people to do so on any British mountain top. We passed a plaque commemorating the event, took a last look at Striding Edge, and then headed onwards.

125. Nethermost Pike

Height: 2920 feet (891m)
Route: South from Helvellyn

A gentle walk soon brought us to the summit of Nethermost Pike. We were only about a mile away from Helvyllyn, but the crowds had gone and we had this summit to ourselves. The summit area is triangular in plan with ridges running to the north, south and east. The actual top is toward the northern corner and set back a little from the drop to Nethermost Cove. Other than northward, where the bulk of Helvellyn intervenes, the views were extensive, with much of the Lake District visible.

126. Dollywagon Pike

Height: 2810 feet (858m)
Route: South from Nethermost Pike, then South-east

We continued heading south, skirting the edge of High Crag as we walked towards Dollywagon Pike. The summit is a small grassy dome and it narrows towards the east. Stopping for a snack and a drink, we realized that our water supplies had just about run out. We had underestimated the heat, our thirst, and the length of the walk. Feeling thirsty, we descended a stepped path to Grisedale Tarn. The tarn is the legendary resting place of the crown of the last King of Cumbria. The crown was allegedly brought here in 945 by soldiers of Dunmail, after he was slain in battle by the combined forces of the English and Scottish kings.

We rested by the beautiful tarn, soaked up the afternoon sun, complemented each other on a great day's walking and generally put off the inevitable start to our long walk home. Return to Glenridding was via Grisedale Beck. The route was delightful, but we were shattered and didn't appreciate or enjoy it as much as we should have done.

Had Helvyllyn lived up to expectations? I think it had - wonderful scenery, delightful weather and fantastic memories - for all apart from Tom that is.

Saturday 23rd April 2011

127. Hartsop Dodd

Height: 2018 feet (618m)
Route: Ascent from the A529

After climbing Helvyllyn we thought that we deserved a physical and an emotional break. Consequently, Thursday was spent swimming and shopping.

Today, feeling slightly more energetic, we decided to head to the Far Eastern Fells before driving back to Devon. The plan was to climb Hartsop Dodd and its near neighbour, Cauldale Moor.

We planned to park at Brothers Water, but many others had the same idea, and they had obviously got up a bit earlier. Brothers Water is a small lake and was formally called Broad Water. The name was changed in the nineteenth century when two brothers drowned here. Interestingly, Brothers Water may be classified in either of two ways; as one of the Lake District's smallest lakes, or one of its largest tarns.

After parking the car in a small lay-by on the A592, we checked our route and then headed up the western slopes of Hartsop Dodd. Wainwright describes this route as "steep, and rather dreary". His description is largely accurate. We trudged our way to the summit, where a timber post marked the highest point.

128. Cauldale Moor (Stoney Cove Pike)

Height: 2502 feet (763m)
Route: South from Hartsop Dodd

Wainwright's description of the next section of the walk did little to heighten our excitement; he describes the walk to Cauldale Moor as "An easy climb on grass…The wall drearily links the two summits". Once again his description was accurate. We followed a wall, on grass, and it was a bit dreary. The walk was beginning to affect our collective frame of mind. We all felt a little lackluster, but our dispositions improved as we reached the summit. Realizing that this would be our final fell top for quite some time, we remembered that we should be making the most of our walk, and we reminded ourselves that we were fortunate to be here.

There's nothing like completing a week in the Lakes with a fantastic walk, and despite our fell top positivity, this was nothing like it! However, we had enjoyed another fantastic week.

If I ever have a better birthday I'll be a lucky man!

THE GLASS IS ALWAYS HALF FULL
October 2011

"The optimist proclaims that we live in the best of all possible worlds; and the pessimist fears this is true." James Branch Cabell

The nice part about being a pessimist is that you are constantly being either proven right or pleasantly surprised. George F. Will, *The Leveling Wind*

When walking is it best to be optimistic or pessimistic?

An optimist, when faced with a problem, tends to find the up side to the situation and starts figuring out ways to solve that problem, or ways to turn it around. These facets are ideally suited to the walker.

A pessimist, however, immediately throws up their hands, and yells, "That's it; it's all over. I can't handle this anymore." Or they will distance themselves from the problem, pretending it doesn't matter. This is denial, and it never works. Such facets are highly unsuitable for the walker.

Can pessimism be a positive force?

My feelings on the matter are that a walker has to approach each day optimistically, but plan pessimistically. I have mentioned before that you need to be positive; you need to be able to see positive outcomes if you are to overcome adversity, but at the same time you have to plan for the worst.

A pessimist sees only the dark side of the clouds, and mopes; a philosopher sees both sides, and shrugs; an optimist doesn't see the clouds at all – he's walking on them. Leonard Louis Levinson

Optimistically planning for cloudless skies, I packed shorts and sun cream, and then pessimistically added my waterproofs. Philosophically speaking – I was ready for anything, apart from another early morning.

Whilst I understand that the function of an alarm clock is to get people out of bed, I despise its efficiency of purpose. Apart from announcing the start of another working day; an alarm clock that interrupts your sleep can damage your memories, your ability to learn, your mood and temper, your relationships with other people, your ability to focus and your overall intellectual performance!

It's no wonder that one of my favourite moments at the start of each holiday is the ritualistic silencing of the alarm. However, this particular ritual was about to be abandoned.

It was the first night of our half term holiday and instead of silencing the alarm, I re-set it to an even earlier and bleaker hour. Memories of our horrendous journey last October, encouraged a decision to head for the Lakes before even the first light of dawn had arrived.

Bleary eyed, dazed and slightly confused, we somehow managed to pack and leave the house in a fairly efficient manner. Fortunately, the journey was without incident; the roads were clear and we made rapid progress. Arriving in the Lake District relaxed and in time for lunch, the trauma of the early morning was forgotten and we eagerly anticipated the holiday to come.

Sunday 23rd October 2011

129. Hen Comb

Height: 161 feet (509m)
Route: Kirkstile Inn – Mosedale Beck – Summit – descent via Little Dodd

Persistent morning rain led to a late start and a decision to tackle a short walk from Loweswater to Hen Comb. Wainwright states that Hen Comb is

"Not an exciting walk, but pleasant enough on a sunny day for anybody who doesn't want to get excited". Well, the rain had stopped, but it wasn't sunny. The state of the weather and Wainwright's unenthusiastic description meant that we approached the walk with 'few' rather than 'great' expectations.

Hen Comb is a linear ridge, beginning in the fields of the Loweswater valley and climbing away southwards. We ascended via Mosedale Beck, and soon faced our first obstacle of the day. With no bridge and no alternative, we had to take off boots and socks and ford the beck. The water was surprising cold; perhaps it was the shock that caused Will to drop his boots into the freezing depths.

Saving what little excitement was promised by Wainwright for the return trip, we followed a valley path to an old mine and then climbed through bracken to the summit. The summit; a small grassy dome, provided some excellent views, especially to the Buttermere valley.

Keeping Wainwright's recommendation in mind, we descended via Little Dodd and we were suitably rewarded. The views were magnificent for just about the whole of the return trip.

Despite his one indisputable commendation of the fell, something tells me that Wainwright really didn't like Hen Comb. In addition to his earlier comments about excitement, he states that the summit has "nothing of interest", and that "It is the sort of fell sometimes climbed, but rarely twice".

Reflecting over a pint at the Kirkstile Inn, we decided that this was a walk we would happily complete again.

Perhaps our initial pessimism had led to a pleasant surprise.

Monday 24th October 2011

130. Brock Crags

Height: 1841 feet (561m)
Route: Hartsop Village car park – Brock Crags

A promising forecast saw us heading out early to Hartsop Village. The plan was to climb Brock Crags, Angletarn Pikes and Beda Fell. The early start proved to be fortuitous as we managed to bag the last space in the village car park. Leaving the eastern side of the car park, we turned right into a lane, then right again across the southern flank of the fell. Climbing up from the west, we passed a series of rocky knolls before we arrived at the summit cairn. Flanked by two small tarns and offering fine views towards the surrounding fells and Brothers Water, the summit was a wonderful place to be.

131. Angletarn Pikes

Height: 1857 feet (567m)
Route: West-north-west then North-east from Brock Crags

The sun continued to shine, but as we walked towards Angletarn Pikes, the wind began to grow in strength. Will and I strode out in front; occasionally crouching down low to avoid being blown off our feet. We looked for a lunch spot that would offer some shelter, but eventually settled for a spot that offered little protection, but did offer a clear view of the very picturesque Angle Tarn.

The wind continued to grow in strength; gusting to gale force as we headed towards the summit. Two rocky towers resembling a miniature Langdale Pikes form the highest points of the fell. Bashed and buffeted, we scrambled to the northern most top. Unfortunately, the high winds forced us from the summit before we could really appreciate all the views on offer.

132. Beda Fell

Height: 1670 feet (509m)
Route: North-east then North and North-east from Angletarn Pikes

The high winds showed little sign of abating; we considered our options, but decided to keep to our original itinerary. Once Bedafell Knott was reached, we could clearly see that a narrowing shoulder of land led towards Beda Fell. The roughly two mile long route would have been fantastic, if it were not for the gales trying to blow us from the thankfully wide ridge.

The summit, sometimes referred to as Beda Head, is a grassy mound with a small cairn. We had a good view of the surrounding high fells, but the wideness of the ridge obscured much of the neighbouring valley.

An enjoyable and a picturesque descent saw us retrace our footsteps to Bedafell Knott, before heading down to Boredale Hause. From here we walked to the impressive falls of Angletarn Beck, and then we returned to Hartsop.

Another day and another great walk (a real hidden gem) was followed by a great meal at the Coledale Inn – why isn't this pub in the Good Pub Guide?

Wednesday 26th October 2011

133. Knott

Height: 2329 feet (710m)
Route: Mousedale Valley – Grainsgill Beck

No walking yesterday, but public recognition of Tom's poetic skills. Whilst listening to the sounds of Radio Cumbria, Tom heard about a competition based on poems starting with the word Cumbria. A quick text letter and Tom was broadcast to the nation (well Cumbria at least).

Cumbria Fells
More magical than spells
Full of bluebells and dingly dells
Oh how I love Cumbria Fells

Wednesday morning saw us head off to the Mosedale Valley. Driving as far as we could, we eventually parked when the road gave way to fellside. From the car we followed a very muddy but enjoyable route beside Grainsgill Beck. The sky was full of cloud, and rain looked a certainty, but fortunately it never arrived. However, as we began our final climb to the summit of Knott, the clouds came down to meet us. Both visibility and temperature were dramatically reduced, and at the same time wind speed increased. Visibility was so poor that we had to use a GPS to reach the summit, and with nothing to look at, we continued to use the GPS to navigate our way to Great Calva.

134. Great Calva

Height: 2264 feet (690m)
Route: South from Knott

As we headed south, the cloud began to lift; as did our fog bound insecurities. Whilst happy to rely on a GPS, it is always a relief when you can see your destination. A distinctive symmetrical pyramid emerged from the gloom, and we were relieved to be so obviously back on track. Arriving at the summit we took a few pictures and then sought refuge in a stone windshelter. Unfortunately, the shelter failed to live up to its intended function. Feeling rather chilled, we soon began our descent. We ambled down a beautiful heather clad slope, and then enjoyed a lovely walk beside the River Caldew. Historically the county watered by the Caldew was Cumberland.

As we headed back towards the car, we passed a magnificently well constructed circular sheepfold. “Idleness builds no monuments” said Wainwright – truer words were never spoken. However, thinking about our plans for the evening, we concurred that sometimes it’s important to be idle.

Thursday 29th October 2011

135. Seathwaite Fell

Height: 1970 feet (632m)
Route: Seathwaite Farm – Stockley Bridge – Styhead Tarn Path – Summit

Seathwaite is listed as having 3552 mm of rainfall annually; this figure makes it the wettest place with rainfall statistics in England. The rain gauge used for this measurement is on the slope of Seathwaite Fell. As we headed towards the fell, the combination of the statistics and the rain laden clouds suggested that we would be unlikely to stay dry.

A slightly pessimistic outlook, but I was hoping to be pleasantly surprised.

The sun may not have been shining as we stepped out of the car, but the absence of any rain, and a slight break in the clouds heightened my optimism.

I actually love this part of the Lakes. A return to Seathwaite Farm is always a time for celebration. I thought about previous visits; my first ascent of Scafell Pike, The boys' first ascent – all wonderful memories, full of never to be forgotten moments.

After a brief nostalgic reverie, we walked to Stockley Bridge. After taking some obligatory photos, we headed along the Styhead Tarn path looking out for an obvious line of ascent. Seathwaite Fell is rarely climbed, usually being bypassed in favour of its more famous neighbours. Consequently, an obvious line of ascent failed to materialise.

Eventually we selected a route beside a beck; it looked a little steep towards the top, but often distance distorts angles and slopes are more gentle than expected. Well, distance certainly had distorted the angle of the slope. The higher we climbed, the more severe the slope became. The boys confidently scrambled towards the summit, but Tania was less than happy with the situation.

Not particularly happy, but full of determination, Tania's struggles were rewarded by some fine views from Wainwright's Northern Summit. This is another of Wainwright's subjective decisions. Whilst acknowledging that the Northern summit isn't the highest point on the fell, Wainwright stated that the one thousand, nine hundred and seventy one foot top, is generally regarded as the true summit.

Friday 28th October 2011

136. Rest Dodd

Height: 2283 feet (696m)
Route: Hartsop – Hayeswater reservoir – Summit

For what would turn out to be the last walk of our holiday, we returned to Hartsop. The plan was to climb Rest Dodd, The Nab, the Knott, Rampsgill Head, Kidsty Pike and High Raise.

Things didn't get off to a great start; Hartsop car park was full and we ended up parking some distance away from our intended starting point. However, 'things' quickly improved. Once back on track, our initial approach beside Hayeswater Gill proved to be extremely scenic, and very easy to follow – a welcome change after yesterday. In fact the whole route to Hayeswater Reservoir is to be recommended. Nonetheless, after Hayeswater Reservoir the climb became more of a slog, and we were exposed to some very cold north-easterlies. Rather frustratingly, we also had to climb almost to the top of The Knott before descending and then climbing to the summit of Rest Dodd. It didn't feel right to turn away from the summit of The Knott when we were so close, but we planned to return.

The summit of Rest Dodd is marked by a substantial cairn, probably due to the close proximity of quite a few old stone walls. The fell top provided a good full length view of the Helvellyn range to the west, as well as a spectacular view of the Ramps Gill valley to the north. We could also pick out our next objective – The Nab.

At this stage we began to realise that today's walk was going to be more ambitious and more strenuous than anticipated.

137. The Nab

Height: 1887 feet (576m)
Route: From Rest Dodd

Wainwright states that "The way of the trespasser is hard, for this route is really unpleasant; the depression is a vast morass".

Whilst anyone visiting The Nab today is no longer a trespasser, the route from Rest Dodd is still a little unpleasant. An initial steep descent from Rest Dodd, and a fall from me, was followed by a walk through some of the boggiest ground I have ever encountered.

Mud-splattered and fairly sodden, we arrived at the grassy and thankfully dry summit. Our view was obstructed by higher ground towards the south, but we had a great view of the Helvellyn range above Angletarn Pikes.

The return towards Rest Dodd heralded an unavoidable return to the morass. I agree with Wainwright, the route isn't particularly pleasant. But,

Will and Tom loved jumping in all the mud (you can guess who has to clean the boots!) and we were rewarded by the sight of a herd of Red deer grazing on the fellside.

To save time on our return, we followed a short cut, cunningly designed to avoid climbing to the summit of Rest Dodd once again. But, cunning failed, and walking further than intended (not for the first time), we inadvertently returned to summit 136.

Our initial plan to continue onwards and visit the Knott, Rampsgill Head, Kidsty Pike and High Raise, was beginning to look hopelessly optimistic. We decided to save these fells for another day, and we realised that sometimes optimism can breed disappointment. However, the disappointment was only temporary. Pushing discontent to one side we enjoyed all that a wonderful afternoon in the Lakes can offer, and we optimistically looked forward to our next visit.

It doesn't hurt to be optimistic. You can always cry later. Lucimar Santos De Lima

DREAMING OF A WHITE CHRISTMAS December 2011

Just about my favourite Christmas ever, was the first I spent in the Lake District with Tania. That Christmas snow had fallen just before our arrival, and the sheer beauty of the Lakes was breathtaking. Crystal clear blue skies, mountains and valleys blanketed in snow, treetops glistening, children listening, sleigh bells in the snow! Well, the last two descriptions may be my memory playing me false, but I still get a warm feeling of satisfaction when I look back and remember.

Quite understandably the boys have always wanted to be at home for Christmas. But this year we tempted them with tales of deep snow, sledging, cosy cottages, log fires and incomparable beauty. Happily, after some reassurance that we wouldn't be walking every day, and 'yes', they would have some time to play with their presents; agreement was reached and we planned our next northern excursion.

We booked an apartment in Thornthwaite; squeezed all our Christmas essentials into the car, and after a journey punctuated with some seasonal family gatherings, we arrived in the Lakes.

I immediately felt a wave of contentment, and I knew we had made the right decision. The valleys may have been free of snow, but the higher fells were festively blanketed. Despite myself and my normally 'scrooge' like disposition, I began to feel a little Christmassy.

Now I love the Lakes, and not surprisingly so do many others; about sixteen million people visit every year, and consequently things can get a little busy. However, driving into Keswick I was pleasantly surprised to find how quiet everything was; deserted car parks and high streets, empty shops and pubs. I can't begrudge the presence of fellow tourists, and I certainly don't underestimate the contribution they make to the local economy, but what a joy! We parked in seconds, we ambled around town, and we were able to choose our favourite table in our favourite pub. I love Christmas!

Full of festive spirit, we eventually journeyed on to Ladstock Hall (a former country house hotel recently converted into ten apartments). Keswick may have been quiet, but we still weren't prepared for the fact that we were Ladstock Hall's only residents. Feeling a little bit like Jack Nicholson in *The Shining*, but hoping that there would be a snow storm, we settled down for the evening.

Wednesday 21st December 2011

138. Birkhouse Moor

Height: 2350 feet (718m)
Route: Glenridding via Mires Beck

The morning was dull and overcast; warming temperatures meant that the clouds threatened rain rather than snow. We decided to aim relatively high and to find some snow before it all melted. We selected Birkhouse Moor, part of the east ridge of Helvellyn. It's actually an extension of Striding Edge, but it is a broad plateau rather than a narrow arête.

The walk started from Glenridding, and we should have simply repeated the initial stages of our Helvellyn route. However, an early navigational error and an unnecessary detour served to confirm our status as poor navigators. Fortunately, more by luck than judgement, we did eventually end up on our intended route – walking beside Mires Beck. Keeping the beck to our left, we followed its course looking out for a safe place to cross, but this turned out to be more difficult than expected. The Beck was in full spate; a mixture of heavy rain and snow melt prevented us from reaching the opposite bank until we had almost given up all hope of doing so.

We reached snow at about twelve hundred feet – a few scattered patches at first, but the covering quickly thickened. From about sixteen hundred feet, the snow became really deep. Drifts accumulated to over a metre and walking became a real effort. But, the effort was worth it. The views were fantastic and the snow itself took on a vivid blue colour. When light passes through snow, red light is absorbed, while blue is transmitted. You can see this effect in snow at fairly shallow depths because the light is bounced around repeatedly between ice grains, losing a little red at each bounce. Progress was slow and we had time for some scientific observations. We could see gradation of colour within the holes made by our feet. Near the opening the snow took on a yellowish colour, as the depth increased the colours changed to yellowish-green, greenish-blue and finally blue.

Worried that our feet might turn blue if we spent too much time sinking into the snow, we continued on our way towards the summits of the fell.

A unique aspect of Birkhouse Moor is that Wainwright mentions two summits, but he neglects to favour one before the other. The true top is on the main ridge to Striding Edge, alongside a dry stone wall. A cairn has been built a little to the west, but the wall appears to cross the highest point. We had passed this point before on our way to Helvellyn, but we choose to visit the spot again. Different conditions always create unique experiences, and today the drifts were so deep that you could walk across the top of the wall. From here we headed north-north-east towards the North top. No walls to walk over, but some fantastic views towards Ullswater.

Descent saw us heading back towards the wall, whilst enjoying a snowball fight of epic proportions. We then followed the wall in an easterly direction towards a saddle above Mires Beck. Here we saw our only other walker of the day, a friendly man with an inquisitive dog. Could this have been the Fell Top Assessor? Working seven days on and seven days off, including weekends and bank holidays, the Fell Top Assessor has to climb from Glenridding to the summit of Helvellyn and report on fell top conditions. The reports are featured in daily weather forecasts. Whilst such a job is probably not everyone's cup of tea – I wouldn't say no.

Mires Beck proved to be almost as much as an obstacle on our return as it had been on our ascent. However, after carefully negotiating the raging torrent, we returned to Glenridding.

What a fantastic way to spend the run up to Christmas.

Thursday 22nd December 2011

139. Seat Sandal

Height: 2415 feet 9736m)
Route: From Dunmail Raise – direct route by the shoulder (not recommended by Wainwright)

On our descent from Helvellyn we had visited Grisedale Tarn, the legendary resting place of the crown of the kingdom of Cumbria. Today our walk would start from Dunmail Raise, the legendary resting place of the last King of Cumbria.

According to legend, Dunmail, the last king of Cumbria and consequently last King of the British, was attacked by the combined forces of Edmund I of England and Malcolm I of Scotland. Dunmail retreated into the heart of the Lake District, and met the kings in battle in the pass that divides Grasmere from Thirlmere. He was defeated and it is said that he was killed in the fight at the hands of Edmund himself. Some of the surviving Cumbrians, taken prisoner by Edmund, were ordered to collect rocks to pile on Dunmail's body. The resulting cairn still exists and gives the pass its modern name, Dunmail Raise.

Hoping that Seat Sandal wouldn't defeat us, we parked the car and started walking. Wainwright recommends the path alongside Raise Beck. It was our intention to follow Wainwright's advice, but with a feeling of déjà vu, we made another early directional error and headed off on the wrong path. We climbed away from Raise Beck, relentlessly slogging up the west shoulder of the fell. Wainwright states that this is "a route not to be recommended", we all agreed. We did have some good views down towards Thirlmere, but in truth they weren't adequate compensation. We were very relieved when we finally arrived at the summit. The summit is a flat grassy plateau with some rock outcrops and a broken down wall. A radio ham reached the top shortly before us and he was broadcasting to the nation. He was the only other person we saw all day.

We decided to descend by the route we should have ascended. Following the broken wall down towards the top of Raise Beck, we enjoyed lovely views towards Grisedale Tarn. However, just as we reached Raise Beck, the clouds descended and the heavens opened. The all-enveloping gloom took the edge off what would have been a beautiful route.

Saturday 24th December (Christmas Eve)

140. Glenridding Dodd

Height: 1425 feet (442m)
Roure: From Glenridding via Blaes Way

Unfortunately, we had to surrender a good walking day yesterday in order to have something to eat on Christmas Day. We spent most of the day in a variety of supermarkets, but I suppose such sacrifices have to be made!

Our enforced inertia made us all the more determined to walk today; determined to such an extent that we braved persistent rain and gales as we heading up the short, steep climb from Glenridding car park to Glenridding Dodd. The inclement conditions provided a real test for our waterproofs – the climb was character building to say the least. If it wasn't for the fact that forecasts predicted even worse weather for the rest of the week, I don't think we would have stepped out of the car. Wainwright states that "On a sunny day in August the summit is a delectable place to be". Well, it was December; the summit was cold, wet and windswept, but still strangely delectable.

We returned by the same route. Tania at one stage was blown over by the wind which screeched to such a level that conversation was practically impossible.

We eat lunch in the rain, standing beside the visitors centre in Glenridding car park. We may have been wet and windblown, but we were all pleased to have completed a walk on Christmas Eve.

The weather continued to defy the season. Warm air and incessant rain dominated the conditions. The papers began to focus on global warming, and our dreams of a white Christmas failed to materialize. However, it's not the weather which makes Christmas, it's the company.

The skies were neither crystal clear nor blue, the mountains and valleys weren't blanketed in snow, but I still get a warm feeling of satisfaction when I look back and remember.

IF AT FIRST YOU DON'T SUCCEED
April 2012

My pulse began to race, my hands clenched the steering wheel and sweat trickled down the back of my neck. "Why have you brought me this way?"

A Land Rover loomed in front of me and I was forced to reverse blindly around a steeply inclined hairpin bend. This was definitely not my idea of fun!

I cast my mind back a few hour and remembered Tania saying "Hardnott Pass is great fun; fantastic views and not as difficult as everyone makes out".

Marriages hinge on moments such as these!

Saturday 7th April 2012

141. Hardknott

Height: 1803 feet (549m)
Route: Direct ascent from Hardknott Pass

Hardknott Pass carries a minor road between the Duddon Valley and Eskdale. It vies for the title of the steepest road in England, achieving gradients of 1 in 3. It is certainly the steepest road I have ever driven on.

The Romans originally built a road over the pass in the second century to link the garrisons at Ambleside and Kendal with the coastal fort at Ravenglass. We were using the road to take us from Amblesdide to Eskdale, with a short stop to visit Hardknott Fell. The short stop and the short cut seemed likely to result in a long drop. At its highest point Hardknott Pass reaches a height of one thousand, two hundred and eighty nine feet. This high point was our initial destination.

The pass itself includes a series of hairpin bends. Drivers should give way to ascending traffic, as advised by the Highway Code, as ignored by said Land Rover.

After parking, applying the hand brake firmly, and clearly asserting my intention not to drive over Hardknott pass ever again, we began our first walk of the holiday.

The climb was more straightforward and certainly less steep than the drive.

Departing from a cairn by the roadside, we followed a grassy path and soon reached the summit. We were rewarded with glorious views towards the Scafell massif. Descent was a simple retracing of our footsteps. However, the road was hidden by the landscape and caused us to momentarily doubt our directional decision making.

Returning to the car, and reassuring myself that the brake pads were relatively new, we began to descend the pass. Our second short stop proved to be a memorable one.

"What have the Romans ever done for us?" – Well, the remains of Hardknott Roman Fort are truly impressive. Well preserved and extensive, situated on a dramatic site and offering stunning long distance views, the Fort proves that amongst other things, the Romans built things to last.

We wandered back in time as we wandered through ancient granaries, a commandants house, and what would have been the former headquarter of the fort.

The fort must have been one of the loneliest outposts of the Roman Empire, but the location was of great strategic importance. The Romans wanted to be able to control the road, so that they could ensure military control of the whole area, thus keeping the Scots and Brigantes at bay. After are historical excursion and my earlier histrionics, we ventured on to Miterdale and our final destination of the day, Bobbin Mill cottage.

Miterdale is a little known corner of the Lake District, tucked away between Eskdale and Wasdale. It runs down from Burnmoor Tarn on the shoulder of Scafell, into the coastal plain in the parish of Irton. The River Mite reaches the sea at Ravenglass. The cottage was delightfully situated on the banks of the River Mite, next door to a working farm.

Running parallel to the River Mite is the river Esk. Eskdale is described by Wainwright as "One of the loveliest of Lakeland's valleys, descends from the highest and wildest mountains in the district to the Sands of Ravenglass in a swift transition from bleak and craggy ridges to verdant woodlands and pastures watered by a charming river".

After so many previous visits to the Lake District, it was fantastic to be staying in another stunningly beautiful and previously unvisited area. What's more, the best was still to come.

Sunday 8th April 2012

142. Middle Fell

Height: 1908 feet (582m)
Route: Direct ascent from Greendale

Our plan today was to visit Wasdale and climb Middle Fell, Seatallen and Bukbarrow.

If Miterdale and Eskdale had been a revelation, Wasdale was an epiphany. The weather could not detract from the fact that this has to be one of the most beautiful places on the planet. Wasdale was voted Britain's best view in 2007, but surely global recognition would be justified? Wasdale is simply stunning. In front of us was England's deepest lake, with the steep screes of Illgill Head plunging down towards its jet black surface. In the distance the silhouettes of Yewbarrow, Great Gable and Scafell, combined to create a captivating, dramatic and altogether unforgettable image.

We began our walk from Greendale, home to the legendary fell runner Joss Naylor. The weather looked far from promising. We emerged from the car in the dry, but rain was threatening. We followed a path to the east of Greendale Gill, before tracking north-east towards the summit.

The walk was a fairly relentless slog. Progress, already slow, was further delayed due to some technical complications arising from Tania's walking poles. Many walkers swear by their walking poles – Tania was swearing at them. They are supposed to aid balance and transfer up to 20% of the walking workload from your legs to your upper body, reducing muscle damage and easing wear and tear on the knees and ankles. Unfortunately, Tania's poles kept retracting; the telescopic mechanism appeared to be fatally flawed. Medical research has shown that using a pair of poles on an eight hour walk will relieve the stress on your knees by 250 tonnes.

If you ask me – stress levels seemed quite high.

Atmospheric conditions mirrored Tania's mood; the cloud lowered, temperatures dropped and the rain arrived. When we eventually reached the summit, the allegedly 'splendid vantage point' (Wainwright) provided a gloom marginally worse than our own.

Instead of an epiphany, we appeared to be facing a depiphany. Our absolute realisation and comprehension of why we walk had descended into self-doubt. We all felt a little negative. Why were we out walking, feeling cold, wet and a little bit miserable? We needed to recapture our positive focus.

Abandoning plans to climb Seatallen and Buckbarrow, we descended Middle Fell and drove to The Wasdale Head Inn.

A drink at the home of British mountaineering did much to restore our collective mood; although Tom was a little disgruntled that I wouldn't buy him any food – I tried to explain that he just hadn't earned it!

Monday was forecast to be a complete wash out. Deciding that discretion is sometimes the better part of valour, we avoided the fells and instead headed for the Ravenglass and Eskdale Railway.

When it comes to completing The Wainwrights, people often ask me what we do to keep the boys motivated. Well, apart from the firmly established pound a summit, the truth is usually nothing. The boys still love walking and approach most days positively, but after yesterday's experience, Tania and I decided that a little 'touristy' treat was in order.

The Ravenglass and Eskdale railway is a narrow gauge railway linking Boot to Ravenglass. The line runs for about seven miles, with seven intermediate stations or halts. One of these stations, Irton Road, was just down the road from our cottage. The railway, affectionately known as La'al Ratty, is owned by a private company and supported by a preservation society. The carriages, some covered, some open, are pulled by both steam and diesel engines.

Despite the inclement conditions, I opted for an open carriage, and consequently ended up travelling alone. A steam whistle heralded our departure from Irton Road, and from the twenty first century. The carriages were pulled by a miniature steam locomotive, beautifully maintained, and like me, practically an antique. Tania and the boys beamed at me from the warm confines of their covered carriage, but I enjoyed the feel of the wind and the rain on my face, and the smell of the smoke. The views were wonderful, the trains were fantastic, the staff friendly and informative. What a delightful way to travel.

Shortly after arriving in Ravenglass, we decided to visit the Roman Bath House. The Bath House is only a short walk from the station, but we were impressed to discover one of the tallest surviving Roman structures in England.

Despite the allure of the Roman Age, the lure of the Age of Steam soon became too much for all of us. After a short mooch around the village, we boarded another train and headed back towards the east. From Dalegarth Station we walked to the Boot Inn, and enjoyed some liquid refreshment before reuniting with La'al Ratty for a final trip back to Irton Road.

We had undoubtedly made the right decision. We had all enjoyed a delightful day, despite the incessant rain. Relaxed, reinvigorated and ready to go, we were ready to tackle some more fells.

Tuesday 10th April 2012

143. Whin Rigg

Height:1755 feet (535m)
Route: Bobbin Mill Cottage – Lorton Fell – Whin Rigg

Maintaining my positive mood from yesterday, today's walk had the added bonus that it started from our own doorstep. I generally enjoy driving, but commuting takes its toll on the soul and on the environment. After yesterday's joyous day of train travel, I was left to reflect on the generally disappointing state of public transport in the UK. Professor Beeching has a lot to answer for, but so do a succession of governments who whilst extolling the virtues of sustainable transport have failed to provide adequate funding to deliver a sustainable future. Professor Beeching proposed a motion to close over half of all railway station and nearly a third of all railway lines. Sadly, most of his proposals were carried out between 1963 and 1970. What a different country we might live in today if either the closures hadn't happened, or a much better bus service had been introduced (as planned) to compensate for the rail closures. We really might have a green and pleasant land, available to all, not just a fortunate few.

Feeling very fortunate to be on holiday, and in the Lake District, we set out walking beside the River Mite. Wainwright assesses Miterdale in the following way – "its floor, threaded by the River Mite and adorned by woodland and copse, is delightful". It certainly is delightful. With little indication of its presence at either end, Miterdale is a quiet, somewhat secretive valley. It has all the qualities of every Lakeland valley, but almost in miniature. After following the river and enjoying its scenic charms, we started to climb up through the plantations on Irton Fell. We enjoyed walking through the woods. The gradient was quite severe, but the sylvan beauty and the views opening up towards the Scarfell Massif compensated for the additional effort involved. However, upon reaching the top of Irton Fell, everything changed. The gradient evened out, which was fine, but the trees had all been felled. Our forested paradise gave to way to a scene of desolation. Tom thought that the area resembled Isengard in *Lord of the Rings.* The change in setting appeared to be reinforced by the change in the weather; sunshine gave way to cloud, the wind picked up and the temperature plummeted. After donning some extra layers, we turned away from the former plantation and headed north-east towards the summit of Whin Rigg. The summit cairn, somewhat precariously perched above the Wasdale Screes, offered excellent views down to Wast Water. However, the view of Sellafield was not quite so appealing.

144. Illgill Head

Height: 1983 feet (609m)
Route: North-east from Whin Rigg – Descent via the Old Corpse Road and Burnmoor Tarn

Turning our backs to the nuclear eyesore, we walked north-east from Whin Rigg. We passed some spectacular gullies, which plunged dramatically down towards Wast Water. Wainwright describes the first half mile of this walk as "a section to linger over as long as time permits". We permitted ourselves more time than originally planned, and then headed towards Illgill Head. The summit of Illgill Head as advocated by Wainwright wasn't the highest point on the fell, but it did provide an excellent viewpoint for Wasdale Head. From the summit we descended a very steep slope to The Old Corpse Road, and the very impressive Burnmoor Tarn; one of the largest and deepest tarns in the Lake District. Our final section of the walk took us over Tongue Moor and concluded with another delightful stroll along the banks of the River Mite.

Wednesday 11th April 2012

145. Kirk Fell

Height: 2630 feet (802m)
Route: Wasdale Head – Beck Head (via Gable Beck) – Summit

Our slightly ambitious plan today was to try and complete The Mosedale Horseshoe. This would entail climbing Kirk Fell, Pillar, Scoat Fell, Steeple, Red Pike and Yewbarrow. We started the walk from Wasdale Head; this allowed another opportunity to marvel at the spectacular scenery as we drove beside Wast Water.

It is possible to climb Kirk Fell directly from Wasdale Head, but Wainwright describes this ascent as "a relentless and unremitting treadmill, a turf clutching crawl, not a walk…" The route looked much as described; consequently we decided to approach the fell by way of Gable Beck. This approach was long, slow and arduous, but the views back towards Wast Water were stunning and we didn't have to clutch the turf.

As we approached Beck Head, we had a great view of our slightly nerve wracking route up Great Gable. From this angle it looked to be as terrifying and ill-conceived a route as we remembered.

The final ascent to the summit plateau of Kirk Fell included a few scrambles over slippery, snow covered rock. A little unnerving at times, but nothing like as bad as our experience on Great Gable.

As we reached the plateau, the amount of snow, patchy at first, soon increased, culminating in an extensive and deep covering. The thick layer of snow slowed progress even further. It seemed to take an age to reach the summit cairn, and all the time the sky was darkening and the wind speed was increasing. Fortunately, the cairn doubled as a wind break, unfortunately it started to hail. We began to discuss our options; The Mosedale Horseshoe was beginning to look hopelessly optimistic, both in terms of time available and the deteriorating conditions. Our final decision was confirmed when another walker told us that the route to Pillar was treacherous. Disappointed, but experienced enough to know that you have to be prepared to change your plans when conditions dictate; we followed our own footsteps back along our route of ascent.

Thursday 12th April 2012

146. Seatallen

Height: 2270 feet (692m)
Route: Greendale – Greendale Beck – Descent to Buckbarrow via Cat Bields and Great How

Our success rate had not been particularly spectacular this holiday. We had only been on four walks, and we had failed to fully complete two of those. Attempting to right some wrongs, we decided to return to Greendale and climb Seatallen and Buckbarrow.

The initial approach up Seatallen proved to be a long and steep, but picturesque slope. After Tongue Gill, the scenic quality of walk diminished, but the gradient of the slope increased. The approach lost some of its charm and more closely resembled a moorland trek. Tired and heavy legged, Tania and I marched resolutely towards the summit, whilst Will and Tom sprinted ahead.

The summit is marked by a massive cairn, possibly a tumulus. Wainwright didn't think much of the views, but we thought they were fairly spectacular. Will and Tom were a little too 'cocky' about reaching the top of the fell first. In an attempt to resurrect my credibility, I challenged them to a race. Unfortunately, the offer of five pounds to anyone who could get to Cat Bields before me, proved to be a big mistake!

147. Buckbarrow

Height: 1388 feet (420m)
Route: Descent from Seatallen

Our route from Seatallen took us to the summits of Cat Bields, Great How and finally Buckbarrow. Although only the latter can be counted as a Wainwright, they all proved to be splendid places to visit; rocky mounds on the edges of crags, all offering superb views, especially those towards Wast Water and the Wast Water Screes.

As we descended from Buckbarrow, the village of Greendale came into view. As mentioned previously, Greendale is home to Joss Naylor. Tania and I discussed where in the village Joss might live.

"It's that house, over there" said Tania. "How can you be sure" I asked. "Because that's him, in the garden".

As we reached the aforementioned house – Joss appeared. He strode towards us with his two dogs running in front of him. Excited and delighted to be in the presence of a real living legend, I said hello and told him what a privilege it was to meet him. Joss was happy to chat; he told us all about his dogs, his running and his love of the Lake District, and then he asked us about our day. He told us that our descent from the summit of Buckbarrow was "the best run in of any fell". Joss was a little more reticent about his next challenge, but he told us it was imminent. It turned out that Joss's plan was to 'beat the bounds' of Wasdale, his own tribute to mark the Queen's Diamond Jubilee. The thirty five mile route around the parish boundaries of Wasdale, encompasses Scafell Pike, Caw Fell, Pillar, Great Gable and Whin Rigg; a total ascent of over eleven thousand feet. A few weeks later Joss completed the run in just less than ten hours, at the tender age of seventy six.

We watched in awe as Joss headed up the lower slopes of Buckbarow, at a frighteningly quick pace. It goes without saying – but we definitely wouldn't have been able to keep up.

Friday 13th April 2012

148. Pillar

Height: 2927 feet (892m)
Route: Wadale Head – Black Sail Pass – Summit

Today we decided to return to the scene of another unfinished walk; it was time to tackle the Mosedale Horseshoe for a second time. After all, if at first you don't succeed, try, try again. Having previously managed to climb Kirk Fell, today's version of the route was slightly shorter. We planned to climb Pillar via Black Sail Pass, and then visit Scoat Fell, Steeple and Red Pike, before returning via Dore Head.

We started the walk from Wasdale Head, passing the farm at Row Head, before crossing Gatherstone Beck and climbing up Black Sail Pass. The walk was delightful; clear skies, moderate temperature and little wind, combined to create near perfect walking conditions. The views took beauty to a whole new level. Pillar looked particularly stunning, if a little daunting.

Standing at two thousand, nine hundred and twenty seven feet, Pillar is the eighth highest mountain in the Lake District. The Fell takes its name from Pillar Rock, a prominent feature on the Ennerdale side, regarded as the birthplace of British rock climbing.

Intoxicated by this heady mix of sun and scenery, a sobering thought was providing by a glimpse or our intended descent route from Dore Head. The route looked to be impossibly steep. Maybe we would have to carry on up Stirrup Crag and over Yewbarrow, and miss out on the descent down the scree. Only time would tell!

The walk along Gatherstone Beck continued to delight, even when we started to climb in earnest. Perspiration and effort were recompensed by the sight of some charming waterfalls, and when we reached the top of Black Sail Pass, we were rewarded with magnificent views into Ennerdale.

Turning towards the summit, and presuming that we had avoided the High Level Traverse, we ended up scrambling towards our intended goal. With the benefit of hindsight, I think we may have gone wrong at this point. We found ourselves struggling over some steep and rocky inclines, too close to sheer drops for comfort. However, Will confidently led the way. Completing his Bronze Duke of Edinburgh Award and training for the Ten Tors on Dartmoor, had boosted his confidence no end. He found a scalable route, and kept Tania calm by cajoling and encouraging in a way that my lack of patience could never have managed.

This fact was pointed out by Tania – more times than was strictly necessary!

Eventually we found our way back to an easier path. With the worst of the climbing behind us, we now had a clear view of the summit. The gradient had eased, and we soon emerged onto the flat, snow covered plateau of Pillar. The views were excellent in some directions, with many of the major fells in sight. However, Scoat Fell was enveloped by a mass of dark cloud. Unfortunately, the cloud was heading towards us, and we were heading towards it!

As we left the summit and descended a rough path towards the narrow col of Windy Gap, which carries a path between Mosedale and Ennerdale, we were enveloped by the cloud and then subjected to a painful bombardment. Hail stung our faces as the wind drove in from the West. Upon reaching Windy Gap, we paused to see how conditions would develop. We were hoping that the conditions would return to those that we had experienced at the start of the day. Unfortunately, conditions worsened. Scoat Fell completely disappeared from view and we only had occasional glimpses of Black Crag. The cloud swirled, temperatures plummeted, and the wind raged.

Surely we wouldn't have to retreat in the face of adversity once again? Surely we would be able to complete The Mosedale Horseshoe this time?

We waited, hoping for some sign of a break in the weather. However, the wind strengthened, the hail continued to hammer at our waterproofs, and the occasional glimpses of Black Crag became rarer. Black Crag finally disappeared from view as completely as Scoat Fell had. It was all very trying. Somewhat reluctantly, we resigned ourselves to the situation and decided to retreat down the screes.

Scree is bits of broken rock piled up at the base of a cliff. Daily heating and freezing of moisture in cracks in the otherwise solid rock causes it to slowly break apart and tumble downhill. A scree slope will pile up to its steepest possible angle. Depending on the size and shape of the rock chunks, that angle may be shallow or steep. The descent from Windy Gap towards Mosedale Beck was steep!

Additional rocks that fall on a scree slope will roll down until they find a resting place or hit the bottom. The same is true for your foot! When you step onto a slope of loose rock it will give way under the weight until the material under it settles with the new weight. In some cases you may be sliding down the slope along with a couple tons of rock, all looking for stable places to rest.

Opinions vary when it comes to advice on the best way to descend a scree slope. You can advance slowly and carefully, or you can try to move rapidly, avoiding sudden stops that may lead to a slide, or you can embrace sliding and take up 'screeing'. If the scree is small enough and deep enough, you can kind of ski down it in your boots. You are actually creating a mini-rockslide and riding it down.

The boy's excitedly 'screed', whilst Tania and I gingerly 'zig-zagged' our way down the slope.

Well, it's better to be safe than sorry, and tomorrow we would be heading for home.

Saturday 14th April 2012

My pulse was slow and even, my hands relaxed and my shirt dry. I nonchalantly spun the steering wheel with one hand.

"This detour is going to take forever" said Tania, "I know, isn't it great?"

SOME FELLS ARE BIGGER THAN OTHERS
July/August 2012

It is difficult to convey to people who haven't visited the Lake District, just how varied the fells are; it is also difficult to convey to people who don't like walking, just what drives you forwards, or indeed upwards.

I have been asked on several occasions "Why do you want to climb 214 Fells? – Surely they are all the same?"

Well, the individual fells are unique, and their variety is related to the complexity of Lakeland geology.

Three broad bands of rock, trending from south-west to north-east, dominate the Lake District. The oldest group of rocks; The Skiddaw Group, were formed about five hundred million years ago. Initially laid down as black mud, but subsequently hardened by heat and pressure, this group forms a triangular mountainous zone in the north. Within this area you can find some rugged edges, but the rocks are more typically smooth. To the South of the Skiddaw Group lies the Borrowdale Volcanics. These rocks are the result of volcanic lavas and ash flows erupted about four hundred and fifty million years ago. The rocks underlie the highest and craggiest part of the Lake District; including Scafell, Helvellyn, Coniston Old Man and the Langdale Pikes. Further south again is a group of less resistant slates, siltstones and sandstones. These rocks are more easily eroded, and they form a belt of lower hills stretching from the Duddon estuary to Kendal.

Since there formation all these groups of rocks have been subject to folding, faulting, and intrusion by magma. They have been raised up and then eroded back down. Finally, about two million years ago, the Earth's climate cooled and glaciers formed. It is the action of these glaciers on the different types of rock which have shaped most of the surface features that we know and love today.

We are the fortunate recipients of a complex geological history, which has resulted in a landscape of beauty, grandeur and great variety.

That's why I want to climb 214 fells, and that's why I was looking forward to our first two week holiday to the Lake District

Sunday 22nd July 2012

149. Knott Rigg

Height: 1824 feet (556m)
Route: Newlands Hause – Knott Rigg

We had discussed the idea of staying in two different locations during our extended visit to the Lakes, but eventually decided that a return to Thornthwaite would allow us to access most areas without suffering the upheaval of moving half way through the holiday.

Apart from looking forward to visiting a variety of fells, after suffering the relentless monotony of the wettest April to June on record across the whole of England and Wales, we were also looking forward to a change in the weather. Fortunately, after days of almost continuous rainfall, the day of our departure witnessed the return of sunshine and clear skies to the south of England. Unfortunately, as we began to travel north we were soon reunited with cloud and rain, and as we travelled further, the frontal systems moved with us. Resigning ourselves to the inevitable, we prepared ourselves for some wet weather walks.

Our first walk started from Newlands Hause, and the skies did look ominous; dark clouds blocked out any signs of summer. When we emerged from the car the winds were so strong that they physically assaulted our senses. The winds were accompanied by a light but all invasive rain, which attempted to breach all defences. The climb should be a straightforward one, but progress was slow. We had to keep stopping, crouching down low to avoid the full force of the gusts.

Wainwright mentions that "An advantage of solitary travel on the fells… is the freedom to perform a certain function as and where one likes", but goes on to state that "The narrow crest of Knott Rigg ridge is no place for indulging the practice…walkers here being clearly outlined against the sky". Wainwright's warning was somewhat unnecessary. We were soon hidden by cloud, but anyway, exposure in such an exposed location, would likely result in frost bite on such a summer's day as this.

Battling our way through the elements, we eventually reached the top of Knott Rigg. The view from the grassy summit was not only restricted by the surrounding higher hills of the Coledale and Buttermere Fells, but also restricted by the swirling cloud and mist. However, our route to Ard Crags was clear enough.

150. Ard Crags

Height: 1906 feet (581m)
Route: North-east from Knott Rigg

A walk of about one mile, descending and then climbing about two hundred feet, brought us to the summit of Ard Crags. The wind was still strong, but at least it had started to break up the cloud. We were rewarded with surprisingly good views, especially towards Catbells and the east. Wainwright mentions that the summit "is delightful to walk upon, and even better as a couch for rest and meditation" – unfortunately the wind mediated against such a leisurely stay. After quickly celebrating fell one hundred and fifty, we decided to return along our outward route. Our decision allowed us to witness an interesting phenomenon. Walking towards Keskadale Beck, we were surprised to see that the hillside resembled a storm tossed sea. The action of the wind on the grass created the illusion of waves running over the land.

Apart from Will losing his hat to the gales, a scene witnessed with serene indifference by the local Herdwick sheep, the rest of the walk was without major incident.

Tuesday 24th July 2012

151. Place Fell

Height: 2154 feet (657m)
Route: Patterdale – via Boredale Hause and Round How

The weather continued in an all too familiar vain. Monday was a complete wash out and today promised little in the way of summer sunshine. The forecast suggested that the best or 'least' worst of the weather would be in the Far Eastern Fells. Consequently, we decided to climb Place Fell. However, as we started our second walk of the holiday, we could see that even here the summits were covered in cloud. Starting the walk from Patterdale, we climbed up towards Boredale Hause. Initially we did have some lovely views; those down towards Brothers Water were particularly impressive. Similarly impressive were the foxgloves that lined our path. Wainwright claims that "Botanists will find much of interest here". Tom's interest turned to concern as I told him about the poisonous properties of *Digitalis Purpurea*. The leaves, flowers and seeds are all poisonous to humans and can be fatal if eaten.

We reached cloud as we arrived at Boredale Hause, and what we thought to be an old sheepfold turned out to be the ruins of an old chapel. From this point onwards visibility rapidly deteriorated, landmarks disappeared, and with vision reduced to a few feet the walk became somewhat eerie. Disembodied voices sounded in the distance, rocky outcrops took on fanciful silhouettes, and small tarns appeared from out of the mist. Eerie, but interesting, we enjoyed the surreal quality of the walk as we carefully climbed a steeply rising path towards Round How. We then completed a more gentle section leading to the summit.

A rocky ridge marks the summit, with a cairn at one end and a triangulation pillar at the other. The latter looked the higher, and after a brief pause, trying and failing to find a view, we returned by our outward route.

Wednesday 25th July 2012

152. Carrock Fell

Height: 2174 feet (660m)
Route: Stone End farm – Rakes Trod – Carrock Fell

Today we would be walking in the footsteps of literary giants, although hopefully not literally. In 1857 Charles Dickens and Wilkie Collins climbed Carrock Fell. Successfully reaching the summit, despite breaking their compass and despite climbing in thick mist, Collins slipped and sprained his ankle on the way down. Dickens had read about "a certain black old Cumberland hill", and was further motivated to visit by an erroneous report by poet Samuel Coleridge, that described the fell top as being adorned by "a vast Druid Circle of Stones".

The Northern Fells are typically smooth, but Carrock Fell is an exception to the rule. Carrock Fell actually means 'Rock Fell', and this angular, rugged, igneous mountain, certainly lives up to its name.

Parking on the road, just past stone End Farm, we started climbing up Rakes Trod. The steep climb up through heather covered slopes eventually brought us to an impressive gully. Pausing to recover from the exertions of the climb, made worse by the hot and humid conditions, we took time to admire the wide, flat, and stunningly impressive expanse of the Eden Valley. It was not difficult to imagine that this area was once an ancient ocean floor.

The summit of the fell is said to be the site of an ancient hill fort; the largest in Cumbria. The site certainly looks impregnable, and a series of tumbled down stones could well mark out the former defensive walls of a Celtic stronghold. However, the walls offered little protection to us. We were driven away from the former fort, not by invading Romans, but by swarming wasps.

153. High Pike

Height: 2157 feet (658m)
Route: West and then north from Carrock Fell - Descent via Driggith Mine

Leaving the swarming wasps behind us, we followed a wide grassy ridge towards High Pike. The route was boggy in places, but the walk proved to be a very pleasant one. We eat lunch on route, and shortly afterwards we arrived at the rather unique fell top. The summit comes complete with a massive cairn (which originally used to be a cottage), a triangulation pillar, a wind shelter, and most unusually of all, a slate bench. We enjoyed the fantastic views towards the Solway Firth and the Scottish Border hills, made good use of the facilities provided, and celebrated the fact that we had completed all of Wainwright's Northern Fells.

Friday 27th July 2012

154. Steeple

Height: 2687 feet (819m)
Route: Bowness Car Park - Low Gillenthwaite - Summit

The weather had returned to its default mode on Thursday, as cloud and rain took hold once again. Abandoning plans to climb any fells, we visited the Whinlatter Centre and went 'Ape' instead. Clinging to ropes and zip sliding some forty feet in the air, Tania and I spent a fantastic afternoon scaring ourselves stupid, whilst the boys spent a fantastic afternoon laughing at our antics.

Forecasts suggested that the weather would be better today, and that the best of the weather would be in the west. Looking at our options in the west, we decided that having previously tried and failed to climb Steeple, Scoat Fell and Red Pike from Wasdale, we would try again, but this time we would start from Ennerdale. This would be our longest walk so far, so we prayed that the forecasts would prove to be accurate.

Ennerdale Water is the most westerly lake in the Lake District, and it provided a beautiful backdrop to the start for our walk. The crystal clear water, shimmering in the sunlight and surrounded by the majestic pines of Ennerdale Forest, gave the area the look and feel of an alpine paradise.

Starting from Bowness Point, we walked towards Low Gillerthwaite; marvelling as Ennerdale Water gave way to what seems like a contradiction in terms – the milky clarity of Liza Beck. Crossing the Beck by way of a footbridge at Char Dub, we began climbing up the drove way. This route is the only section of the lower slope of the fellside that is free of trees (the route was made to allow for the passage of sheep). The route was steep and muddy, but some well-placed benches allowed us to rest our already weary legs. Eventually emerging at the top of the plantation, we headed through the heather covered slopes towards the babbling waters of Low Beck.

It was well after mid-day by this point, so we stopped for a quick bite to eat beside the beck, and prepared ourselves for the steep climb to come. Steeple is really part of Scoat Fell, being the rocky northern projection of that fell, but its prominent peak and steep sides justify its individual status. Rested and resolved, we headed onwards and upwards; a boulder field, a rocky barrier and a succession of rock towers led us towards the narrow summit. With little room for a family of four, we somewhat nervously enjoyed the views, and then cautiously headed towards Windgap Cove. Heading in this direction, the ground falls away sharply on all sides; I began to feel nervous again.

155. Scoat Fell

Height: 2759 feet (841m)
Route: South from Steeple

An arête leads the way from Steeple to Scoat Fell, and it provides a short, but an exciting walk. Wainwright states that "every step is a joy" – I would say that it was only the last step from the arête to the summit plateau which was a real joy (I was relieved to reach the other side). Showing little such apprehension, I was impressed by the boys' sure footedness, and their cautious, but nerveless approach to walking in the mountains. Smiling broadly and obviously proud of their achievements, Will and Tom followed the solid stone wall of the Ennerdale Fence until they reached the summit cairn. It was difficult to miss; the cairn is actually perched on top of the fence.

156. Red Pike (Wasdale)

Height: 2710 feet (826m)
Route: South-south-east from Scoat Fell

To reach our next destination, we crossed the Fence, descended a boulder strewn slope and then picked up a path which traverses the base of Red Pike. From this path a steep climb leads towards the summit cairn. Perched on the very edge of Mosedale Crags, this is not a cairn that can be walked around. Standing a respectful distance away from the edge, we surveyed the magnificent views towards Wastwater and the Wastwater Screes.

157. Haycock

Height: 2618 feet (797m)
Route: North-north-west to the Ennerdale Fence – West-south-west to Summit

Our original plan for the day had been achieved, but as we tracked back towards Scoat Fell, we realised that Haycock was tantalisingly close. Tempted by the prospect of reaching an otherwise isolated fell, Tania and I made the decision to keep walking. The boys were less than impressed. They pointed out the strengthening wind, the darkening skies and the first drops of rain. They also reminded us that our original plan included a firm intention to be back in time to watch the opening ceremony of the 2012 London Olympics. "Let's put it to a vote" exclaimed Tom. Recognising that democracy has no part to play in family politics, but desperate not to miss the Olympics, I turned a deaf ear to Tom's pleas and strode ever more purposefully towards Haycock.

Reaching the summit first (a rare occurrence these days), I watched as Tania, Will and Tom, trudged slowly, and in the boys case reluctantly uphill. It was at this point that I had to concede that the boys had a point about the weather. I searched in vain for a view, and when I was joined by the others, the clouds burst and the wind forced us to seek refuge in a purpose built shelter.

Fortunately, the frankly miserable conditions didn't last for too long. The skies cleared and the sun began to shine. Our legs were weary, but the weather and the wonderful views ensured that our return to Bowness Point was delightful. We had completed our longest walk to date (walking over thirteen miles), and we arrived back in time to watch the Olympics.

Perhaps we should have walked to Caw Fell as well!

Sunday 29th July 2012

158. Sheffield Pike

Height: 2215 feet (675m)
Route: Glencoyne NT Car Park – Nick Head – Summit

The plan today was to climb Hart Side and then visit Sheffield Pike, but like so many of our plans things didn't work out quite as expected. Things started well enough; the walk towards and then through Glencoyne Farm was simply idyllic. The sun shone, lambs gambolled, and any problems in the world could have been a million miles away. Just past the farm itself, we passed the aptly named 'Seldom Seen' cottages. Screened by trees, the cottages also appeared to be hidden from the twenty first century; it appeared as if the whole area had been untouched by time.

Admiring the views and lost in our own thoughts, we failed to notice the gathering clouds. People talk about experiencing three seasons in one day; today we would experience four. As we headed towards Nick Head, black clouds, heavy rain and strong winds suddenly appeared, and at the same time landmarks disappeared. Fearing the unknown, we abandoned our original plan to climb Hart Side first, and headed for Sheffield Pike instead. Crossing rocky outcrops and deep bogs in driving wind and rain, we struggled our way to the summit. Conditions were far from idyllic, but the impressive rocky summit must be a wonderful place to be on a sunny day. Thankful (not for the first time), that some industrious people had created a windshelter, we hunkered down and began eating our lunch. At first we were accompanied by rain, and then by hail.

As autumn turned to winter, we waited for spring to arrive. However, spring seemed a little reluctant to put in an appearance, so we made a move anyway. Leaving the higher ground behind us, conditions did at least become a little less biblical. Hail turned back into rain, winds turned from strong to fresh, and the cloud became less opaque. I thought I could make out our next destination.

159. Hart Side

Height: 2481 feet (756m)
Route: Nick Head – Summit

A short steep climb followed by an easy walk brought us to the summit of Hart Side. Views were limited, blocked not by cloud this time, but by the Helvellyn Range to the west and slightly higher ground to the east. The cloud had all but disappeared. Spring had finally arrived and summer promised a visit. With waterproofs well and truly consigned to rucksacks, soft shells and mid layers soon followed suit.

Walking back towards Glencoyne Farm, we basked in glorious sunshine and marvelled at the wonderful views towards Ullswater. Today's walk had been rather special; tomorrow heralded a special event

Monday 30th July 2012

160. Mellbreak

Height: 1676 feet (512m)
Route: Loweswater (Kirkstile Inn) via valley path beside Mosedale Beck

The dulcet tones of Clare Grogan sang out as the Altered Images song 'Happy Birthday' reverberated around the kitchen. Yes, the forever gorgeous Tania was twenty one again. Celebrating each advancing year in July, Tania was no stranger to birthdays away from home, but this was to be her first one in the Lake District. Sharing similar views when it comes to the idea of a perfect birthday, the plan was to complete a good walk, and then find some good food and drink. Prioritising these simple requirements we based our day around lunch at the Kirkstile Inn. Providing food and drink since Tudor times, and coming both highly recommended and complete with its own brewery, we were looking forward to our visit.

Parking in Loweswater (somewhat later than anticipated), we called in at the Kirkstile Inn to check the food serving times. Consequently, we set forth knowing that we couldn't afford to dawdle. We headed along Grassy Lane, avoided the direct path to the lower North Top, and then walked along Valley Path. Mellbreak is relatively low lying, but it is an impressive fell, standing in splendid isolation and surrounded by steep slopes. Our pleasant, if slightly hurried stroll, turned into a slow, steep climb as we headed up towards a slight depression between the North and South Top. Tania struggled on the climb, her calves were aching and consequently progress for her was not only slow, but painful. However, Tania was determined to continue, and when we eventually reached easier gradients, walking became slightly easier for her. Tracking south we soon reached the higher, but less acclaimed South Top. The grassy summit provided some good views, but we had little time to really appreciate them. We were hit with the sudden realisation that we might well be too late for lunch.

Tania was in no fit state to hurry, so half running and half walking; I headed off down the fell. I managed to reach the pub in time, but only just. Winded and gasping for breath, I stood panting at the bar. I was unable to utter a single coherent sentence, but at least I had the Landlords attention.

My timing was fortunate; the culinary delights of The Kirkstile Inn were second to none. Tania loved her meal, and the sumptuous fare was accompanied by terrific ale – we will definitely return.

Tuesday 31st July 2012

161. Causey Pike

Height: 2035 feet (637m)
Route: Stonycroft - Ellas Crag - Rowling End- Sleet Hause - Summit

Today we decided to try and complete all of Wainwright's north western fells; this would involve climbing Causey Pike and Scar Crags. Tania's aches and pains had been seemingly soothed by rest, relaxation and wine, so with sun shining and our boots gleaming, we headed to Stonycroft. We decided to take Wainwright's recommended route, and started heading along a path leading towards the low rocks of Ellas Crag. After climbing a couple of hundred feet we crossed another more distinct path, but we kept heading up in our original direction. The route was a delight; we walked through red, purple and pink heather, and we walked under clear blue skies. Unfortunately, however, it wasn't long before Tania was suffering in a similar fashion to yesterday. With her calf muscles screaming, and a slightly sore Achilles, progress was once again slow and painful. We discussed the idea of abandoning the walk and returning to the car, but also just like yesterday, Tania was determined to continue.

Tania, valiantly struggled onwards, and eventually we emerged onto the grassy top of Rowling End. Despite her present predicament, I think that even Tania considered that the views justified the effort involved. Revealed was the full splendour of the Newlands Valley, and the distinctive, if somewhat daunting summit of Causey Pike. A short ridge route leads towards the summit, and from the distance, Causey Pike resembled an insurmountable mass of rock. We set forth full of anticipation, mixed with a little bit of fear. Wainwright states that the final climb involves "a bit of real mountaineering" - unfortunately, we did not feel like real mountaineers. However, on a more positive note, Tania felt much better on the more or less level surface of the ridge, and as we walked towards the Pike it did at least begin to look surmountable.

The final climb was actually quite exhilarating; using hands as well as feet, we slowly inched our way towards the summit, and for a few moments at least, we did feel like real mountaineers. Once again the ascent was well worth the effort – Wainwright states that "in all directions the scenery is of the highest order", we had to agree.

162. Scar Crags

Height: 2205 feet (672m)
Route : From Causey Pike

Reluctantly leaving Causey Pike behind us, we traversed the 'bumps', which characterise the summit, and then climbed a rising path towards the flat top of Scar Crags. Unimpressed by the summit cairn, Tom and I increased its height and significantly improved its style. We had now completed all of Wainwright's north western fells. Descent involved a walk to Sail Pass and a final return to the car at Stonycroft Gill. The walk brought back fond memories of our first 'round' – the Coledale Round. Scar Crags continues the line of the ridge from Eel Crag, and our return route was initially the same as our route from Sail to Outerside.

Thursday 2nd August 2012

163. The Knott

Height: 2423 feet (739m)
Route: Low Hartsop – Hayeswater Reservoir – Summit

After a much needed rest day we decided to return to Low Hartsop; our plan was to climb The Knott, High Street, Kidsty Pike, High Raise and Rampsgill Head. Apart from the addition of High Street, and the subtraction of Rest Dodd and The Nab, this plan was similar to a previously over optimistic one – hopefully we would be more successful this time.

Reassuringly things got off to a positive start. On our last visit we hadn't been able to park at Low Hartsop, but this time the car park was almost empty. Then it was October, now it was August. Interestingly, although the towns had been really busy this summer, there seemed to be fewer people on the fells.

Just like meeting up with an old friend, one of the joys of repeating a walk is the expectation of renewed acquaintance. I was really looking forward to walking beside Hayeswater Gill again, but just like meeting up with an old friend, I hadn't forgotten that some aspects of a reunion can be a little trying; I certainly wasn't looking forward to the steep climb up from Hayewater reservoir.

Happily, Hayeswater Gill was a delight, even better than last time. The river was almost bankfull and consequently the cascades and waterfalls were particularly thunderous and impressive. Even better, the walk up from Hayeswater Reservoir seemed far less steep than I remembered, and this time we climbed all the way to the summit of The Knott rather than detouring towards Rest Dodd. Sometimes these get-togethers can be a good thing!

After a quick photo call at the summit, we retreated to the shelter of a nearby wall. Here we listened to live Olympic rowing on my wind up radio. Hayswater Gill and The Knott had delivered, and so did the Men's Lightweight Four (although they were edged into silver by a determined South African crew).

164. High Street

Height: 2718 feet (828m)
Route: South from The Knott

Tracking south from The Knott, we followed the wall and headed towards High Street. The views were impressive, especially those into the Straits of Riggindale. We looked out for signs of a Golden Eagle (the only bird of its kind left in England nests in Riggindale), but we had about as much luck as we have had with spotting Ospreys.

The broad, flat and barren summit of High Street has historically been put to good use by the local, and not so local inhabitants. The Romans built a road across the fell, the same road that we had followed when we walked from Loadpot Hill to Wether Hill, and in more recent times, the summit has been used as a site for local fairs and as a racecourse.

165. Kidsty Pike

Height: 2560 feet (780m)
Route: North then East from High Street

After enjoying the views from the summit of High Street (good in all directions, but especially towards the west), we retraced our footsteps. Flanked between wall and escarpment, we headed north, back towards the straits of Riggindale. From here we took a right turn, heading east towards Kidsty Pike. The fell's distinctive peaked profile looked impressive, and it didn't disappoint. The small cairn is perched on grass, surrounded by boulders, and stands next to sheer crags. It provided a spectacular stage from which to observe the mountains to the north and west.

166. High Raise

Height: 2634 feet (802m)
Route: East from Kidsty Pike

"Exit stage left" – we turned towards the east, and headed off towards High Raise. Quietly contemplating the beauty of the surroundings, my reflective reverie was interrupted by the sounds of urgent shouting. Cries of anguish, laced with fear, echoed over the fell tops. We stopped and surveyed the scene. We heard more yelling and screeching, and we noticed that several other walkers had stopped, and like us, they were attempting to locate the source of the commotion. We now heard several distinctive cries for help. Increasingly worried that a real emergency was taking place, I reached for my phone. Seconds later the cries for help were interrupted by screams of laughter, and then in the distance I spotted a large group of extremely boisterous walkers. The walkers were definitely the origin of the commotion and they definitely weren't in trouble. Not so silently cursing their antics, but remembering our experience on Robinson, we continued to High Raise. Whilst the stony and rocky summit provided a contrast to those already visited; the glorious views continued a constant theme.

167. Rampsgill Head

Height: 2581 feet (792m)
Route: South-west from High Raise

Walking south-west from High Raise, we followed a path to a grassy depression and then climbed towards our final summit of the day. Wainwright states that "On the right sort of day, the top is a pleasant place to linger awhile". Blessed with clear skies and good views in all directions, we decided that this was definitely the right sort of day.

Friday 3rd August 2012

168. Sergeant's Crag

Height: 1873 feet (571m)
Route:Rosthwaite - Stonethwaite - Greenup Gill - Summit

The plan today was to climb Sergeant's Crag and Eagle Crag from Rosthwaite. The initial stage of the walk followed the Cumbria way to Stonethwaite; this was a welcome repeat of the initial stages of our walk up Rosthwaite Fell. Now as then, the walk beside Stonethwaite Beck was an absolute delight. The only thing that interrupted the beauty and the tranquillity of the experience was the sound of a helicopter landing in a nearby field. The helicopter was being used by 'Fix the Fells' to transport boulders and stones to construct paths further up the valley. I have previously mentioned that I don't particularly like these man-made intrusions on the landscape, but they are an unavoidable consequence of the popularity of the fells. Lakeland paths are fragile and the sheer number of visitors often leaves scars on the landscape. Over time grass is compacted by scores of booted walkers, the compacted grass dies, exposing the soil. Heavy rainfall then washes the exposed soil down the steep slopes into streams, rivers and eventually the lakes. Hopefully, by designing and creating paths that are resilient to wear and tear, foot path erosion can be drastically reduced. The work being done by 'Fix the Fells' is essential to the long term sustainability of the Lake District, and the volunteers who carry out the work should be singled out for special merit.

Perhaps we should all try to follow Wainwright's advice and be 'good walkers' – "A good walker is a tidy walker. He moves quietly, places his feet where his eyes tell him to, on beaten track treads firmly, avoids loose stones on steep ground, disturbs nothing. He is, by habit, an improver of paths".

Trying to tread carefully, we continued on our way. Our second objective – Eagle Crag, loomed in front of us. The vertical crags and cliffs looked spectacular, and spectacularly unassailable at that. A direct route to the top does exist, but we had already decided to bypass this frontal assault, so we headed towards Greenup Gill instead. Our intention was to climb up behind Eagle Crag, visit Sergeant's Crag, and then double back to Eagle Crag.

Our walk continued to delight; we followed a path, possibly constructed by 'Fix the Fells', and passed a succession of beautiful waterfalls and rock pools. When we thought we were about half way between the base of Sergeant's Crag and Eagle Crag, we climbed up over some wet and boggy land until we reached a wall which links the two fell tops. Following the wall to the south we soon came upon the summit of Sergeant's Crag.

The rocky top of the fell provided a safe environment within which the boys could practise their free climbing skills, and it also provided excellent views towards Bowfell and Esk Pike.

169. Eagle Crag

Height: 1650 feet (520m)
Route: North-north-east from Sergeant's Crag

Retracing our footsteps and following the wall northwards, we soon reached Eagle Crag. A small cairn, balanced on a tilted slab of rock marks the summit. We enjoyed impressive views to the North, and we watched with interest as the 'Fix the Fells' helicopter unloaded its cargo in the very picturesque Langstrath Valley. Descent was basically a reversal of ascent, after which we concluded our walk, and indeed our whole holiday, with a hearty meal at the Scafell Hotel.

Over the course of two weeks we had managed to climb twenty one highly individual and unique fells; we had visited different geographical and geological areas, and we were already looking forward to returning. The Lakes truly are a landscape of beauty, grandeur and great variety.

Why wouldn't anyone want to climb 214 fells?

CHANGES
October 2012

Idly musing that eight years had passed since we first visited the Lake District as a family, and that over five years had passed since we first climbed a Wainwright together, I asked the following – "I wonder what has changed since we first visited the Lakes?" "I've got taller and the mountains have got smaller" replied Tom. Relatively and geologically speaking, Tom was correct.

The boys have not only got taller, they have become stronger and faster. Will and Tom often lead walks now, and instead of trying to speed them up we often have to slow them down. For them the fells are no longer as daunting or as demanding as they used to be, whereas speaking for myself, the reverse is probably true. We tend to visit the Lakes more frequently now, and although our walks have generally got longer, the relative isolation of the remaining fells means that we climb fewer fells per day and per holiday. Venturing further afield means that we now have a far greater knowledge and understanding of the Lake District, and although this is by no means complete, it has heightened our enjoyment and appreciation of the experience. The experience was also changing in another way; our initial optimistic dream was slowly becoming a reality – it was beginning to look like we might actually be able to complete all 214 summits featured in Wainwright's *Pictorial Guides.*

A change of another sort now – in an attempt to focus on the Eastern and Southern fells, we decided to stay in Ambleside. Arriving shortly before lunch, after another early, pre-dawn start, we escaped the crowded streets and headed for the oasis of calm and luxury that is the Salutation Hotel. We wouldn't be staying in the Hotel, we would be staying in a cottage close by, however non-residents were not only welcomed, they were warmly welcomed (the Hotel certainly lived up to its name). We enjoyed some fabulous food and drink in the very comfortable lounge bar, served by the very attentive and friendly staff. Feeling far too full and far too comfortable, we did eventually manage to rouse ourselves. We then set about the less relaxing tasks of buying some provisions for the week, and buying some new walking boots for Will.

Sunday 28th October 2012

170. Troutbeck Tongue

Height: 1191 feet (364m)
Route: The Mortal Man – Ing Lane – Summit

Yesterday had been an almost perfect autumnal walking day; clear, bright, dry and calm. However, our early start, relaxing lunch and unavoidable shopping excursion, combined to legislate against a first walk of the holiday. Today, waking rested and revived, we decided to head out on to the fells, unfortunately the rain had decided to head out on to the fells as well.

Some things never change!

With the rain forecast to last all day, and the cloud low and threatening, we decided to aim low. Having previously abandoned an ascent of Troutbeck Tongue because of poor weather, today we decided it was our only viable option. Starting the walk from The Mortal Man in Troutbeck, we headed north along Ing Lane, crossed Trout Beck via Ing Bridge, and then approached the base of the fell via Troutbeck Farm. Rain was our constant companion, but it little to dampen our spirits. We were suitably attired and we enjoyed walking through the leafy lanes. Troutbeck Tongue was clear, but cloud hovered just above the summit, obscuring the surrounding higher fells. We climbed up the southern slopes of the fell, hoping that we would get higher before the cloud got any lower. The ascent was quite steep, but the modest height of the fell meant that it didn't take very long to reach the summit. Fortunately, the summit was still free of cloud; unfortunately, cloud still dominated the surrounding scene.

Monday 29th October 2012

171. Yoke

Height: 2316 feet (706m)
Route: Kentmere – Garburn Pass – North to summit

Be careful what you say – be even more careful what you write. After clearly stating that our walks were becoming longer and that we were completing fewer fells per day – today we planned to follow our short walk of yesterday with an eight summit trek. Our plan was to climb Yoke, Ill Bell, Froswick, Thornthwaite Crag, Mardale Ill Bell, Harter Fell, Kentmere Pike and Shipman Knott – thereby completing The Kentmere Horseshoe.

The forecast for the week was horrendous, but the forecast today was promising; our only real dilemma was the amount of daylight available. Having just stepped back into autumn, the clocks had gone back and we had effectively lost an hour of daylight. We decided to set out early, and we allowed ourselves a good eight hours to complete the twelve mile walk.

Driving towards Kentmere, the cloud laden skies appeared to contradict the forecast. However, as we parked beside Kentmere Church, the fells began to emerge from low cloud and the sun began to shine. The improving conditions and the anticipation of completing our last major 'round' saw us heading off full of optimism and excitement.

We actually started walking at half past eight in the morning, probably our earliest ever start.

We began by walking along the Garburn Road. Shortly after setting off we caught sight of Kentmere Hall, complete with its distinctive fourteenth century Pele tower. Pele towers are small defensive fortifications. In the Lake District they were they were designed to resist attack from the Scots. Kentmere Hall is a particularly fine example, complete with a tunnel-vaulted tower, turrets and five-foot thick walls. The next point of interest along the way was a massive boulder lying in an adjacent field. Known as Badger Rock or Brock Stone, the vast erratic is often utilised to practise rock climbing. Resisting the temptation to have a go ourselves, we continued onwards, the gradient steepening as we headed towards the top of the pass. As we climbed higher we reminisced about the Land Rover we had seen attempting to drive over the pass some five years before (and the woman in fluffy pink slippers). Leaving the pass at almost its highest point, we headed north, following a wall whilst climbing the very marshy southern flank of Yoke. When we arrived at the summit we were rewarded with lovely views across to Crinkle Crags, Bowfell, Scafell Pike and Great Gable.

172. Ill Bell

Height: 2484 feet (757m)
Route: North from Yoke

Heading north from Yoke, we descended and then climbed towards the summit of Ill Bell. Tom thought that a bridge constructed between the two fell tops would have provided a more direct and certainly a more level approach. The summit is small, but it is dominated by three large cairns which stand proud like a trio of stone sentinels. Taking some time to work out which sentinel guarded the highest point of the fell, we spent the rest of our summit stop basking in sunshine and enjoying the wonderful view towards Windermere, and the wondrous view of a cloud filled Kentmere Valley.

173. Froswick

Height: 2362 feet (720m)
Route: North then North-west from Ill Bell

Heading north then north-west, a rough descent and then an easy rise brought us to the summit of Froswick. Our arrival meant that we had managed to climb three fells before half past eleven – a bit of a record, but we were already behind schedule. We stopped for a quick snack and enjoyed clear views towards our next destination. However, in the time it took us to eat a granola bar – temperatures dropped, cloud rolled in from the north, rain began to fall, and despite the apparent presence of a tall 'obelisk' – Thornthwaite Crag completely disappeared from view.

174. Thornthwaite Crag

Height: 2572 feet (784m)
Route: North from Froswick

I know I shouldn't sound surprised, but the change in the weather was truly remarkable. In the space of just a few minutes a warm autumnal morning of sunshine and clear skies, had been transformed into a cold, wintery morning of dense cloud, heavy rain and strong winds. With visibility reduced to a few feet we could no longer see where we were heading, but with three hours walking already completed, we decided to plough on. In most conditions the walk between Froswick and Thornthwaite Crag is completely safe, but dense cloud can be very disorientating. In the mountains it always pays to be cautious. Informed by our map, guided by GPS and compass, and reassured by occasional glimpses of the 'obelisk', we followed a northerly bearing and hoped we were heading towards Thornthwaite Crag.

Fortunately our aim was true; the 'obelisk' turned out to be Thornthwaite Beacon – a fourteen foot summit cairn. But, we didn't linger. Views restricted by cloud, we headed along the High Street path, regularly checking our position before tracking east towards Mardale Ill Bell.

175. Mardale Ill Bell

Height: 2496 feet (760m)
Route: East – East-north-east – East and then south from Thornthwaite Crag

The path towards Mardale Ill Bell was narrow and fairly indistinct, but in poor conditions paths do at least provide a sense of security. However, paths don't always go exactly where you want them to go. Reluctant to leave our directional security blanket too soon, and keen to avoid Bleathwaite Crag and a sudden descent into Hall Cove, we ended up tracking too far to the south. Our GPS began to indicate that we were walking away from, rather than towards Mardale Ill Bell. Checking both map and GPS carefully, but still with that lingering doubt that a lack of visibility can bestow, we abandoned our path and headed north. Fortunately, all doubt was eventually eliminated by the welcome sight of the summit cairn.

After a somewhat hurried lunch we had to trust in the GPS once again; this time we headed south-east, hoping that we would pick up a path that would lead towards Nan Bields Pass. Visibility was dreadful, but very occasionally the cloud lifted and we had a few tantalising glimpses of Hawswater and Small Water.

176. Harter Fell

Height: 2539 feet (778m)
Route: East-south-east then east from Nan Bields Pass

"Hope springs eternal" said Alexander Pope. We hoped, we prayed, we plotted a course and things did turn out the way we wanted – we successfully negotiated our way to Nan Bields Pass. However, after descending to the pass, hope became more ephemeral, and just about the only thing springing forth was despair – the six hundred foot climb to the summit of Harter Fell was not what we had hoped for. Increasingly tired and increasingly frustrated by the lack of views on offer, we admired the mixture of stone and iron that makes up the summit cairn, and then headed south towards Kentmere Pike.

177. Kentmere Pike

Height: 2397 feet (730m)
Route: South from Harter Fell

Visibility was still poor, but at least visibility was no longer a navigational issue. A fence linking Harter Fell and Kentmere Pike clearly indicated our route. The presence of the fence meant that we no longer needed to keep stopping to check our position. Taking full advantage of this fact and the downhill terrain, we strode out confidently. Nevertheless, I was beginning to become a little anxious about the amount of daylight remaining. The day was advancing rapidly and with over four miles still left to walk, I began to think that our early start wasn't early enough!

An increasing sense of urgency resulted in some speedy walking and only a brief summit stop. We admired Morecombe Bay, illuminated in the midst of a sea of gloom by a small patch of sunlight breaking through the clouds, and then we headed on towards Shipman Knotts.

178. Shipman Knotts

Height: 1926 feet (587m)
Route: South-east then east from Kentmere Pike

Heading south-east, walking over easy but boggy ground, we managed to maintain a fairly quick pace. Another brief summit stop, this time involving a climb from the west side to the east side of a wall, was followed by a final descent to Kentmere. The descent took longer than originally anticipated. After checking that our route was fairly straightforward and that our torches were functioning, we abandoned our race to beat the setting sun and slowed our pace accordingly. We realised that such a wonderful spectacle was too good to miss. As we slowly headed towards Stile End, we knew that we had made the right decision. Vibrant light filled the sky and reflected off the clouds - red, violet and orange hues heralded the approaching night, and an orange haze was cast over the landscape as a golden sun hovered and then finally disappeared behind Yoke.

Guided by torchlight, under cover of the night, we finally arrived back at the car nine hours after setting out. Happy and unhurried, we had learnt an important lesson. Sometimes in life you have to slow down and embrace the moment.

Thursday 1st November 2012

179. Dow Crag

Height: 2555 feet (778m)
Route: Walna Scar Road - Goats Water - Goat Hause- Summit

Slowing down even further, we spent a lazy Tuesday wandering around Ambleside. Any ideas about serious walking were thwarted by a combination of tired legs and torrential rain. By Wednesday our legs had recovered, but our planned walk was thwarted by dodgy forecasting. Our intention had been to climb Grey Crag and Tarn Crag from Longsleddale. Wainwright and a variety of guide books suggested that this was a relatively easy walk, but a walk that shouldn't be contemplated in mist. Forecasts suggested that the Far Eastern Fells would be free of mist and cloud, so placing our faith in meteorology, we headed out. More often than not these days meteorologists get it right, but when we arrived at Longsleddale, after a fairly tortuous drive along a series of narrow lanes, Grey Crag was covered in grey cloud. Forced to abandon our plan, and with no viable alternative within striking distance, we headed into Kendal.

After four days of rain I would like to be able to report that Thursday morning saw the return of clear, dry and sunny weather, but the reality was somewhat different. Cloud and heavy rain dominated the scene. After two days of relative inactivity, one voluntary and one forced, we decided to head out anyway.

Just over two years ago we had attempted a Coniston Round. We successfully climbed Wetherlam, Swirl How, Great Carrs, Grey Friar and Brim Fell, but rather frustratingly we ran out of time and we failed to climb Dow Crag. Our plan today was to return and complete this unfinished enterprise.

Parking at Banishead Quarry, we emerged from the car into thick mist. Setting out, we couldn't see much, but at least the rain had stopped. Initially heading north-east, before turning towards Cove, we then walked beside Goat's Water. At this point the weather started improving. Cloud and mist slowly dispersed revealing a quite magnificent spectacle. Goat's Water, nestling in the shadow of the mighty flanks of Dow Crag, is surely one of the Lake Districts finest scenes. Unfortunately, the clear skies proved to be only a brief interlude amidst the general gloom. Climbing towards Goat's Hause, cloud and mist returned, this time accompanied by snow. At first only a few scattered snowflakes, but as we began our final approach to the summit, snowflakes merged and a blizzard blasted in from the south-west.

The conditions were horrendous - heads bowed, eyes blinking in the face of driving snow, we walked and then we scrambled our way almost blindly towards the top of the fell. It's only a short hike from Goat's Hause, but the conditions and the proximity of sheer drops caused moments of doubt, discomfort and dread. Tania briefly became 'cragfast', panicking as we walked close to the edge. Will and Tom were beginning to get cold, and despite their usual stoicism, they were beginning to raise their concerns. Their concerns were more than justified. Thinking that we might have to abandon Dow Crag for a second time, I looked ahead for one last time; surely we couldn't be that far away? Anxiously searching through the swirling snow storm I finally spotted the rocky summit - it was tantalising close. After a brief family conference to confirm our intentions, we edged our way forward, the summit itself providing some shelter from the worst of the weather. Edging our way around the base of rocky top, we discovered and then climbed a short gully to reach Wainwright's "airy perch".

Our original intention had been to head off the fell by walking south towards Walna Scar Pass. But, I had had enough of walking into driving snow, and I didn't particularly want to walk into the unknown. Working on the principal that it's 'better the devil you know, than the devil you don't', we headed back towards Goat's Hause. Despite the doubt, discomfort and dread, we were all suitably attired and suitably equipped for the conditions. However, as we began to descend from the summit we met a somewhat less well prepared family. A couple with two very young children emerged from the gloom. "We're a bit lost", they said. It turned out that they thought they were walking beside Goat's Water, heading towards Cove. Their children looked freezing, they didn't have an accurate map and they didn't really have a clue. Worried about their safety and worried that they might require the services of a mountain rescue team in the not too distance future, I urged the family to follow us back down the mountain. Somewhat reluctantly they agreed.

Returning to Goat's Water, the skies began to clear, but the summit of Dow Crag was still shrouded by storm clouds. We had made the right decision. Warming in the weak but welcome afternoon sunlight, I was surprised and somewhat confused by what I saw next. In the distance were a group of nineteenth century walkers. Dressed in tweed jackets, woollen shirts, plus-fours and deer stalkers, the men and even the women sported fine Victorian moustaches. I thought I might be suffering from some kind of hypothermic hallucination. Surely we hadn't got that cold? My anxieties were fortunately unfounded. It turned out that we were sharing the fells with some very cheerful and friendly members of the 'Eccentric Walkers Club'. How do I join?

Friday 2nd November 2012

180. Grey Crag

Height: 2093 feet (638m)
Route: Ascent from Sadgill

Today would be the final day of our holiday, so it was with a sense of disappointment that we awoke to the sound of rain hammering on glass. Disappointed but determined to complete a final walk, we checked the forecasts carefully. Rain and cloud were predicted to remain all day, but the far eastern fell tops were predicted to be free of cloud. Once again placing our faith in meteorologists, we headed back towards Longsleddale. After a less tortuous drive than last time (a long drive via Kendal avoided some of the narrow country lanes) we parked beside Sadgill Bridge. It was still raining heavily, but the fell tops were free of cloud. Deciding that we wouldn't be thwarted a second time, we headed up a steep, pathless slope towards Great How, and then followed a more gentle approach to Grey Crag. Contrary to the forecast, the clouds descended and arrived at the summit shortly before we did. All views and landmarks were quickly obliterated.

181. Tarn Crag

Height: 2176 feet (664m)
Route: North then north-west from Grey Crag

Lost in a sea of mist, we trusted our GPS and followed Wainwright's advice "to skirt the marshes of Grey Crag Tarn". Trust well placed – we kept our feet reasonably dry and successfully navigated our way to Tarn Crag. Wainwright states that "anyone who climbs Tarn Crag for a view of Lakeland will be very disappointed" – such words today provided comfort. We obviously weren't missing much. In mist the most hazardous section of this walk is the descent, so once again we followed Wainwright's advice. We kept "strictly to the fences" and after a long and winding route we safely returned to the car. Our efforts today may not been rewarded with fine views, but after a long and winding drive to the Watermill at Ing, they were rewarded by some fine food and drink.

Idly musing that six days had passed since arriving in Ambleside, and that on each of those six days it had rained – I asked the following – "when's it going to stop?"

THE BEGINNING OF THE END
December 2012/January 2013

I know that in reality one year is the same as the next in terms of passage of time, but it is an accepted truth that our perception of how quickly time passes changes as we age, and in accordance with our circumstances. Driving up to the Lakes at the end of December I found myself reminiscing about 2012. Overall it felt as if the year had gone quickly, but in another way, literally and metaphorically, a lifetime had passed. Notching up a personal half century meant that for me time was definitely speeding up, but the recent loss of my father to a sudden and unexpected illness meant that for a while time stood still, and then time replayed itself endlessly in a series of emotional flashbacks. I owe my love of walking, geography, history, literature and music to my father – he was a source of inspiration in many ways. I still find it hard to believe that he has gone. Life as I knew it had changed. Realising that it was probably still too soon to be reminiscing, I locked away the memories and focused on the road ahead.

Sunday 30th December 2012

182. Grike

Height: 1601 feet (488m)
Route: Forestry track from Heckbarley Gate near Kinniside Stone Circle to the Summit

Before driving up to the Lakes, Tania and I made a list of our remaining unclimbed Wainwrights. Linking some summits together, and allowing for a mixture of walks in terms of length, height, degree of difficulty involved and location, we planned a series of seventeen walks that would allow us to complete our challenge. The majority of these walks could be completed from a base in or around Keswick, so once again we decided to stay in Thornthwaite, our favourite location. Only seventeen more walks - it really was the beginning of the end.

The first walk of our planned final seventeen involved linking Grike and Crag Fell. We drove towards Ennerdale and started walking from Heckbarley Gate. A fairly straightforward walk along a forestry track led us towards Wainwright's most westerly fell. Initially heading east along the forestry track, we crossed over to an old mine road before tracking north to the summit. The summit provided extensive views, a wind shelter, and 3G reception - probably due to the close proximity of a communications mast.

183. Crag Fell

Height: 1716 feet (523m)
Route: East, then North-east from Grike

Heading east and then north-east from Grike, we completed a gentle descent and then a gentle climb to reach the summit of Crag Fell. Although it was windy and cold, the skies were reasonably clear, so we were able to enjoy the lovely views down towards Ennerdale Water. Our return route was basically a repeat of our ascent; although this time we bypassed the summit of Grike as we returned to Heckbarley Gate. This first walk of our holiday had been an ideal one; it provided good views without any exhaustive effort.

After returning to the car we made a short detour to visit Kinniside Stone Circle. The circle is composed of eleven stones, with a diameter of about eighteen metres. Although the site looks Neolithic, it was reconstructed in 1925 and the bases of the stones are now set in concrete. We soaked up the ambience created by the atmospheric setting and then headed for home.

New Year's Eve

Our resolve failed on New Year's Eve. With winds blowing at up to eighty miles an hour at ground level, we had little desire to see what the wind speeds were doing at altitude. Abandoning a planned trip to Gray Crag, we attempted to walk around Derwent Water instead. This plan had to be abandoned as well. Water levels in Dewent Water were so high that circumnavigation was impossible. Not only were the foot paths submerged, so were the iconic landing stages. Later on in the day this visual evidence of heavy rainfall was backed up by statistical evidence – 2012 was now officially the wettest year since records had begun. Hopefully things would be better in 2013. Our resolve may have failed, but we still made some resolutions. With only sixteen walks left to complete, we resolved to complete all our remaining Wainwright's by the end of the year.

Tuesday 1st January 2013

184. Ullscarf

Height: 2382 feet (726m)
Route: Watendlath via Blea Tarn

It would be nice to report that the New Year brought new weather, but it wasn't the case. With the wind howling and the skies leaden, we set forth from Watendlath. Initially heading east as we followed Wythburn Pass, we then tracked south towards Blea Tarn. Conditions, poor to start with, gradually deteriorated. Rain, hail, and finally snow, blasted in from the west. By the time we reached Blea Tarn, conditions were decidedly unpleasant. Rather heretically, Tania began to think that there might be better ways to spend New Year's Day. I began to think she might have a point. Just to add to our woes, our route became uncertain and we inadvisably climbed up the steep central face of Standing Crag. We were tired, cold and frustrated, but at least when we reached the top of the crag, our route became clear. From here onwards we would be able to follow a fence and then a ruined fence to reach the summit. The final route of the ascent may well have been obvious, but it was still unpleasant. Struggling in the face of driving snow, the walk was rapidly turning into a war of attrition. However, surrender wasn't an option. We slowly but resolutely marched to the top. A large cairn greeted us, but we didn't stay long. Wainwright's description of the summit was unfortunately accurate – "a cheerless place, even in sunshine; in storm there is no vestige of shelter". In desperate need of some shelter, we headed back down the fell by our outward route.

Thursday 3rd January 2013

185. Gray Crag

Height: 2286 feet (699m)
Route: Hartsop – Wath Bridge – direct climb to summit

Moods dampened by our experience on Ullscarf, we avoided the fells and the forecast rain on Wednesday, and we headed into Carlisle instead. England's northernmost city was initially founded by the Celts, before being strengthened and fortified by the Romans. Known by the Romans as Luguvallum, the settlement acted as a frontier town, protecting the rest of Roman Britain from invasion by the Picts and Scots. Over the course of time Carlisle was abandoned by the Romans and then reclaimed by the Celts. Subsequently, amongst other events, Carlisle was sacked by the Vikings, captured by the Jackobites, and then recaptured by the English. All in all, Carlisle has had a long and interesting history. Many aspects of this history are brought back to life at Tuille House Museum and Art Gallery. We spent an interesting afternoon looking around the delightfully eclectic museum, and then spent the rest of our time exploring the Lanes. Even I had to concede that shopping in the Lanes was therapeutic. Later that evening, feeling rested, revived and revitalized, we planned another attempt on Gray Crag.

In the morning the skies were overcast, but at least it was dry. Rain was forecast to arrive, but not until midday. We set out reasonably early and parked at Hartsop. Initially following Hayeswater Gill, we aimed for Wath Bridge. From here we headed directly up the grassy northern ridge of the fell. The route was really steep and progress was slow. We walked and then we crawled, scrambling on all fours and grasping the turf as we climbed towards the summit. Unfortunately, we were still climbing when the rain arrived. Once again we hadn't managed to stay dry, but the summit, a fairly level plateau of grass between steep cliffs, provided some great views down towards Hayeswater reservoir. Descent was a reversal of ascent, but our progress was far from slow. Sliding down the now wet and slippery slopes on our backsides, we fairly flew down the mountainside. Our descent may well have been somewhat unorthodox and undignified, but it was far quicker and far safer than walking. The boys may never walk down a mountain again!

Friday 4th January 2013

186. Selside Pike

Height: 2142 feet (655m)
Route: Haweswater – Old Corpse Road – Selside End – Summit

Today would mark the end of our latest trip to the Lake District. Pressures of work and a very unfavourable weekend forecast encouraged a decision to head for home after one final walk. Hopefully today would also mark the end of another chapter in our Wainwright odyssey, or more accurately another book. If we could climb Selside Pike and Branstree, we would complete all of Wainwright's Far Eastern Fells.

We parked beside Haweswater reservoir, at the start of the Old Corpse Road. The road, or more accurately the mountain pass, was formally used to take the Mardale dead for burial in Shap. Although Mardale used to have a church, it was only allowed its own cemetery in the seventeen hundreds. I say Mardale used to have a church advisedly. The church has now disappeared. The site was drowned somewhat controversially when the whole valley was flooded in the 1930s. Despite the fact that the valley was considered to be one of the most beautiful in the area, and included the villages of Measand and Mardale Green, Manchester Corporation was given permission to create a reservoir in 1929. All the buildings in the villages were demolished, including the church, and the stone was used to construct the dam that would herald the end of a century's old way of life. Few traces of that way of life still remain, but if water levels are low enough, the remains of stone walls and the village bridge can still be seen.

Turning our backs on Haweswater, we headed east following the Old Corpse Road. At first the gradient was severe; it was hard to believe that it had ever been possible to use this route for its original purpose. Perhaps the passage of time was catching up with us. Puffing and panting, Tania and I struggled, but Will and Tom effortlessly raced ahead. Thankfully, after passing some ruined cottages, the ground leveled out and we were able to regroup. After allowing a few moments for the oldest members of our party to catch their breath, we tracked east and then north-east, initially bypassing our destination before heading south-west towards Selside Pike.

The weather today had been the best of the week so far, but as we closed in on the summit, the weather closed in on us. Blue skies disappeared as the cloud lowered and the air chilled. By the time we reached the large cairn that marks the summit, we could see little else.

187. Branstree

Height: 2333 feet (713m)
Route: South-west from Selside Pike

Visibility was poor, but we were able to follow a fence towards Branstree. We kept as close to the fence as possible, although occasionally we were forced away from our lifeline as we bypassed some completely waterlogged areas. Thrown marginally off course by one such morass, we stumbled upon the impressive cairns of Artlecrag Pike. After this interesting, but inadvertent detour, we returned to the fence and continued heading south-west until we reached a junction between the fence and a dry stone wall. A short distance away from this junction, we located the summit. A small cairn next to what looked like the base of triangulation column marked the top of the fell. The top of the fell also marked our successful completion of Wainwright's Far Eastern Fells.

After a quick celebration and a photo call, we continued heading south-west. We walked towards Gatescarth path, and then turned towards Mardale. As we descended beside Gatescarth Beck, we finally emerged from the cloud and we were blessed with glorious views towards Haweswater reservoir. Once again, I found myself agreeing with Wainwright – "If we can accept as absolutely necessary the conversion of Haweswater (to a reservoir), then it must be conceded that Manchester have done the job as unobtrusively as possible. Mardale is still a noble valley".

Driving back to Devon, I found myself looking forward rather than back – probably advisable on a motorway. We now had only thirteen walks left to complete, and although part of me didn't want our Wainwright challenge to end, another part was excited and exhilarated about the prospect. I was looking forward to climbing the remaining fells, and I was looking forward to exploring new areas. I also understood that completing the Wainwright's wouldn't be the end our love affair with the Lakes – completion would open up new opportunities and new challenges. Personally speaking, our week in the Lakes had been a cathartic experience – I realised that in life every ending leads to a new beginning – life depends upon it.

SENSES WORKING OVERTIME
February 2013

Humans have five main senses that allow perception of the environment - sight, hearing, taste, smell and touch. In theory, when we focus on our senses, and consequently focus on the current moment, we maximise our potential for happiness. Life is meant to be lived in the present, experienced for the reality that it can be. If the experience of the present is maximised by a full scale assault on all five senses, the 'here and now' becomes everything and life is being lived to the full. Obviously, when walking it is wise to pay close attention to what you can see and hear, but your other senses appear to be heightened as well. Walking forces your senses to work overtime, whether you want them to or not. Perhaps that's why walking makes so many people so happy.

Sunday 17th February 2013

188. Base Brown

Height: 2120 feet (646m)
Route: Seathwaite - Sour Milk Gill - Green Gable Path - detour to Summit

A truly memorable day began with truly fantastic weather. Clear blue skies, little wind and relatively mild temperatures, resulted in the best walking conditions that we had experienced for a very long time. Parking close to Seathwaite Farm, we headed towards and then through the farm, before crossing the River Derwent and heading up on a path beside Sour Milk Gill. The route was delightful. A stepped path, interspersed with a few rocky scrambles, delivered extensive views, and also allowed us the opportunity to witness a number of picturesque, tumbling cascades. The appropriately named 'Top Waterfall' proved to be a particularly impressive and thunderous cascade. We edged as close to the vertical torrent as we dared – spray rose high into the air, we could feel moisture on our faces; water tumbled and plummeted, emitting such a crashing roar that we could hardly hear ourselves speak; there was a freshness in the air, and you could almost smell the aroma of the highly oxygenated water. Standing, transfixed and immersed in the beauty of the moment, we concluded that this particular assault on our senses had definitely optimised our potential for happiness.

Eventually and somewhat reluctantly, we dragged ourselves away from the falls and headed along Green Gable path. After carefully negotiating some patches of ice, we avoided the steep, direct ascent of Base Brown, and walked around the back of the fell instead. From here we began our final climb to the summit. This approach was still fairly steep, and the top of the slope was almost completely blanketed by a carpet of frozen snow. However, treading cautiously we managed to reach the summit without any major problems. We were rewarded with some simply stunning views. Scafell Pike and Great Gable could be seen to the south, Hellvelyn to the east, Skiddaw and Blencathra to the north. What's more, the major summits were revealed in all their winter glory. Snow-capped peaks glistened in the bright afternoon sunlight. We surveyed the scene in awed silence. I'm not sure that I have ever spent so long admiring the view from a summit, but this was the sort of day when you run out of superlatives.

Descent proved to be just as delightful as ascent. Not only we were able to enjoy all the spectacular views for a second time, we were also able to practise some glissading and some rock climbing. Glissading is the art of descending a steep snow covered slope on one's backside in a controlled manner – we weren't very controlled, but we did descend on our backsides. Our rock climbing was the result of a visit to Seathwaite Slabs.

The 'Slabs' are used for rock climbing practice by novices, so we were amply qualified. We spent an exciting few minutes trying to find a route to the top. Tom was our trail blazer; he nervelessly discovered a route that Will and I managed to follow.

Heading back to the car, I remembered an epigram by Oscar Wilde – "To live is the rarest thing in the World – most people exist, that is all". Well, today we had lived. We had experienced the present and we had stored up wonderful memories for the future. And whilst I have never fallen out of love with walking or the Lake District, today my love was confirmed beyond doubt – reasonable or otherwise.

Monday 18th February 2013

189. Great Borne

Height: 2019 feet (616m)
Route: Buttermere – Scale Force – Scale Beck – Gale Fell – Summit

Worried that yesterday's weather might have used up our quota of good luck for the week, I was pleasantly surprised when the forecast predicted, and then the morning delivered, even better weather. Not only did the skies retain their unseasonal blue hue, but the wind had died away and temperatures had risen. Nevertheless, just to be on the safe side, I donned thermals and multiple layers before heading out of the door – after all, it was still February.

The plan today was to climb Great Borne and Starling Dodd. Parking at Buttermere, we walked towards Scale Bridge and then turned right, heading north-east on a path beside Crummock Water. When we reached Scale Beck we headed upstream, pausing when we caught sight of today's impressive waterfall – Scale Force. Considered to be the highest waterfall in the Lake District at one hundred and seventy feet, with one single drop of one hundred and twenty feet, we found ourselves agreeing with Wordsworth – "A fine chasm, with a lofty, though but slender, fall of water". Eager to get a closer look at the falls, we walked into the gorge cut by Scale Force. Slipping and sliding on damp, algae covered rocks, but fortunately remaining upright, we enjoyed another full scale assault on our senses before heading back to the path and climbing towards the top of the gorge. Some of the higher sections of the path were eroded. In some places we were forced to walk along narrow ledges, and in others, our continued progress necessitated negotiating scrambles next to dramatic vertical drops. Just to add to the general feeling of unease we were dazzled and blinded by bright sunshine, usually at the most inopportune of moments. But, the walk was delightful, and when our situation became a little less precarious, we stopped for lunch.

After a welcome bite to eat, we crossed Scale Beck and started climbing out of the steep valley. Progress was slow and not particularly pleasant. The angle of the slope, a thick covering of heather and very uneven ground, all served to hamper progress. Dragging ourselves ever more slowly to the top of the valley, spirits were eventually revived by the first sight of our first objective - Great Borne. However, we still had to cross the extremely marshy expanse of Gale Fell. From a distance the route looked direct, level and straightforward, but conditions were so wet underfoot that it was hard to keep on a direct line. Attempting to skirt the worst of the bogs, we spotted several sink holes. We could see rivulets disappearing underground and we could actually hear water flowing beneath the boggy surface of the fell. The cool, trickling sound of the water, contrasted with the warmth provided by the afternoon sun. It became increasingly apparent that my decision to wear thermals was not a good one, and even though I took off as many layers as modesty would allow, I still felt like I was overheating. As a result, the final steep climb to the summit was fairly tortuous, but at least the summit was a nice one. A triangulation pillar and a wind shelter crowned the heights, and the top provided extensive views towards the Loweswater Fells.

190. Starling Dodd

Height: 2085 feet (633m)
Route: East-south-east from Great Borne

After cooling down a little, we followed a straightforward route towards Starling Dodd. With the smooth grassy summit always clearly in sight, we made rapid progress. As we closed in on the fell it appeared to be topped by a modern work of art. Closer inspection revealed that stone and iron had been crafted to form a unique and striking cairn.

Despite our recent rapid progress, daylight was rapidly running out. Conscious that time was against us, we choose the most direct route of descent. Heading north-east, we walked downhill towards Scale Beck. Forsaking any recognisable paths, heather and hidden scree conspired against us. Walking was awkward and progress was not as rapid as we would have liked, but at least we had time to admire the view. Crummock Water, framed by the surrounded fell tops and bathed in the red glow of the setting sun, looked simply magnificent.

Tuesday 19th February 2013

191. Tarn Crag

Height: 1810 feet (550m)
Route: Grasmere – Sour Milk Gill –Easedale Tarn –Old Path – Summit – Descent via East Ridge

Implausible as it sounds; clear morning skies heralded yet more fantastic weather. Today, not only were the skies blue, but temperatures had risen and there was no wind, even at altitude.

The plan today was to climb Tarn Crag via Easedale Tarn. Having completed the walk to Easedale Tarn on a previous occasion, Tania promised that Will, Tom and I would love this walk – she wasn't wrong.

We started walking from Grasmere, and after passing the house of a well-known rock star, we looked out for 'fields of gold' as we made our way towards Sour Milk Gill. Climbing up beside the Gill, we were privileged to witness another series of impressive and thunderous waterfalls. White water was rapidly becoming the theme for the week. Climbing higher, we followed the crowds up a well-worn path towards Easedale Tarn. Crowded, but beautiful, we spent some time admiring the view, and then spent some more time skimming stones across the frozen surface of the water.

Wainwright recommends a direct route from Easedale Tarn to the summit of Tran Crag, but from our position it was difficult to identify whether or not any such route existed. When we did finally manage to spot Wainwright's indistinct and aptly named 'Old Path', it looked steep and daunting. Hesitantly, we decided to go for it anyway. Fortunately, on closer inspection the route proved to be both obvious and easy. The route also offered fantastic views back towards Easedale Tarn. We should have more faith!

Tania, feeling relaxed and in her element, began to lecture the boys (and me) about glaciation. Didn't I mention that Tania was also a Geographer! Glazing over, I spent my time trying to photograph Herdys. Herdwick sheep are the hardiest of all British sheep; they can survive the winter months at high altitudes. They are a quintessential feature of the Lakeland landscape. Managing to capture a few good pictures, we headed onwards and upwards, with tales of arêtes, pyramidal peaks and hanging valleys, ringing in our ears.

All was plain sailing until we reached a steep, snow filled gully, which blocked our route of ascent. Successive freezing and thawing of the snow had caused it to transform into solid ice. Side stepping the snow where we could, and literally walking in other people's footsteps when we couldn't, we cautiously made our way to the top of our final Central Fell.

The summit, a sharp peaked outcrop surmounted by a small cairn, offered amazing views. Not only could we see a whole range of fells, but the sun shone, and the moon reflected in its glory. Celebrating the moment, we took a few photos, nostalgically remembered other favourite walks and climbs in the Central Fells, and then headed back to Grasmere by way of the delightful East Ridge.

Thursday 21st February 2013

192. Caw Fell

Height: 2288 feet (690m)
Route: Heckbarley Gate – Old Mine Path – South-east to Summit

After three days of walking, a family conference came to the conclusion that Wednesday should be a day of rest – the decision was not unanimous. Forsaking mountains and lakes, we visited 'The Puzzling Place' in

Keswick. Home to an anti-gravity room, a hologram gallery and many interesting optical illusions, we spent an enjoyable afternoon not quite believing our eyes.

Not quite believing that I had been outvoted yesterday, at least today I had the satisfaction of knowing that we would be returning to the hills. Our main aim was to climb Caw Fell. Wainwright describes the fell as "a rolling upland of modest height…But this is a fell that should not be underestimated. It is remote from shelter or habitation". Wainwright goes on to state the following – "Good advice is to divide the time available by two, and if the top is not gained by half time, turn back". It was clearly apparent that whichever way we planned the walk it would involve a long trudge. Our decision came down to a choice between two alternative routes. We could either complete Caw Fell on its own from Ennerdale, a walk of about five miles each way, or we could combine Caw Fell with Lank Rigg, a walk of about six miles each way.

Our final decision was influenced by the weather. Although temperatures had plummeted, hovering just above freezing, the skies were clear and the air was still. With the weather on our side, we decided that we should have just about enough time and energy to complete both fells. This would also mean that we would be keeping to our original schedule in terms of our final planned walks.

Starting the walk from Heckbarley Gate, we followed a forestry path before picking up an old mine road. This was the same route that we had used when we climbed Grike and Crag Fell. Thinking about our need for rapidity, and heeding Wainwright's advice and dividing the time available for the walk by two, we were relieved to discover that our progress was remarkably quick. The landscape more closely resembled moorland than mountainside, and the lack of steep or awkward climbs worked to our advantage. Keeping to the old mine road we bypassed the summits of Grike and Crag Fell, before entering woodland and heading south-east. Our trajectory led us towards a dry stone wall, a wall which we could follow almost all the way to the top of Caw Fell. The route was not only direct, but the gradient was fairly gentle, and even though we had to walk into a bitterly cold easterly wind, progress was still rapid. The only real hard work was the final climb to the summit, but we still managed to reach the summit thirty minutes ahead of schedule. The top of Caw Fell, a rather flat and featureless plateau, provided good views towards Pillar and Steeple

193. Lank Rigg

Height: 1775 feet (541m)
Route: North-west from Caw Fell – then west to Whoap and south-west to Summit

Leaving Caw Fell, we were faced with more choices. We could either head directly west towards Lank Rigg, a shorter route, but one which would involve a steep descent followed by a steep ascent, or we could take a longer route, backtracking along our outward route before heading over Whoap, then approaching Lank Rigg. We choose the latter route – I think wisely. Once again we were able to keep moving quickly, and we passed some Neolithic stone circles as we followed the almost level terrain. Our rapid progress was also aided by frozen bogs which made a satisfying crunching sound as we walked over rather than through them. Once again the only section of the walk that put the 'brakes' on our progress, was the final climb to the summit of the fell.

Lank Rigg was the final fell that Wainwright completed for his *Pictorial Guide to the Lakeland Fells*. In honour of the occasion he buried a two shilling coin under a stone on the summit. Tradition now dictates that visitors to the fell top who find Wainwright's buried treasure take a coin and replace it with another. Tom set about the task of finding the coin in true piratical style. X didn't mark the spot, but a small stone about four feet away from a triangulation column did. Mission accomplished, we took a last look back towards Caw Fell, and then headed directly down to the confluence of Stinking Gill and the River Caldew. From here we skirted the base of Blakely Raise, climbing until we met Cold Fell Road. A walk of about a mile, heading north and passing Kinniside Stone Circle, brought us back to Heckbarley Gate and the car.

Later that evening after enjoying a well-earned meal at the Coledale Inn, we calculated that we had walked over thirteen miles – no wonder we all felt so tired. We had enjoyed the walk more than we thought we would, but all the same, it had been a good one to get out of the way – no disrespect intended.

Friday 22nd February 2013

194. Hartsop above How

Height: 1870 feet (580m)
Route: Deepdale Bridge – path beside Low Wood – Gale Crag – Summit

Today, the clear skies that had been such a bonus all week finally disappeared. Without the sun's warmth temperatures dropped even further. With temperatures now hovering around freezing and snow clinging to any ground above eighteen hundred feet, our options were limited. In theory we had only nine walks left to complete, but most of these were either impossible to do in the present conditions or too remote to reach from Thornthwaite. One of our final planned walks involved linking Arnison Crag, Birks, St Sunday Crag and Hartsop above How, but this route meant that we would also have to visit Cofa Pike and Fairfield – not a wise choice today. Realising that we would have adapt our plans to match the conditions, we decided to climb Hartsop above How from Deepdale, and leave the other higher fells for another day. After all, it was bound to be warmer at Easter.

Parking next to a bus stop, just after Deepdale Bridge, we started heading along a direct path towards Hartsop above How. We enjoyed lovely views back towards Deepdale, and we enjoyed the easy, gradual climb. Enjoyed that is until ice underfoot caused a few problems. Slipping and sliding, and thinking that we should have invested in some micro spikes, we detoured away from the main path just before we reached Gale Crag. Climbing around the side of the Crag, we managed to avoid the worst of the ice before regaining the main ridge. The final stage of the walk provided dramatic views towards Dove Crag and Hart Crag. The summit, an airy perch, surrounding by steep vertical drops, provided some more dramatic views, but the exposed location was bitterly cold and the arrival of snowflakes heralded the beginning of our descent.

Perhaps appropriately, we ended the final walk of our holiday beside yet another waterfall. The babbling beauty of Deepdale Beck serenaded our senses and confirmed our belief that walking does indeed generate happiness.

WALK OUT TO WINTER
March/April 2013

It would be fair to say that the weather in March was not what we or anyone else had expected. Just when we thought that we should be saying goodbye to winter and welcoming spring, the coldest March in fifty years brought unseasonably wintry weather to most parts of the UK. In the Lake District, temperatures hovered around freezing and snow accompanied by strong easterly winds built up huge drifts, causing problems for farming, power supply and transport. The conditions would also provide problems for us. Many roads were impassable and some of our final summits looked to be too dangerous to climb.

We arrived in the Lake District at the same time as the clocks went forward and British Summer time started, but if we were going to climb any fells we would have to get kitted out for winter. Advice from 'Mountain Rescue' suggested that people shouldn't venture out onto the fells without crampons or an ice axe. Having previously discovered that hiring such items is impossible, we ended up purchasing some light and sturdy trail crampons, but somewhat unwisely we didn't buy any ice axes.

Sunday 31st March 2013

195. High Hartsop Dodd

Height: 1702 feet (519m)
Route: The Brotherswater Inn – Hartsop Hall – Summit

Full of excitement and confident that our newly purchased crampons would allow us to 'boldly go where we hadn't been before' – we headed off to climb High Hartsop Dodd, Little Dodd, Red Screes and Middle Dodd. We initially planned to drive along Kirkstone Road, but this route was blocked by snow. Heading towards Windermere, we picked up the Kirkstone Pass instead. Kirkstone Pass is the highest pass open to cars in the Lake District. Driving over the pass is always an experience, but today it was more of an experience than normal. Snow ploughs had cleared the pass, but snow banks encroached onto the road and towered above our car.

We parked at the Brotherswater Inn, and then walked through Sykeside campsite. We were impressed to observe, that despite the fact that there was snow on the ground, some hardy campers had pitched their tents. Heading towards Hartsop Hall, we turned left and began to climb the steep, snow covered north face of High Hartsop Dodd. The snow, patchy at first, soon thickened. Worried that we might start slipping and sliding, we stopped to attach our crampons. Our concerns were immediately alleviated. Not only did our crampons allow us to walk with confidence, but they made us feel like Alpine adventurers.

The climb which had been steep all the way, became even steeper towards the summit. The top was marked by a small cairn, but it provided a big view. We admired the brooding magnificence of Hartsop valley, and then we headed onwards.

196. Little Hart Crag

Height: 2091 feet (637m)
Route: South-west from High Hartsop Dodd

Heading onwards involved climbing a ridge towards Little Hart Crag. The gradient was less severe than it had been, but the snow was even deeper, so walking was still hard work. Fortunately, hard work generally reaps rewards. The summit of the fell, a rocky platform with two distinctive tops, provided more impressive views of Hartsop valley.

197. Red Screes

Height: 2546 feet (776m)
Route: Decent to Scandale Pass - South-west - Summit

We enjoyed a pleasant lunch, picnicking on a small patch of grass - an island of green in a sea of snow. Satisfied and satiated, we briefly headed west before picking up a path that descended towards Scandale Pass. I say path, but we had little evidence of its actual existence - we followed a fence and footprints in the snow. After crossing Scandale Pass, we began to climb up the steep western face of Red Screes. Periodically blinded by reflected sunlight, we could hardly see where we were going, but we were able to follow a dry stone wall. Soft snow sapped our energy and the climb was a hard slog, but we eventually reached the crest of the ridge. From here we tracked away from the dry stone wall and walked towards the summit itself. Our crampons had made us feel like Alpine adventurers, now the wintry landscape made us feel like Arctic explorers. The skies were clear and the views from the summit were excellent. The Eastern Fells, The Old Man of Coniston, Bowfell and Scafell looked spectacular.

198. Middle Dodd

Height: 2106 feet (654m)
Route: South-west then North-east - Summit

Heading south-west we walked towards another dry stone wall, which we then followed towards Middle Dodd. I say followed, but at times the wall was completely buried by drifts. We alternated between following the wall, walking on top the wall and wondering where the wall had gone! Nevertheless, we soon found ourselves on the summit. We enjoyed yet more spectacular views, especially those back towards Red Screes and down towards Brothers Water.

Today's walk was rapidly becoming one of my favourites. The use of crampons had allowed us to access the high mountains on a day when ice and snow meant that the landscapes and vistas were even more breathtakingly beautiful than normal. However, one of my favourite walks was soon to become one of my least favourite. Our original intention had been to backtrack from Middle Dodd to Scandale Pass, and then to descend beside Caiston Beck. The rationale for this route was avoidance of the steep northern face of Middle Dodd. Unfortunately, we ignored our original plan, and with what would turn out to be misplaced confidence, we began to descend the northern face of the fell.

Tom was a few feet behind Tania and a few feet in front of me. One minute I was happily chatting to him, but then all of a sudden he slipped and began to hurtle downhill. Shocked, frightened and unable to help, I watched as Tom reached out towards Tania. Fortunately Tom managed to grab one of Tania's walking poles, effectively checking his own descent. Tom came to a halt, but Tania was knocked off balance. Tania fell on to her front and began to slide – things didn't look good. Within seconds Tania was sliding at a rapid rate. Scanning the ground in front of her I could see that the precipitous slope did eventually level out, but only for a short while before it plunged downhill again. My worry was that Tania's momentum would not allow her to stop in time. Glancing back I could see that a bad situation had got worse. Tania had spun round and was now sliding headfirst towards some rocks. Putting her hands in front of her to protect her face, Tania's shoulder smashed into one of the rocks. Hearing a shriek I watched as Tania was spun round again, thankfully this time she came to a stop. The collision had checked her descent, probably averting a worse fate, but Tania lay on the snow, worryingly still and strangely quiet. I shouted to Tom, he said he was OK. Heading downhill I shouted to Tania, she answered, but she didn't look OK.

Fortunately, Tania was only bashed and bruised, but understandably she was shocked and stunned. In the space of a few seconds she had slid about a hundred and fifty feet down a mountain side. We waited, perched on the mountain side for quite a considerable time. Will and I did our best to look after Tania and Tom, but their nerves were somewhat shredded.

Once Tania and Tom felt able to continue, we descended slowly and carefully, making our way back to the Brotherwater Inn. We were safe, but it had been a traumatic event. Tania and Tom both looked haunted by the experience. However, things could have been far worse.

Accidents do happen and safety in the mountains can never be guaranteed, but we had made some fundamental mistakes. We had planned a safe descent based upon the prevailing conditions and the terrain, but we had ignored this option and chosen a shorter, more direct route. We were well aware that Wainwright described the northern face as 'excessively steep' but we went for it anyway. We shouldn't have attempted this route when it was covered by snow and we shouldn't have contemplated the route without ice axes. In an attempt to save some time we had accepted an unnecessary level of risk. After all we aren't Alpine adventures and we aren't Arctic explorers.

Tuesday 2nd April 2013

199. Green Crag

Height: 1602 feet (489m)
Route: Seathwaite – Stepping Stones – Grassguards Gill – Ulpha Fell – Summit

I have never had anything but complete admiration for Tania, William and Tom's resolve and resilience, but today they surprised even me. Tania's shoulder was still aching, and Tania and Tom wanted to avoid any steep, snow covered slopes, but after only one day of rest and recovery, they were determined to start walking again. In an attempt to ease ourselves back into walking, we looked for a relatively easy climb. However, with only eight walks left to complete our options were limited. Pondering over maps and guidebooks, we eventually decided that our best bet would be to climb Harter Fell and Green Crag from Eskdale. The quickest way to reach Eskdale is to drive over the Hardknott Pass, but the Pass was closed. We would have to drive to Eskdale via Ulpha. Whilst I was secretly pleased to have an excuse not to drive over Hardknott Pass, I was also a little disappointed – our new route would involve a lengthy detour. As it transpired, not only did we have to drive about half way around the whole of the Lake District, but when we reached Ulpha, we discovered that the road to Eskdale was ice bound, so we ended up driving to Seathwaite instead. Starting our walk from Seathwite meant that our planned walking route was now obsolete, so we had to design a new one. We had never visited this area before, so we planned without any real knowledge of which routes would be good, bad or indifferent, but we hoped to be pleasantly surprised.

Walking from Newfields Inn, we headed towards Stepping Stones and then followed the River Duddon upstream. Talk about being pleasantly surprised. The initial stages of the walk were delightful enough, but then we walked through Wallowbarrow Gorge. The deep wooded ravine, dusted with a light covering of snow, and enclosing a series of cascades and falls, was simply wonderful. Following a path that wandered between boulders and over scree, we appreciated the beauty of our surroundings as we gradually climbed up and away from the river. When we reached Dunnerdale Forest, we headed north-west, skirting Fickle Crag as we headed towards Grassguards. From Grassguards we followed a faint path beside Grassguards Gill; this route guided us through a coniferous plantation and brought us to Ulpha Fell. With our first objective now clearly in sight, we headed west towards Green Crag. Although the summit was only about a mile from the edge of the forest, this part of the walk seemed to take forever. The summit, impressive and rocky, provided magnificent views towards the Southern Fells – we could also make out Blackpool Tower. We enjoyed the views, but we began to realise that time was against us. We had started walking at half past eleven in the morning and now it was three o'clock in the afternoon. Although we were only about a mile and a half away from our next destination, we knew that we didn't have the time or energy to climb the steep and somewhat intimidating western face of Harter Fell.

With an element of frustration, but with an overwhelming belief that today we had made the right decision, we headed back to the car.

Wednesday 3rd April

200. Raise

Height: 2889 feet (883m)
Route: Stannah - Sticks Pass - Summit

When we set out on Tuesday, we had set out with the knowledge that we only had to complete eight more walks to complete all our remaining Wainwrights. Today when we started walking, we had nine walks left - something didn't add up. We weren't mathematically challenged, but we were meteorologically challenged. Yesterday, roads blocked by ice and snow delayed the start of our walk and led to a decision to miss out Harter Fell, which we would now have to climb on its own. Today, ice and snow meant that we had to make the decision to split another walk into two. We had planned to link Raise, White Side and Catstycam, but a walk from White Side to Catstycam, would necessitate a visit to Swirrel Edge. Not as fearsome or dangerous as Sriding Edge, Swirrel Edge is still a daunting prospect; under a covering of ice and snow, with cornices and steep drops - it was too daunting for us. Decision made, we saved Catstycam for another day, and we set out to climb Raise and White Side.

Climbing Raise and White Side would take us back into the high mountain, but our route from Stannah was one that we knew well, and it was one that we knew to be relatively safe. Parking at Stannah, we climbed up towards Sticks Pass. The route is steep and it was snow covered, but we used crampons and we were never troubled. Confidence regained, Tania and Tom were back to their old selves, and even a cold easterly wind couldn't dampen their spirits.

Raise is home to England's only ski resort, founded in 1936 by the Lake District Ski Club. Ski resort might be a slightly grand description and skiing is only possible on rare occasions, but we were delighted that our climb coincided with one such occasion. Walking and watching, we spotted several skiers slaloming down the slopes. Suitably distracted from our own efforts, we made short work of the final climb to the summit. The summit was marked by an intricately patterned ice encrusted cairn. It was bitterly cold on top of the fell, but the views were extensive and we were thrilled to have climbed our two hundredth Wainwright

201. White Side

Height: 2832 feet (863m)
Route – South-west from Raise

An easy walk heading south-west across the summit plateau of Raise, brought us to White Side. The top was marked by a small cairn, but the views were impressive, especially towards Helvellyn, Catstycam and Swirrel Edge. The view towards Swirrel Edge confirmed that our decision not to cross the arête had been the correct one.

A straightforward descent saw us heading north-west towards the delightfully picturesque Fisher Place Falls. Taking some time out to enjoy this spectacle, we also noticed another one – temperatures had risen and the surface of the snow now glistened with a watery sheen.

Perhaps spring had finally arrived?

Thursday 4th April 2012

202. Harter Fell

Height: 2140 feet (653m)
Route: Grassguards – Dunnerdale Forest – North-east to Summit

Well, spring hadn't arrived and if winter could talk it would have said "rumours of my demise are greatly exaggerated". Yesterday, temperatures had risen to the sultry heights of seven degrees centigrade, but today winter reasserted its grip.

Wrapping up warmly we headed towards Seathwaite. Our last visit to Seathwaite had resulted by chance rather than by design, but today we planned to return. Captivated by the peace, tranquillity and beauty of the area, we were happy to head back.

On this occasion we drove slightly beyond Seathwaite, parking under the shadow of High Tongue. From here we picked up a footpath that led towards Fickle Crag and Grassguards. Repeating the initial stages of our previous walk beside Grassguards Gill, we then headed north-north-east, walking through Dunnerdale Forest. The coniferous trees of Dunnerdale were being actively felled, with a view to re-establishing deciduous woodland. Emerging from the forest, we headed north-east towards the summit of Harter Fell. The western face of the fell was almost as intimidating as we thought it was when we viewed it from Green Crag. The fell was steep and snow covered, so crampons were the order of the day. After a long hard slog, we headed towards a triangulation pillar and prematurely celebrated climbing another Wainwright. Unfortunately, the highest point of the fell is not the one occupied by the triangulation pillar, but rather a steep sided rocky outcrop close by. Ascent looked to be problematic, but after one large step and an easy climb up a groove in the rocks, we perched ourselves on the highest point.

Friday 5th April 2012

203. Arnison Crag

Height: 1424 feet (433m)
Route: Patterdale - West to wall - South - Summit

Today we decided to return to the Eastern Fells and climb a trio of mountains - Arnison Crag, Birks and St Sunday Crag. After another drive over the Kirkstone Pass, we parked in Patterdale. Walking behind the Patterdale Hotel, we headed west until we came to Glemara Park. Turning left and following a wall south, we headed towards our first peak of the day. Once again the climb was steep and snow covered, but we used the wall to pull ourselves up the slope. A rock tower blocked our path to the actual summit, so we walked around the back of the tower and eventually climbed up from the east. The highest point provided lovely views down towards Ullswater.

204. Birks

Height: 2041 feet (622m)
Route: SW from Arnison Crag - Trough Head - Summit

Leaving Arnison Crag, an easy walk to Trough Head was followed by a long, slow trudge up towards Birks. As we climbed higher, the weather which had been clear and cold all day became even colder. As temperatures plummeted, we raided our rucksacks for some extra layers. Feeling slightly warmer, we reached the summit and contemplated the view towards St Sunday Crag.

205. St Sunday Crag

Height: 2756 feet (841m)
Route: South-west from Birks

The summit of St Sunday Crag looked terrific, but it also looked a little terrifying. A combination of steep slopes, crags, sheer drops and snow, led to a degree of natural reticence on our part – after all, we didn't want a repeat of our experience on Middle Dodd. Thinking about our options, a family conference ensued. After carefully considering our options, we decided to continue, but we included the proviso that we would turn back if we felt in any real or immediate danger. Fixing crampons, we headed onwards. Initially climbing up the north-east ridge of the mountain, we then traversed the eastern face. Our final climb to the summit was steep and a little unnerving, but the deep snow gave our crampons something to bite into. We were never in any real or immediate danger, but our anxiety resulted in one of the quickest ascents that we have ever made.

Conditions at the summit were a little cold and blustery, but once again we were blessed with stunning views. Snow-capped peaks could be seen in all directions, with Helvellyn, High Street and Fairfield looking particularly spectacular. We enjoyed the views and then headed back to Birks. From Birks we descended to Patterdale via Thornhow End and Glemara Park.

A lovely day out was rounded off by a great meal at the White Lion.

Saturday 6th April 2013

Our original intention this holiday had been to complete all the Wainwrights. To facilitate this plan we had organised a two week stay in the Lake District. One week in Ambleside followed by another week in

Thornthwaite. When we saw the forecasts and then experienced the conditions, we knew that completion would be a tall order. However, at the end of week one, completion was still a possibility.

In an effort to keep our plan alive, we decided to keep walking. On Saturday morning we packed up all our possessions, loaded the car and headed for Thornthwaite via Wasdale Head. Our route may not have been the most conventional one, but our massive detour would allow us to climb Yewbarrow.

Yewbarrow is often described as one of the most difficult Wainwrights to climb. Although smaller than other fells surrounding Wasdale Head, its shape resembling the upturned hull of a boat, offers no easy routes to the top. The two most traditional routes of ascent, via Great Door or Stirrup Crag, involve some scrambling. Tania and Tom had largely regained their confidence, but discussion forums and photos on the internet persuaded them against these options. Although there is no easy route to the top, we did discover that an easier route existed. Starting from Overbecks, we planned to head towards Dore Head, and then climb the steep grassy western face of the fell.

We set off optimistically, but perhaps not confidently. In much the same way that looking up illnesses on the internet can fuel hypochondria, looking up and reading about dangerous routes can feed acrophobia. Too much research can be a bad thing. We followed our intended route and got to almost within touching distance of the summit ridge. However, just as the slope was at its most precipitous, grass gave way to snow and Tania could go no further. Tania had done fantastically well to keep going after her fall on Middle Dodd, but Yewbarrow caused her fears and worries to resurface. Understandably anxious, Tania was not really concerned about her own safety, but she was worried about the boys. Taking everything in to consideration, we decided to retreat back down the mountain. After two hundred and five Wainwrights, we had found our nemesis – its name was Yewbarrow.

Tuesday 9th April 2013

206. Slight Side

Height: 2499 feet (762m)
Route: Wha House Farm – Terrace route – Summit

Having failed to climb Yewbarrow, we realised that it was now extremely unlikely that we would be able to complete all the Wainwrights on this holiday. Completion was still theoretically possible, but it would mean that we would have to walk every day, regardless of the conditions. The prospect of even theoretical completion disappeared on Sunday. Taking a rest day was a sensible decision in many ways, but we ended up even further behind schedule. Just to add to our woes, the wintry conditions were now forecast to last for another week, and this meant that at least one of our walks would probably be impossible to complete. Matters were made even worse on Monday. We spent so much time trying to decide which walk to do, that by the time we made a decision, it was too late to walk anywhere. But, thinking back to our original reasons for trying to climb all the Wainwrights, we came to the conclusion that it didn't really matter; what mattered was enjoying our final fells and not rushing them just because of some self-imposed timeframe.

Back with the correct mind set, we made an early decision over the breakfast table and we headed off to climb Slight Side and Scafell. Parking in a National Trust Car Park, close to Wha House Farm, we began walking along the terrace route. This route climbs steadily and easily, and it provided impressive views, especially towards Harter Fell. As we approached Cat Crag, views opened up towards Slight Side. This view was a little daunting. Slight Side rises dramatically from Quagrigg Moss, and the mountain looked to be anything but slight. We crossed over the level and boggy terrain of the moss, and then started climbing up the steep, mostly snow free, southern face of the fell. The ascent confirmed our suspicions – it was hard work. Not only did we have to climb over nine hundred feet of ascent, but we also had to complete a final rocky scramble to reach the highest point. Wainwright includes the summit in his top six summits, describing the top as "rocky, shapely and well defined" – we were tired, but we had to agree.

207. Scafell

Height: 3162 feet (964m)
Route: North via Long Green

The weather had been fairly benign so far, but as we crested the summit of Slight Side, ferocious north-easterly gusts threatened to knock off our feet. Battered and chilled by the gusts, the snow cover also increased, and we attached crampons for the final stage of the walk. We crossed over a level area of frozen ground, and then we climbed a steep slope towards Long Green. From Long Green we completed a short climb to reach the summit of Scafell. We were thrilled to be on top of the second highest mountain in England, but conditions were horrendous. Increasingly cold and windblown, we appreciated the views and then looked for some shelter. A wind shelter close to the summit cairn looked like it might offer protection from the elements, but the wind shelter was so full of snow that its primary function failed. We took a last look across to the summit of Scafell Pike, and then somewhat reluctantly, cut our stay short and headed for home.

Wednesday 11th April 2013

208. Fleetwith Pike

Height: 2126 feet (648m)
Route: Honister Pass - Drum House - Summit

Today, we decided to climb what we had originally intended to be our final fell - Fleetwith Pike. Feeling tired after yesterday's outing and with options limited by ice and snow, we felt that we had to change our Wainwright bagging schedule. Wainwright bagging, I don't particularly like the term; it makes me think of a memorable quip by Eric Robson, who described Wainwright baggers as "trainspotters with altitude" - I like to think that we and most other so called 'Wainwright Baggers' are primarily concerned with walking rather than ticking lists, but I do know what he means. One thing that Wainwright baggers are definitely concerned about is the question of which fell to complete on. We had certainly spent a long time discussing the subject. After much debate, Fleetwith Pike was chosen because it would allow us to complete on a single fell, and it would also allow us the opportunity to visit Haystacks and pay tribute to Wainwright. Changing our original plan was necessary, but it was a little bit disappointing.

Walking from Honistor slate quarry, we followed the old tramway (signposted Great Gable and Haystacks) to Drum House. From here we headed north towards Hopper slate quarry, and then Wainwright's perched rock. The rock, still perched, led us to a path that led to the summit of the fell. An impressive large cairn marked the highest point and a slender artistic cairn marked a fine viewpoint. The highest point provided marvellous views towards Great Gable and Pillar; whist the viewpoint provided fantastic views towards Buttermere and the High Stile range. Thinking that this would have been a great fell to complete on, we reflected upon what might have been.

Friday 12th April 2013

209. Ling Mell

Height: 2649 feet (800m)
Route: Brackenclose NT Car Park – East-north-east – Direct route up the shoulder of the fell

Conjecture is all very well, but in reality we still had six fells left to complete. After a trip to Carisle on Friday, today we decided to climb Ling Mell. Starting from Brackenclose Car Park, we climbed directly up the western shoulder of the fell. The route was steep all the way, but the route could be divided in three distinct sections. A grassy slope was followed by a scree slope and then a stepped slope. After the stepped slope, the route levelled out, but just before we reached the summit, the clouds descended and visibility was reduced to just a few feet. Utilising map, GPS and compass, we carefully plotted a course to the summit. A large and impressive cairn marked the highest point, but with no views whatsoever, we didn't hang around. We touched base (cairn) and then returned by our route of ascent. Perhaps we are trainspotters – I hope not.

Saturday 13th April 2013

210. Yewbarrow

Height: 2058 feet (628m)
Route: Overbecks - North-east towards Stirrup Gap - climb to depression on summit ridge - Summit

Starting our day with another massive detour, we decided to return to Devon via Wasdale. It was time to face our nemesis. Setting off with a sense of grim determination, we actually ended up loving this walk. It's amazing the difference a day (or a week) can make. Heading towards Stirrup Gap, under clear skies, we tracked north along the contours below Long Crag. After walking for about a mile and a half, we saw some walkers descending from the summit ridge. Logically thinking that if they could descend, we could climb, we headed up the steep, grass and heather covered slope. Ascent was far easier than last time; clumps of heather provided a steeped route up the steepest sections of the climb. Attaining the ridge, we turned right and headed for the higher southern summit of the fell. The southern summit provided fantastic views, but in all honesty, the whole elongated ridge provided fantastic views. It was hard to know where to look - magnificence abounded in all directions.

Eventually managing to drag ourselves away from the summit, we headed back towards the car. We were delighted to have finally climbed Yewbarrow and we were pleased to have completed the Western Fells, but we were disappointed that another holiday was sadly over. There's more to life than fells you know, but not much more.

COMPLETION
May 2013

"It's a truth universally acknowledged, that a family in possession of walking boots must be in want of a mountain" – well, fortunately in our case that's true. Some people seem to think that I drag Tania, Will and Tom to the Lake District, forcing them to follow my dreams and ambitions, but this couldn't be further from the truth. Tania and the boys love the Lake District and they love walking, and it was Tania and I, who jointly came up with the idea of completing all the Wainwrights. Coercion has never been necessary – even the pound a summit for the boys turned out to be a needless incentive.

Completing the Wainwrights has been a family affair, and completing the Wainwrights together has made the challenge more enjoyable and more satisfying. Family and the Lake District, it's not like any other kind of love. Together, we have shared wonderful never to be forgotten moments; we have walked, talked and laughed, we have experienced highs and lows, successes and failures, and we have worked and acted as one. If I'm feeling down, there are always three other people willing and able to pick me up and drive things forward. It's like having your own support team, both emotionally and physically.

You may wonder, therefore, why on our latest journey up to the Lakes, I was feeling quite so full of trepidation. With only four fells left to complete in two walks, our journey was nearly over. Whilst part of me was excited about the prospect of completion, another part felt deeply apprehensive. Walking the Wainwrights has been such a big part of our lives for so long, that the idea of final completion just felt strange. I shared my thoughts with the rest of the family. Tania and Will understood what I meant, but Tom just wanted to finish – he said he had really enjoyed the experience, but he was looking forward to holidaying in sunnier climes.

Saturday May 4th 2013

211. Great End

Height: 2984 feet (910m)
Route: Seathwaite – Stockley Bridge – Ruddy Gill – Esk Hause – Summit

Tom, may well have had a point about sunnier climes – Saturday morning revealed leaden skies and ominous cloud. But, the conditions did little to dampen our spirits. Despite yesterday's concerns, today we felt upbeat and positive – it's amazing what a good night's sleep can do! We realised that completion would be a fantastic achievement and the realisation of a dream. I wondered how many other families had climbed all the fells – not many from Devon I suspect. I think we also realised that completion wouldn't mark the end of our association with the Lake District. I was already thinking about the fells that I would like to climb again, the new places that I would like to visit and the adventures that I would like to share.

Eager to get out and about, we headed off towards Seathwaite. Our plan today was to climb Great End, Allen Crags and Glaramara. Our penultimate walk started from Seathwaite Farm, and I think we all realised that we should make the most of every second of the experience. Today was not a day for any doubt or despondency. Repeating the route that we had used when we first climbed Scafell Pike as a family, I was also repeating the initial stages of the first walk that I had ever completed in the Lake District. The walk took on a new level of poignancy. Heading towards Stockley Bridge, we immersed ourselves in the moment, but we also began building up a list of Lakeland family favourites – favourite walks, fells, summits, ridges, meals and pubs. Recollections brought back wonderful memories, and reminded us of just how lucky we have been. If you're interested by the way, my personal favourites were as follows: The Coledale Round; Helvellyn; Coniston Old Man; Scope End; the Kirkstile Inn; the Dog and Gun. Mind you, ask me again tomorrow and I will probably come up with a different set of responses.

From Stockley Bridge, we headed south, climbing up beside Grains Gill. This approach is beautiful and our eyes darted between the tumbling cascades of the gill, and the strikingly impressive bulk of Great End. Crossing Ruddy Gill, we headed towards Esk Hause. Some footpaths in the Lake District are difficult to discern, but the path leading from Esk Hause towards Scafell Pike, is the fell walking equivalent of a motorway. Staying in the inside lane, a walk over level ground was followed by a steep climb up Calf Cove. From here we departed from the Scafell Pike path, and headed north-north-east towards Great End. Unfortunately, just as we had the summit in our sights, cloud swirled in from the west and the summit disappeared. We have actually been quite lucky in terms of achieving views from summits – one hundred and eighty nine, from the two hundred and eleven visited so far, but not today – well, not so far. Thankful for our map and our GPS, we negotiated our way to the top of the fell. We used our *Pictorial Guide* to paint a picture of what might have been.

212. Allen Crags

Height: 2572 feet (785m)
Route: Esk Hause – North-east to Summit

Backtracking to Esk Hause, we emerged from the cloud and headed north-east towards Allen Crags. A straightforward level walk, followed by a short steep climb, brought us to our second summit of the day. The top of the fell has three cairns, and the one in the middle is the highest. The summit was cloud free, so we didn't require Wainwright's assistance to recreate the view.

213. Glaramara

Height: 2560 feet (783m)
Route:North-north-east from Allen Crags

Heading north-north-east, we walked downhill, knowing full well that we would have to climb again. The route from Allen Crags to Glaramara consists of a series of rises and falls, with minor summits interspersed by marshy depressions and glorious tarns. The route between the two fells was quite beautiful. We stopped frequently, not because we were tired, but because we wanted to make the most of the experience. We enjoyed the views towards the north-eastern fells, we rested beside the still waters of the tarns, and we continued to reminisce about past walks. One particularly stunning tarn resembled an infinity pool – we marvelled at what nature can create, and people can only imitate. Eventually reaching the top of the fell, we thought that Wainwright's second summit appeared to be higher than his main summit, so we visited both. We had now completed all of Wainwright's Southern Fells, and after six years of Wainwright Bagging (I still don't like the term) we only had one fell left to climb.

Sunday 5th May 2013

214. Catstycam

Height: 2917 feet (890m)
Route: Glenridding – Glenridding Road – Red Tarn Beck – Path to Swirrel Edge – Summit

My first real introduction to Wainwright was his guide to *The Eastern Fells*. I remember standing in a bookshop and devouring his chapter on Helvellyn. It seemed apt therefore, that as I helped to plan our final walk to complete our final Wainwright, I was using the very same book that I had first 'devoured' and then purchased. Now a little used and abused, I looked at the chapter on Catstycam. Wainwright suggests that "Walkers with red blood in their veins should give their attention to the north-west ridge". Thinking carefully about Wainwright's suggestion, I immediately planned a different route. Well, we needed to save some routes for the future!

After packing my rucksack carefully – GPS, map, compass and Cava, we left our holiday cottage in Portiscale, and headed towards Glenridding. It certainly felt strange to be heading off to climb our final fell – emotions were high and moods 'rollercoastered' between joy, regret, excitement and apprehension.

Leaving Glenridding Car Park, we headed along Greenside Road, before turning south-west and climbing the path beside Red Tarn Beck. If we had thought for a single moment that the sun would come out to bless our final walk, we would have been completely mistaken. The clouds that had filled the sky all morning, lowered, and heavy rain began to fall. In a strange way, the rain itself felt like a fitting tribute to our final walk. Nothing in life that is worth having is ever gained easily. Battling the elements and immersed in cloud, as we had been so many times before, we missed Wainwright's route up the east shoulder of Catstycam. It was slightly disappointing, but edifying to think that after two hundred and thirteen fells, we could still go the wrong way. Missing our intended route, we walked on towards Red Tarn and then headed towards Swirrel Edge. As luck would have it, our unplanned detour provided an easy route to the top of the fell. Branching off from the midpoint of Swirrel Edge, we soon reached the summit of Catstycam.

Any lingering doubts about completion completely disappeared. We were elated, we were ecstatic, we were delighted. After six years and one hundred and ninety five thousand, six hundred and sixty five feet of ascent; and after five hundred and ninety nine miles, and ninety eight walks – we had finally completed our Wainwright challenge.

Retreating to the shores of Red Tarn, we popped open the Cava and drank in what little was left of the views – it was all a bit misty and murky. With a shared sense of disbelief, mixed with a great sense of satisfaction – we laughed, we joked, we talked about our adventures and we celebrated our achievement. Our family challenge was over, but our memories would last for a lifetime.

Heading back to the car, Will suddenly asked "What's next Dad, The Munros, The Corbetts, The Hewits, The Donalds or The Marilyns?" – I thought carefully before replying "I think the pubs of Cumbria would be a good idea".

Acknowledgements

Thanks to Tania, Will and Tom, without whom this book would not have been possible.

Thanks also to the following people for their direct or indirect contributions towards my first book:

Clare Salkeld and Mark Sutcliffe for their early support and encouragement; Jane Evans at Sigma Press for taking a chance and following it through; Francis Lincoln Publishers for their kind permission to quote from the great man himself; John Manning at Lakeland Walker for his continuing support; and Alan Hinkes, OBE, for taking time out of his hectic schedule to write the foreword.

Thanks must also go to fellow members of the Wainwright Society and my followers on Twitter for their support, advice and feedback.

INDEX

A

Allen Crags 241
Angletarn Pikes 155
Ard Crags 181
Armboth Fell 101
Arnison Crag 232
Arthur's Pike 142

B

Bakestall 126
Bannerdale Crags 92
Barf 38
Barrow 33
Base Brown 215
Beda Fell 155
Binsey 80
Birkhouse Moor 162
Birks 232
Black Fell 104
Blake Fell 124
Blea Rigg 57
Bleaberry Fell 94
Blencathra 90
Bonscale Pike 141
Bowfell 61
Bowscale Fell 92
Brae Fell 76
Brandreth 36
Branstree 213
Brim Fell 108
Brock Crags 154
Broom Fell 40
Buckbarrow 175
Burnbank Fell 124

C

Calf Crag 114
Carl Side 69
Carrock Fell 183

Castle Crag 46
Catbells 37
Catstycam 242
Caudale Moor 150
Causey Pike 190
Caw Fell 220
Clough Head 140
Cold Pike 111
Crag Fell 209
Crinkle Crags 111

D

Dale Head 42
Dodd 67
Dollywagon Pike 149
Dove Crag 55
Dow Crag 204

E

Eagle Crag 195
Eel Crag (Crag Hill) 32
Esk Pike 62

F

Fairfield 55
Fellbarrow 99
Fleetwith Pike 236
Froswick 200

G

Gavel Fell 125
Gibson Knott 51
Glaramara 242
Glenridding Dodd 165
Gowbarrow Fell 30
Grange Fell 83
Grasmoor 97
Gray Crag 211
Graystones 121
Great Bourne 217
Great Calva 157
Great Carrs 107
Great Cockup 75
Great Crag 82
Great Dodd 140
Great End 240
Great Gable 34
Great Mell Fell 94
Great Rigg 56
Great Scafell 76
Green Crag 228
Green Gable 35
Grey Crag 206
Grey Friar 108
Grey Knotts 36
Grike 209
Grisedale Pike 31

H

Hallin Fell 122
Hardknott 167
Harrison Stickle 19
Hart Crag 55
Hart Side 188
Harter Fell (Eskdale) 231
Harter Fell (Mardale) 202
Hartsop above How 223

Hartsop Dodd 150
Haycock 186
Haystacks 24
Helm Crag 52
Helvellyn 146
Hen Comb 153
Heron Pike 56
High Crag 78
High Hartsop Dodd 225
High Pike (Caldbeck) 184
High Pike (Scandale) 54
High Raise (Langdale) 58
High Raise (Martindale) 193
High Rigg 117
High Seat 93
High Spy 42
High Stile 79
High Street 192
High Tove 101
Hindscarth 43
Holme Fell 64
Hopegill Head 31

I

Ill Bell 200
Illgill Head 173

K

Kentmere Pike 202
Kidsty Pike 193
Kirk Fell 173
Knott 156
Knott Rigg 180
The Knott 191

L

Lank Rigg 222
Latrigg 81
Ling Fell 44
Ling Mell 237
Lingmoor Fell 64
Little Hart Crag 225
Little Mell Fell 95
Loadpot Hill 142
Loft Crag 60
Long Side 69
Longlands Fell 77
Lonscale Fell 72
Lord's Seat 39
Loughrigg 84
Low Fell 100
Low Pike 54

M

Maiden Moor 41
Mardale Ill Bell 201
Meal Fell 76
Mellbreak 188
Middle Dodd 226
Middle Fell 169
Mungrisdale Common 91

N

Nab Scar 56
The Nab 159
Nethermost Pike 149

O

Old Man of Coniston 20
Outerside 33

P

Pavey Ark 18
Pike O'Blisco 110
Pike O'Stickle 59
Pillar 176
Place Fell 182

R

Raise 230
Rampsgill Head 194
Rannerdale Knotts 98
Raven Crag 88
Red Pike (Buttermere) 79
Red Pike (Wasdale) 186
Red Screes 226
Rest Dodd 158
Robinson 145
Rossett Pike 62
Rosthwaite Fell 143

S

Sail 32
Saint Sunday Crag 233
Sale Fell 45
Sallows 115
Scafell 236
Scafell Pike 26
Scar Crags 191
Scoat Fell 185
Seat Sandal 164
Seatallan 174
Seathwaite Fell 157
Selside Pike 212
Sergeant Man 58
Sergeant's Crag 194
Sheffield Pike 187
Shipman Knotts 203
Silver How 138
Skiddaw 70
Skiddaw Little Man 71
Slight Side 235
Sour Howes 115
Souther Fell 89
Starling Dodd 218
Steel Fell 113
Steel Knotts 143
Steeple 184
Stone Arthur 67
Stybarrow Dodd 120
Swirl How 107

T

Tarn Crag (Easedale) 219
Tarn Crag (Longsleddale) 207
Thornthwaite Crag 201
Thunacar Knott 59
Troutbeck Tongue 198

U

Ullock Pike 70
Ullscarf 210

W

Walla Crag 74
Wandope 97
Wansfell 127
Watson Dodd 139
Wether Hill 143
Wetherlam 105
Whin Rigg 171
Whinlatter 83
White Side 231
Whiteless Pike 98
Whiteside 96

Y

Yewbarrow 238
Yoke 199

Walking In Eden

Ron Scholes

The definitive guide to walking in the Eden Valley, a unique part of Cumbria nestling between Kendal and Carlisle. The walks, both circular and linear, range from 2 to 15 miles and are peppered with fascinating accounts of the history and culture of the area. Outline route maps, inspiring photographs and absorbing background information all add to the value of this unique guide to walking in the Eden Valley – the closest that walkers will get to a paradise on earth!

£8.99

Walking the Wainwrights

Stuart Marshall

This book links all 214 peaks in the late Alfred Wainwright's seven-volume Pictorial Guide to The Lakeland Fells. Clear route descriptions are presented with two-colour sketch maps.

"An excellent, concise manual on how to tackle the 'Wainwrights' in an intelligent way." – A. Harry Griffin MBE

£8.99

Waterside Walks in the Lake District 2nd Ed

Colin Shelbourn

25 stunning walks along the shores of some of the most beautiful lakes to strolls beside rushing rivers and wild water- falls. Whatever the length or location you choose you'll meet with stunning scenery, a richness of wildlife, and many interesting places to visit.

£8.99

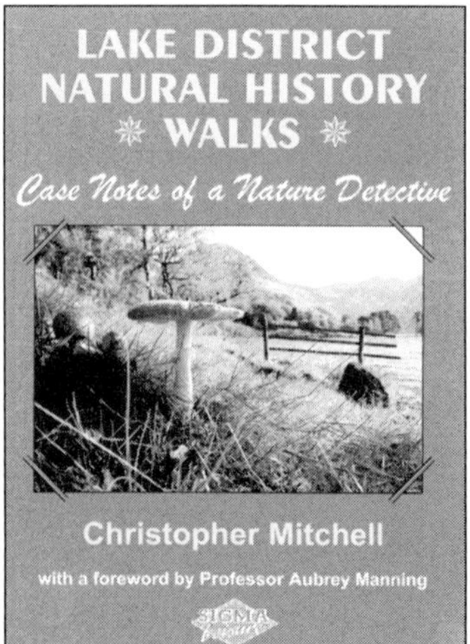

Lake District Natural History Walks

Case Notes of a Nature Detective

Christopher Mitchell

18 walks suitable for all ages and abilities Fascinating facts help you interpret the country- side by looking at the effects of geology and plant life on the animal population of the area.

£8.99

35 Really Good Lake District Walks

Peter Bowker

This book describes 35 quality outings in the mountains of the English Lake District. The walks, which all visit at least one 'Wainwright' summit, have been specifically chosen to appeal particularly to those who prefer to travel at a leisurely pace on straightforward routes which avoid more challenging and demanding situations.

£8.99

Lost Lakeland

In the footsteps of Thomas Pennant

Christopher Mitchell

Thomas Pennant was an eighteenth-century travel writer, antiquary and naturalist. Travelling on horseback with a group of friends and servants including his own artist, he was one of the first to explore the Lake Counties. This book follows Thomas Pennant's historic journey. It revisits what has become familiar ground and in the process discovers a 'lost' Lakeland **£8.99**